The King's Book

of

Numerology II

Forecasting - Part 1

Richard Andrew King

2

The King's Book of Numerology II

Forecasting - Part 1

by

Richard Andrew King

Richard King Publications

4

© by Richard Andrew King
Published by Richard King Publications
PO Box 3621
Laguna Hills, CA 92654

Library of Congress Cataloging-in-Publication Data

King, Richard Andrew
The King's Book of Numerology II: Forecasting, Part 1
ISBN: 978-0-931872-05-1

DEDICATION

To

Helena Davis for her humility, generosity and courage
in sharing her understanding of numbers.

~

To

Frank Monahan and Lewis Hunter Stowers:

Genuine Seekers

of Truth Through Numbers

APPRECIATION

Many thanks to Shannon Yarbrough,
author of Stealing Wishes and The Other Side of What,
for his cover design.

THE KING'S BOOK OF NUMEROLOGY II

FORECASTING: PART 1

Table of Contents

Author's Forward		9
Chapter One	Into The Looking Glass	13
Chapter Two	Life Cycle Patterns	29
Chapter Three	Pinnacle/Challenge Timeline	89
Chapter Four	Epoch Timeline	123
Chapter Five	Voids	135
Chapter Six	Case Studies	149
Chapter Seven	Name Timeline	163
Chapter Eight	Letter Timeline	185
Chapter Nine	Decade Timeline	201
Chapter Ten	Age Timeline	209
Chapter Eleven	Universal Timeline	237
Chapter Twelve	Personal Year Timeline	255
Chapter Thirteen	Annual Cycle Pattern	265
Chapter Fourteen	The Chart	275

AUTHOR'S FORWARD

The Future - it has concerned us, disturbed us, frightened us, mystified us, challenged us, occupied our thoughts, fortified us and given us pause, even hope. We think it is unknowable. It is not. God knows it because He is omniscient. He created it, as well as the Past and Present. Those who have merged with Him also know it because they have become One with Him. But the rest of us, who are not spiritually evolved enough to be at that level where all can be known, still have not been left totally in the dark. God did not drop us here without a plan, a plan we can know, decipher and use for our benefit.

Our lives and destinies are known quantities. In fact, Perfect Living Masters tell us our lives are destined to the breath, that what we will get in any life experience, in any incarnation, is established long before that life is given birth. Not only are the hairs on our head numbered--a statement Christ made to inform his disciples of this predestined aspect of life--but every step we are to take in our life's journey, every dollar we are to earn or lose, every breath we are to breathe, every relationship we are to have, and even every morsel of food we are to consume in our entire life is likewise established prior to our moment of birth. If these things were not established, they could not be known, and because God knows all, He knows these things, too. If we had the ability to choose and exert total free will and somehow alter or generate our own life plan, and if our steps and breaths were an unknown quantity, this would invalidate the omniscience of God, for then God would not be all-knowing. In fact, He would be unknowing, or, at best, He would have a limited knowing, a finite understanding. He would not, therefore, be omniscient. He would not be God. Not hardly.

> *The total number of breaths which one is to take till death, the morsels which one is to eat and the steps which one is to walk are all preordained at birth and no one can alter, decrease or increase them.*
>
> ~ Sawan Singh, 19th/20th Century Saint

God is real and He is omniscient. Furthermore, He has established a blueprint for each of us throughout each of our incarnations. That plan is also a known quantity, at least to a limited degree. It is visible through our name and date of birth as extraordinary, fantastic or absurd as it may seem. Through these natal vehicles - the name and birth date - we can know what our life's destiny is. Through them, we do not have to stumble in the dark or behave as ignorant beasts unwilling to accept the mantle of knowledge and responsibility for ourselves and our life. Through them we can become more in tune with our life's plan. Henceforth, we can become more self-realized.

The King's Book of Numerology II: Forecasting - Part 1 is dedicated to opening the door to the divine blueprint of our lives. When the principles set forth herein are studied and learned, one will begin to see there is definitely a life plan for each of us and that it is exact, precise, unchangeable, unalterable and . . . knowable. We are all so very unique--like snowflakes--no two are alike, but each snowflake is similar because en-masse they combine to form that which we universally recognize as 'snow,' just as we, as humans, combine to form that which we recognize as humanity.

Once this awareness becomes established, our understanding and consciousness of life will, no doubt, change. We will begin to see ourselves as part of an immense spiritual super-structure far beyond our current ability to comprehend, understand or perceive. Life will take on new meaning and, perhaps, we will even begin to awaken to greater spiritual truths, one of which is that we are prisoners entangled, ensnared and incarcerated in a Great Cosmic Web of restricting, constricting and limiting energy fields whose interweaving intricacy is so perfect and binding that we are, seemingly, hopelessly bound and doomed to suffer in this dimension of polarized darkness forever. Good. Perhaps then we will begin to raise our heads and voices in defiance and revolution and initiate the great battle for our spiritual freedom and liberation from this nether land, this negative pole of creation.

Additionally, and most profoundly, we will move closer to God. There will be no way any sentient soul, once he sees how perfectly each of our lives has been designed and structured, cannot bow his head in utter reverence and respect for the power that created this creation. The word "Awe" does not do justice to our perception of His work. After all, the very second a person is born, a numerology chart can be constructed outlining every individual's destiny! What Power is there that has the capacity to create such things? One can only shake his head and wonder what He is and how powerful He is, for truly He is beyond profound. It is this infinite Power we call God.

It is with this understanding that this book is offered. Knowing our life's blueprint for this incarnation can have extremely beneficial ramifications. But we must not become too absorbed, mesmerized or hypnotized by it all because all of this worldly knowing is still--and will remain forever-an aspect of *this* creation. The purpose of human life, as Saints tell us, is God-Realization, and we must never lose sight of this goal lest we lose the precious and priceless opportunity to rise above and beyond this dimension, liberate our souls from it, gain eternal freedom and return Home . . . forever.

A caveat: all arts and sciences need continued study, research, analysis, and refinement in order to reveal deeper truths and realities. It is no different with numerology, and it is no different with the principles outlined in this book. Continued research and development are encouraged in order to further elucidate the truth regarding the divine blueprint of our lives and destinies.

God Speed.

Richard Andrew King

Chapter One

INTO THE LOOKING GLASS

For now we see through a glass, darkly.
~ Bible: I Corinthians 13:12

The very hairs of your head are all numbered.
~ Bible: St. Matthew 10:30

To every thing there is a season and a
time to every purpose under the heaven.
~ Bible: Ecclesiastes 3:1

All men come into this world with a destiny of
their own which goes on pushing them relentlessly
on the course already marked out for them.

In fact, we do not see things as they are;
we see things the way we are.
~ Charan Singh, Twentieth Century Mystic

What destiny has planned for you will come
to pass without any planning on your part.
Your destiny will cause you to act and
make effort according to its plan.
~ Jagat Singh, Twentieth Century Mystic

Everything is determined, the beginning as well as

the end by forces over which we have no control.

It is determined for the insect, as well as for the star.

Human beings, vegetables or cosmic dust - we all dance

to a mysterious tune, intoned in the distance by an invisible piper.

~ Albert Einstein, Nobel Laureate, Physics, 1921

God himself forces his creatures into destined paths of karmas

over which they have no control and which cannot be effaced.

Whatever is destined to take place must take place.

~ Guru Amardas, Sixteenth Century Saint

Welcome to the world of the future . . . and the past . . . and the present. In this volume of *The King's Book of Numerology* we deal with time - the measurable construct of our existence. Through this aspect of numerology we are granted the special privilege of looking into the cosmic crystal ball of our lives. . . scientifically.

Each of us has a destiny - a predetermined course of life far beyond our power to manipulate or control. That destiny, as strange as it may seem, as fantastic as it may seem, as profound as it is, exists. Of this there is no doubt. As Mystics tell us, before we exit our mother's womb our lives are not only destined as to the total number of hairs on our head (Bible: St. Matthew 10:30) but also to the very number of heartbeats and breaths. As 19th and 20th Century Saint, Sawan Singh corroborates:

The total number of breaths which one is to take till

death, the morsels which one is to eat and the steps

which one is to walk are all preordained at birth

and no one can alter, decrease or increase them.

Such is the enormous precision by which our lives are constructed. It is this precision which generates a blueprint of life for each of us, a framework of supernal origin giving each of our lives its own special and magnificent divine design.

The King's Book of Numerology II: Forecasting - Part 1

In mystic terms our destiny is our karma coming due. It is the reconciliation of debts incurred from prior lives, a balancing of the books, an adjustment of accounts, the reaping of the seeds we have sown in the past and the harvesting of its crop. Destiny is the reaction of past deeds of former lives which we have to fulfill in this life and . . . there is no escaping it. Believe it or not. Destiny is factual and inexorable.

Knowing Our Destiny

As profound as it is that our lives have a destiny, it is equally profound that we can know it, not in specific terms but certainly in general terms. Not only did God not drop us here without a plan, He also did not leave us without a way of knowing that plan. Through numerology we can, indeed, know that plan . . . if we choose.

It is, however, not necessary that we know our fate. It's a matter of choice and acquiring the knowledge. If we do choose to look into our lives, it is best we maintain a spiritual focus to ground us. Knowledge is power, but it can destroy as well as edify. Sometimes it may be best not to know some things, especially when we cannot change them, and we may worry unnecessarily over things and events beyond our control. Therefore, to look into our future requires spiritual balance, poise and the detached understanding that we are simply actors on a stage, reading a script and giving a performance during one of many incarnations.

There are those who neither believe we have a destiny nor the capability of understanding it. Such is their belief, but belief neither validates nor invalidates reality. Belief is simply an accepted thought. It is not fact, and the fact is that destiny is a matter of fact. Experience in these matters is the best teacher. It would be impossible for anyone with an open, unbiased, dispassionate, inquisitive and scientific mind to study the science of numerology and arrive at a different conclusion. To reiterate, God did not drop us here either without a distinct plan for each of our lives or without the means of knowing that plan. The plan exists . . . for each of us. Whether we choose to know the basic blueprint of that plan or not is our choice, but disbelieving does not invalidate the reality of the road of destiny which each of us is forced to follow. States Charan Singh: "All men come into this world with a destiny of their own which goes on pushing them relentlessly on the course already marked out for them."

To be sure, it is not necessary for us to know our fate in general terms. Knowing our destiny will not change it. We can't push the river any more than we can control the flow of our lives. Events, conditions, relationships, fortunes - the tides of our lives - will present themselves to us in their own manner, at their own time, by their own volition. The best we can do is adjust to their

King

flow and flow with them, grow from them, learn from them and, hopefully, acquire a deeper sense of spirituality in the process.

However, in the cosmic gazing methodology of numerological forecasting, we must know that we will only be able to see what is in our destiny to see. For all of our looking, for all of our searching, for all of our intelligence, our ability to analyze, our intuition, our depth of understanding - for all of it, we are helpless to change what has been written. Mystics tell us that what has to happen has already happened and that whatever happens, had to happen in order to fulfill the script of our lives and destinies, destinies which cannot be altered.

It is also beneficial to know that our vision to see clearly is obscured by design, defect or divine directive. If it is in our destiny to fall into a ditch, for example, we will be made blind, deaf, dumb, even stupid, so that our destiny of falling into the ditch can be fulfilled. If it is in our destiny to inherit a fortune, then we will do so without any effort on our part. Destiny happens of its own accord as naturally as leaves fall from a tree and no thought, person or event can change it. Therefore, there is no use in worrying about anything. The choices we make are the ones we were destined to make. "Karma will take care of our choice automatically," says Charan Singh.

Benefits

If we do choose to peer into the looking glass of our destiny, there are benefits. Perhaps one of the greatest is simply in knowing that there is order to the journey, that each of our lives has a structure, a framework, a blueprint, a divine design created by a power far more vast than our minds can possibly imagine. Our destinies are not random happenings. Our lives and destinies are karmically sculpted works of Godly art, created by the Artisan of Artisans, the Creator Himself.

Embracing this knowledge can be quite comforting because when things happen in our lives beyond our control, as they certainly will, we can take solace in the fact that such occurrences were in our fate. We can then adjust and accept life and all of its twists, turns, ups, downs, joys, sorrows, smiles and tears with greater ease, peace and grace knowing the divine hand of God moves all . . . perfectly, precisely, fairly.

Another benefit of looking into the Glass (the crystal ball of our destiny) is that we may be able to foresee the oncoming spiraling mass of a tumultuous hurricane bearing down on the quiet comfort of our lives and, thereby, be able to prepare for it spiritually so we are not blind-sided by it. We can batten down the hatches, secure the house, sandbag the property, obtain the appropriate amounts of food, clothing and supplies needed to weather the storm and lessen its impact. However, unlike an actual hurricane, we cannot run away from the winds of destiny or vacate the premises until they pass. We cannot change our destiny or the events they bring, or escape from them, whether those events are thunder storms, hurricanes, sunny days or summertime vacations. No one can outrun his destiny. However, with foreknowledge we can prepare for oncoming circumstances - psychologically, emotionally, spiritually. Consequently, their effects, if seemingly negative, can be mitigated and our discomfort from them lessened, if not obviated altogether.

This is, truly, one of the great gifts of studying the numbers of our lives - the ability to see ahead so we may not be caught off guard, so we may be aware of our future and, therefore, be better able to prepare or relax as circumstances dictate. But then again, this too is fated -- our having foreknowledge of oncoming energies. Should we be given foresight of destiny's doings we can, and should be, grateful for such vision. It is not given to all, only to the grateful few who seek to know, understand and appreciate such a gift, a gift whose violation will result in revocation.

It is not just knowing the future which can help us adjust to life. By knowing our past, if we are old enough to have a substantial number of years behind us, we can better understand the full design of the blueprint of this lifetime. When we see, for example, by looking back, that 'this or that' was in our destiny, we can more easily realize, respect and accept that whatever it was, it was meant and made for us. In fact, it was created by us in previous lives via the Law of Karma. The fabric we are now wearing is indeed karmic fabric, sewn from the seeds of prior deeds and motives generated in prior lives, just as the fabric we will wear in future lives is being woven by the motives, deeds and seeds planted in this very life. Such is the Law. We sow; we reap. We plant; we harvest. Inescapably, we are forced to eat the fruit of the very seed we scattered upon the fertile soil of life. Bad see; bad life. Good seed; good life. Pretty simple.

The experiences of this incarnation, especially the negative ones, are not the result of someone else doing bad or rotten things to us devoid of our involvement. Others may be the vehicle for our pain, suffering, tragedy or joy but we, by karmic law, are the root cause of all we experience. As 15th/16th Century Mystic, Guru Nanak, stated: "I blame not another, I blame my own karmas. Whatever I sowed, so did I reap." So it is for each of us.

The acceptance of this awareness releases us from blaming others for our present life and its distasteful, and sometimes poisonous, fruit. Through this awareness we can move into the spiritually mature ground of personal accountability, releasing us from the negative pall of future entanglements. Easy to do? No. Spiritually necessary if we're to grow? Yes.

As much as we would like to think otherwise, there is no such thing as an innocent victim in this world. What we get in this life or in any life, we deserve - purely and simply. Such is the Law of Sowing and Reaping, Cause and Effect, Compensation and Adjustment, Karma. If we have sown bad seed in the past, then it is bad seed we will get in the future, and vice-versa. And if the future happens to be 'now' and it is bitterly delivered to us through the hands or acts of another or others, we would be well-served to accept it, work with it, endure it and, hopefully, not resent it but rather forgive it and learn from it so we do not further entangle ourselves in it by untoward reactions on our part. Says Saint Dadu of the 16th Century, "What thou hast not done will never befall thee; only what thou hast done will befall thee." In modern language this reads, "What you have not done will never befall you; only what you have done will befall you."

Turning the proverbial finger of blame around and pointing it directly at us where it belongs is certainly one of the first major steps on the road to spiritual evolution and liberation. How grateful we should be if this awareness is given to us now while in this life, in this human body, in spite of any discomfort we may experience, so we may acquire the golden opportunity to pay our karmic debts, balance the scales, reconcile the books and gain our freedom so we may move onward in our spiritual ascent, obviating an otherwise certain fall from the great height of human attainment.

Another major benefit of knowing forecasting principles and precepts is that we can guide ourselves and others, especially our children, more efficiently. Having studied the self in *The King's Book of Numerology, Volume I, Foundations & Fundamentals*, and having gained insights on a personal level through an analysis of the Extended Basic Matrix, we can now assist ourselves and others on a personal level. No journey is without its challenges and conflicts, and if one is aware of these, he is better prepared to overcome them, manage them, and not be negatively impacted by them.

Time Periods: AKA-Timelines

From a numerological standpoint, each of our lives passes through very specific time periods and energy fields which are quite calculable. The transitions between these fields can be quite dramatic. During any of our lives it is not uncommon for an energy shift to move to its exact opposite polar field, creating a shift of painful or pleasurable proportions.

For example, shifts from a 1 vibration to a 2, a 4 to a 5 or a 7 to an 8 bring major changes in one's life because the individual numbers in these three pairs are diametrically opposed to their counterparts. Knowing when these shifts are destined to occur can be of immense help in preparing for the new energy or even celebrating the passing of the old. Not knowing of these changes can be devastating, like being overwhelmed and destroyed by a hurricane you never knew was coming as opposed to securing your property, moving to safer ground, and thereby avoiding disaster by virtue of being able to look ahead. The tools of numerology forecasting are much like the satellite tools of weather forecasting. We can't change the storms descending upon us, but through proper forecasting instrumentation we can prepare for them.

Then there is the benefit of knowing and living in the <u>present</u>. The past is dead and gone, the future never really comes. We live, constantly and forever, in the 'ever-present, present' - the Eternal Now. Our minds may be elsewhere - dwelling in the past or daydreaming in the future - but the present never escapes us, for it is in the 'ever-present, present' that all living takes place. The present is the critical tense of life. Within its eternal embrace, we think, act, react, create, sow, reap, laugh, cry, suffer, live and die. It's where we need to be if we're to be Self-Realized. It is the skin which clothes us, and we cannot step outside it until we learn, spiritually, to rise above it. Therefore, it is crucial to understand it and work carefully within it.

The Past is history;

the Future, a mystery,

but the Now is a gift,

and that's why it's called --

the Present.

~ Anonymous

One of the great advantages of seeing and knowing where we are in the present is that we can work with the energies as they unfold daily in our lives. We can see precisely how numbers and their accompanying vibrations are manifested. We can learn about our personal cycles and the recurring lessons, energies, circumstances and situations they bring as well.

Speaking of events and cycles, we cannot change or control them, but we can control our reactions to them. . . as they happen, something we cannot do with the past or the future. It is in the present that our learning and sowing take place, so knowing the precise energies in our lives at any given time can help to facilitate our personal life-education process by giving us instant feedback.

In consideration of our reaction to life's events, if, through our forecasting awareness and skill, we know that our current day, month or year is going to be potentially filled with conflict with others, for example, we can focus more carefully and acutely on patience, tolerance, kindness, discipline, restraint and self-control so when the circumstances of the conflict present themselves and we feel the heat of the moment, we can, as a result of our knowledgeable expectation, breathe deeply, count to ten or a hundred if need be, remain calm and controlled, and not let the situation or its energies throw us out of a balanced focus and run away with us, thereby possibly generating a

King

negative karmic reaction which could return to envelop and haunt us later in this life or some future life.

In effect, to be forewarned is to be forearmed. Preparation is the key to success. Our reactions to events which blind-side us or hit us unsuspectingly are often much different, in a negative way, than those generated as a result of our being prepared and ready. Therefore, by being forewarned, we can fortify ourselves and weather the storms of our lives more easily.

The Theory of Perfect Placement

Another prominent aspect of understanding the time and times of our lives is that we soon learn, through sincere and open-minded study, that we are never out of place in this world, and, in fact, that we are perfectly placed at all times, at every second of our existence. This spiritual principle is called, *The Theory of Perfect Placement.* Simply, it states that we are never in front of where we should be, nor are we ever behind where we think, or society thinks, we ought to be. We travel at the speed of our destiny and we exist exactly where that destiny wants us to exist at every millisecond of our lives. We cannot run faster. We cannot walk slower. We move at Divine Perfect Speed - that speed at which is accomplished all that our fate has designed for us. By learning to live in this theory of Perfect Placement, we can step outside the structures which imbalance us, which make us tense and potentially neurotic. We can get out of the way of our lives and allow them to flow, as we flow with them. We can then choose not to fight the currents of our destiny, nor force them, nor swim against them. Rather, we can flow with them and achieve a sense of wisdom and peace in the process.

To be sure, this life skill of flowing, not fighting or forcing our lives, is difficult to learn. We are brought up to push against the force of our lives, to take what we want when we want it. And do we ever pay for our pushing and lack of spiritual insight! Thinking we are in control of our destiny, and being driven by our selfish desires and motives, we push and shove and huff and puff and, in the end, often end up blowing our own house down, the house of our spiritual well-being, while simultaneously planting negative seeds, the fruit of which we will have to harvest in a future life and time. And whom do we blame for all our trouble? Where does the proverbial 'finger of blame' point? Where does the focus of our rage rest? If we look around, it is sadly and painfully easy to see. God pity and have mercy on us all.

By fighting our destiny and not flowing with it, we generate more ills than we know. Our physical health suffers - maybe not in the beginning but certainly in the end. Our emotionally imbalanced states of being cause untold suffering and hardship for us as well as others. Our psychological health becomes jeopardized. Our social relations bear tension. Our financial status causes grief. But most of all, our spiritual well-being suffers tragically, for the acts and violations we commit by pushing, shoving, huffing, puffing, growling and howling create an enormous mountain range of karmic debt which may take lifetimes to pay off. By not flowing, we end up sowing the seeds of future turmoil, boiling in the oil of our own creation.

When we become aware of the blueprint of our lives and we understand its inescapable design (our destiny) we have the opportunity to learn and live by this theory of Perfect Placement. We may not like what our destiny has given us (in effect what we created for ourselves) but, nonetheless, we are stuck with it, and the sooner we adjust to it and flow with it, not fight it, the more content we will be. This is the essence and essential beauty of the following maxim:

> God, grant me the serenity
> to accept the things I cannot change;
> the courage to change the things I can,
> and the wisdom to know the difference.

Free Will

When we talk of the destiny of life, the question of free will always arises, especially when we are beginning on the path of self-realization. When we 'see' and eventually experience our destiny through our numbers, our point of view becomes much more defined in favor of a predetermined principle underlying all life.

Mystic Masters tell us that life is fixed to the breath, that not only are the hairs on our head numbered, but the steps we are to walk, the breaths we are to breathe, every cent we are to gain and lose, the heartbeats allotted to us, and the morsels of food we are to eat in life are established long before we are born into this incarnation. Any free will we have is, at best, limited free will in as much as we can control our reactions to the events of our lives but nothing else. All else is fixed and beyond personal manipulation.

For those scientists and academics skeptical of a predestined life, Albert Einstein, the preeminent scientist of the 20th Century, Nobel Laureate and Time Magazine's Person of the Twentieth Century, confirms what mystic masters have always taught:

King

> *Everything is determined, the beginning as well as the end, by forces*
> *over which we have no control. It is determined for the insect, as well*
> *as for the star. Human beings, vegetables or cosmic dust - we all dance*
> *to a mysterious tune, intoned in the distance by an invisible piper.*

And here's an eerily similar quote from 15th Century Mystic, Guru Amardas:

> *God forces his creatures into destined paths of karmas over which*
> *they have no control and which cannot be effaced. Whatever is destined*
> *to take place must take place.*

Interesting, isn't it? Here we have the most famous scientist of the 20th Century and a mystic master who lived five hundred years before him stating almost word for word the same basic concept of a fated existence. In speaking of the predetermination of life, Einstein uses the phrase, "over which we have no control," and Amardas uses the phrase, "over which they have no control!" The only difference in these two phrases is between the pronouns "we" and "they." Amazing.

The analogy Masters often give to explain free will is that of a chess match. When we were placed in this creation, our very first thought and action expressed as much free will as we would ever have, and at that time it could be said we had total free will, even though it was not our will that sent us here in the first place but His. That was eons ago, millions of lives in millions of forms, spanning millions of years.

Our first action, like the first move in a chess match, created a condition causing a reaction in the chess game of our existence. The manifesting reaction to our initial action generated another action which limited our freedom to choose, causing us to make a choice with limited scope. Every new action of ours created yet another reaction and counter action in the universal scheme of things, creating further limitation to our free will and, eventually, like the chess game, bringing us to a place in time and space where we found ourselves being ever restricted and constricted in our movement and choices with a total lack of any free will whatsoever. Ultimately, our lives checkmate us by placing us in an inextricable position.

And so it is in life, except we have been playing this cosmic chess game for so long, generating so many actions, reactions and counter-actions, that we now find ourselves in a precarious situation where we are indelibly bound by the actions we have generated within the entirety of our prior existence and we, for all intents and purposes, have no free will at all. Escape from this creation becomes nearly impossible, let alone the exercise of a free and unrestricted will to do as we please, when we please, where and how we please.

The Great Cosmic Web

The action-reaction process of initiating cause and rebounding effect has, over the course of our existence in this creation, woven a web of beautifully exquisite, inescapable, incarcerating intricacy for each of us. When we see, truly *see*, our life as it is represented in our numerology charts, we cannot help but accept the principle of fate - the pre-determination and pre-destination of life. This may seem to place us in a predicament of hopelessness, but not so. This awareness, coming to the conclusion that we are truly bound to this creation, will, hopefully, serve as a catalyst for us to seek a way out and, as we know, *the way out is in*. This is why Mystic Master Maharaj Charan Singh has admonished us to, "Just live in the creation and get out of it." As the famous Old English writer, Geoffrey Chaucer, stated in his Ballade of Good Counsel, "Here is no home; here is wilderness."

This dimension will never change. It is the proving and purifying ground for the soul. We are all incarcerated in it, and until we are delivered from it, we will never be free. If numerology serves any true spiritual purpose, it is to elucidate the incarcerating framework of this polarized dungeon in which we are held prisoner and point us in the direction of spiritual purification and ultimate soul liberation. This is its greatest purpose and service.

Looking Into The Glass

Numerology does give us the ability to see beyond what we would otherwise know or perceive. It especially allows us to see time and, hence, we can forecast the future in general terms, understand the past and comprehend the present. However, a caveat must be given here. If we do not want to know our future, then we must not look, nor ask someone else to look for us. We may like what we see but, then again, we may not, and what we do see may disturb us more than living in a state of ignorance and unknowing. And, if we acquire the ability to look into the glass, never do we have the right to tell someone else what is in their destiny without their consent. Such wanton and irresponsible behavior will surely bring disastrous results to us karmically.

We cannot change what is in our destiny or anyone's destiny and, therefore, if we are to look into the glass, into the cosmic crystal ball of our lives, there are three main qualities we must possess: responsibility, acceptance and adjustment. The first characteristic, *responsibility*, is vital. Our chart represents our life, and our separate life is our separate responsibility and no one else's.

King

What is there, is there because we put it there, and it is our duty and responsibility to understand this and blame no others. The second is *acceptance* because since we cannot change or alter what we see, we must accept it and work with it. To fight it will only bring discomfort. The third is *adjustment*, for therein lies the way to our private and personal peace. The maxim is: *once we know, we can never not know*, so we will have no option but to adjust to our fate if we are to live a contented and harmonious life.

One final caveat--numerology is only a tool. It can help us understand the way things are, but it cannot help us change them or, more importantly, climb Spirit Mountain and attain our soul's liberation. This we must do by ourselves. We cannot become so involved in the process of foretelling the future or looking into it 'to see what we can see' that we loose sight of the supreme goal of life - God Realization. This human birth is very special but it is also ephemeral. We cannot waste its precious time in being awed by the web of life and destiny. We must, quite the contrary, do our best to extricate ourselves from it by continually striving to lead as pure a life as possible, for if we do not, then it will surely keep us imprisoned for untold eons and further incarnations.

The Timelines

Our lives are interwoven tapestries of cosmic vibration. In The King's Numerology System there are nine major *timelines* at the beginning level which create the warp and woof, the fabric of our lives. These interconnecting *timelines* create layers of vibratory fields of specific (but varying) duration through which we are moved during the course of our destiny. Each of the basic timelines is interlaced with every other timeline, yet each is separate in itself. This intertwining shows how complex our existence truly is and, at the same time, reveals the seemingly unknown secrets and mysteries of our lives and destinies and our journey through them. These nine major timelines are:

The Nine Major Timelines

1	LP	Lifepath Timeline
2	PCTL	Pinnacle/Challenge Timeline
3	ETL	Epoch Timeline
4	NTL	Name Timeline
5	LTL	Letter Timeline
6	DTL	Decade Timeline
7	ATL	Age Timeline
8	UTL	Universal Timeline
9	PTL	Personal Year Timeline

Science & Art

It is these nine major *timelines* which we will engage in the forecasting process and, truly, this is what *numerological forecasting* is - a process of both science and art, the science and art of calculating future influences through the study and analysis of available, pertinent numerological data.

The science of numerology is expressed through its calculations and formulae. The art of numerology is interpreting how the variegated vibratory energy fields of our life and destiny interact with each other as we interact with them.

For example, let's say we were sitting barefooted in a square room with an open roof, one door (closed), and four windows centered on each side of the room, all of which are open. There is no actual floor covering to this room except for the ground, which is soaking wet from the previous night's rain. The sun is high overhead, but the atmospheric temperature is quite cold. Storm clouds come and go spilling rain drops on the umbrella we are using to protect ourselves. Intermittent winds blow through the windows, circling and swirling around on the inside of the room in various directions and patterns. There is a small campfire in the middle of the room to help keep us warm, and we are draped with a very thin wool blanket as we sit barefooted on a large stone block close to the fire.

Given all these variables, how comfortable will we be? What effect will the sun, wind, rain, fire, floor, temperature, blanket, umbrella and stone chair have on us as we seek solace, sans shoes,

King

within our roofless abode? How will all these factors interact with each other and act on us at any given time? To know these things is not science. It is interpretation and speculation. It is art.

So it is with numerology forecasting. The interwoven energy fields of our lives create a myriad of factors, circumstances, situations and events, the outcome of which at any given time is left to the art of diagnosis and prognosis, the former being the examination of the intertwining energy fields represented by the numbers in our lives and the latter being the extension of thought to future moments in time where events can be reasonably determined by previous vibrational archetypes and patterns.

Knowing all this is art. Knowledge and experience will help us in our predictions, our forecasting, but in the end it is still a process of educated guesswork. Knowing the future is tricky because there are an infinite number of vibrational combinations involved at any one time. However, given study, thought, analysis, introspection, reflection, experience and intuition, we do have the capability of getting in the ball park.

It is a fascinating journey looking into the Glass. To be sure, our lives are richly interwoven tapestries of cosmic energy. Like snowflakes, no two lives are identical, nor are any two numerology charts exactly the same. Each person, each entity, each life is an extraordinarily unique work of divine art, and knowing the destiny attached to each is challenging, exciting, stimulating and rewarding.

It is now time to embark on our journey into time. Our first step in forecasting our destiny is in the field of Life Cycle Patterns, the subject of the following chapter. Best wishes, peace and balance to all who choose to make this journey, a thought for which is offered in the following poem on the next page.

Cards of Life

(C) Richard Andrew King

These are the cards your life has dealt,

so these are the cards you play.

There's no use weeping over cards

that were not dealt your way.

Life is destined to the breath--

a truth we must accept

if we're to find some peace of mind

and live without regret.

We all are actors on a stage,

but the Director sets our role.

Our life performance is a script--

it's the nature of the show.

Therefore, we mustn't be distressed:

no two hands are just the same.

When all is finally said and done,

in the end, it's just a game.

So play the cards your life has dealt,

but play them strait and true,

remembering from His own hand

your cards were dealt for you!

And remember, too, it's just a play,

but the secret of the game,

is to gain your Liberation

by remembering His Name.

28

Chapter Two

LIFE CYCLE PATTERNS

It's not true that life is one damn thing after another;

it is one damn thing over and over.

~ Edna St. Vincent Millay

Stone walls do not a prison make

nor iron bars a cage,

minds innocent and quiet

take that for an hermitage.

~ Richard Lovelace

Life is circles and cycles. As the seasons cycle from Spring to Summer to Fall to Winter and back again; as the moon circles and cycles the earth; as the earth circles and cycles the sun; as the tides ebb and flow; as the sun pulsates in its own expansion/contraction phases . . . like hearts; as empires rise and fall; as females endure their personal monthly menstrual flux; as the Wheel of Life and Transmigration go round and round circling and cycling, so does our destiny. These circles and cycles of life, of destiny, are Nature in manifestation. They are inescapable, intransigent, unrelenting and . . . astonishingly, predictable.

Numerology gives us one method of understanding and predicting the circles and cycles of our own lives. How is this so? Because numbers follow their own cyclic flow from zero to nine and back again. As it is no mystery that the new birth of Spring follows the death of Winter, so it is also no mystery that the specific energy patterns comprising our lives (as represented through numbers) flow with the same constancy and sequential perfection. Order is the first law of the universe, and the establishment of order is as specific to human destiny as it is to nature.

In fact, American poetess and playwright Edna St. Vincent Millay correctly surmised, "It's not true that life is one damn thing after another; it is one damn thing over and over." How numerologically precise was her percipient sagacity. In fact, life is the same thing over and over again. Why? Because nature circles through her cycles.

Human life is no different. The divine design present in each of our lives is comprised of recurring cyclical energy patterns manifesting through numbers. In each incarnation God wants us to experience certain situations and learn certain lessons privy only to Him but specific to us alone. This is why we keep experiencing the same things, issues and problems over and over and over again during our lifetime. It's also why we are totally incapable of judging another person's life. To do so, we would have to live within the cyclical energy patterns of that person's destiny. Impossible. Each of our destinies is vibration specific and, therefore, specific only to us. Hence, mystic Charan Singh's comment: "In fact, we do not see things as they are; we see things the way we are," i.e., through the vibrational veils and cycles of our own life blueprint.

In a very real way these circles and cycles imprison us, entrap us in a framework of natural origin and design, a framework that is truly inescapable in a mundane sense. Seventeenth Century poet Richard Lovelace writes in his poem 'To Althea form Prison': "Stone walls do not a prison make nor iron bars a cage; minds innocent and quiet take that for an hermitage." It is true. Stone walls and iron bars are not the only materials incarcerating us. Cosmic energy fields, invisible to the naked eye and lying beyond the realm of general understanding, also incarcerate us in a prison of vibratory form, perhaps making us wish we did live in a prison made simply of stone walls and iron bars. To be sure, the prison of our destiny is composed of material far stronger and more powerful than brick, iron, steel or any man-made substance.

The Nine Life Cycle Patterns (LCPs)

In understanding the many intricate circles, cycles and timelines of our lives, we first need to understand the nine Life Cycle Patterns - the recurring, measurable, definable, describable, cyclic archetypes of our existence. These LCPs create a structure of Influence and Outcome, Cause and Effect, Action and Reaction, Theme and Reality within each of our lives as they play themselves out on the great life stage. LCPs are critical to our forecasting ability, as well as to our basic understanding of how each of us responds generally to specific energies in our lives.

Life Cycle Patterns are a major construct of our destiny and there is no varying from them. They are present in every major timeline within the destiny blueprint. When we know a person's LCP we gain many valuable clues as to how he may generally behave under certain conditions and in response to certain stimuli. We can also determine how people will behave toward each other and how interpersonal relationships will be effected. Assets and liabilities in individuals and their relationships become known factors which can be utilized to achieve greater understanding and harmony between the parties concerned. To be sure, possessing a working knowledge of Life Cycle Patterns is acutely important to the accuracy of numerological forecasting analyses.

Life Cycle Patterns (LCPs) have two fields: an influencing, incoming, causal energy defining the issues and themes to be managed, and an outgoing, outcome or effect energy which defines the realities, eventualities and performances the individual will create and come to know through direct experience. These patterns, all originating with the number One (Causal vibration) have nine components each. The labels of the patterns are:

Life Cycle Pattern Labels

Top row - Influencing energy	1	1	1	1	1	1	1	1	1
Expression	[+9]	[+1]	[+2]	[+3]	[+4]	[+5]	[+6]	[+7]	[+8]
Bottom row - Outcome energy	1	2	3	4	5	6	7	8	9

The first pattern is called a 1/1 pattern, the result of a 9 Expression. The second in sequence is a 1/2, the result of a 1 Expression. The third, a 1/3, the result of a 2 Expression and so forth. How is each pattern formed? As we see, simply by adding the individual's Simple Expression to the number One.

For example, if a person's Simple Expression is a Two, then his LCP would be a 1/3 (1 + 2 = 3). If a person's Simple Expression is a Five, then his Life Cycle Pattern would be a 1/6 (1 + 5 = 6). If his Simple Expression is a Seven, then his LCP would be a 1/8 (1 + 7 = 8). All nine LCPs are listed in the following chart.

King

The Nine Life Cycle Patterns

If your Expression is a	Your Life Cycle Pattern is a
1	1/2
2	1/3
3	1/4
4	1/5
5	1/6
6	1/7
7	1/8
8	1/9
9	1/1

Within the basic structure of the nine life cycle patterns there are a total of eighty-one combinations referred to as IR Sets (Influence/Reality) - nine LCPs each comprised of nine influencing ciphers and nine outcome ciphers (nine times nine equals eighty-one). In other words, each LCP contains nine IR sets. These Life Cycle Patterns and their IR sets are charted below. Following each LCP is a discussion of how to interpret them.

In the chart below, notice that the top row of each LCP will always have the numbers one through nine in sequence (1-2-3-4-5-6-7-8-9). These numbers represent the energies of varying timelines in each person's destiny. They identify the influences, issues, causes and themes of the timeline in question, timelines which we will study in due course.

The bottom row of each LCP will be sequential but not identical to the top row (except for Nine Expression people). As stated earlier, the numbers in the bottom row will be determined by the addition of the Simple Expression cipher to the basic number in the top row above it. These bottom row ciphers identify the outcome, effect, reality and experience created by the individual when the influencing cipher (top) combines with his/her Expression cipher. The 9 Life Cycle Pattern will always have identical rows because 9 plus any number always equals that number (1+9=10>1; 2+9=11>2; 3+9=12>3 and so forth). This may be confusing but it will become clear when we actually put the theory to use in studying the Pinnacles, Challenges and Epochs later on in this text.

The Nine Life Cycle Patterns and their I/R Sets

(I-I-C-T Field [top] = Influences-Issues-Causes-Themes)
(O-E-R-E Field [bottom] = Outcome-Effect-Reality-Experience)

1/2 LCP	1 Expression								
I-I-C-T	1	2	3	4	5	6	7	8	9
+ 1 Expression	[1]	[1]	[1]	[1]	[1]	[1]	[1]	[1]	[1]
O-E-R-E	2	3	4	5	6	7	8	9	1

1/3 LCP	2 Expression								
I-I-C-T	1	2	3	4	5	6	7	8	9
+2 Expression	[2]	[2]	[2]	[2]	[2]	[2]	[2]	[2]	[2]
O-E-R-E	3	4	5	6	7	8	9	1	2

1/4 LCP	3 Expression								
I-I-C-T	1	2	3	4	5	6	7	8	9
+3 Expression	[3]	[3]	[3]	[3]	[3]	[3]	[3]	[3]	[3]
O-E-R-E	4	5	6	7	8	9	1	2	3

1/5 LCP	4 Expression								
I-I-C-T	1	2	3	4	5	6	7	8	9
+4 Expression	[4]	[4]	[4]	[4]	[4]	[4]	[4]	[4]	[4]
O-E-R-E	5	6	7	8	9	1	2	3	4

1/6 LCP	5 Expression								
I-I-C-T	1	2	3	4	5	6	7	8	9
+5 Expression	[5]	[5]	[5]	[5]	[5]	[5]	[5]	[5]	[5]
O-E-R-E	6	7	8	9	1	2	3	4	5

1/7 LCP	6 Expression								
I-I-C-T	1	2	3	4	5	6	7	8	9
+6 Expression	[6]	[6]	[6]	[6]	[6]	[6]	[6]	[6]	[6]
O-E-R-E	7	8	9	1	2	3	4	5	6

1/8 LCP	7 Expression								
I-I-C-T	1	2	3	4	5	6	7	8	9
+7 Expression	[7]	[7]	[7]	[7]	[7]	[7]	[7]	[7]	[7]
O-E-R-E	8	9	1	2	3	4	5	6	7

1/9 LCP	8 Expression								
I-I-C-T	1	2	3	4	5	6	7	8	9
+8 Expression	[8]	[8]	[8]	[8]	[8]	[8]	[8]	[8]	[8]
O-E-R-E	9	1	2	3	4	5	6	7	8

1/1 LCP	9 Expression								
I-I-C-T	1	2	3	4	5	6	7	8	9
+9 Expression	[9]	[9]	[9]	[9]	[9]	[9]	[9]	[9]	[9]
O-E-R-E	1	2	3	4	5	6	7	8	9

King

Reading the Life Cycle Patterns

Reading a life cycle pattern is done by beginning with the influencing energy (represented by the top number in the pair) which defines the influences, issues, causes and themes at hand. These numbers will be found in the varying timelines as we will see in our forecasting studies. This influencing cipher can be likened to a mist, cloud or wave of energy encompassing us and/or moving through us.

As the influencing timeline energy filters, funnels, passes through, mixes or combines with each of our Expression numbers, a second energy is created (the bottom number) which identifies the outcome, effect, reality and experience operating in our life. This whole process is simply a mixing of energies - our own with the enveloping vibration. *Energy in* (top number); *reality out* (bottom number).

LCP FORMULA

Influencing Energy [top row] **+ Expression = Outcome Energy** [bottom row]

Individuals or entities with the same Expression will share the same Life Cycle Pattern. For example, all Four (4) Expression individuals will share things in common, just as all Seven (7) Expression people will view life much like their own numerical kind. A Four Expression person will see life and its issues much differently, however, than a Seven Expression individual and vice-versa. And so it is for the entire nine set life cycle spectrum. Yet, there will be differences among people sharing the same LCP because each person's life and numbers are different and, like snowflakes, no two lives are exactly the same. Because there are only nine basic numbers and LCP sets, one ninth of the world's population will have a 1/1 LCP; one ninth will have a 1/2 LCP; one ninth will have a 1/3 LCP etc.

When reading the LCP, use keywords associated with each number, remembering to define the number in the top position - the INFLUENCE cipher - as the issues and themes at hand, and describing the number in the bottom row - the OUTCOME cipher - as the realities and performances to be experienced. In effect, this is the same process used to create the Basic Matrix which was the subject of *The King's Book of Numerology, Volume I: Foundations and Fundamentals* (KBN1) where the Expression plus Lifepath equals the PE (performance/experience).

As a note for simplicity sake, in the LCPs only single ciphers are used. However, for deeper insight the Transition, General and Specific root structures of the numbers can also be applied. Again, these were described in KBN1. To give extensive attention to root systems and their affect on the LCP at this time, however, would cloud the lesson and place the cart before the horse, so the root structures are not treated here other than to say they can and should be used to gain as thorough an analysis as possible when the practitioner is schooled enough to apply them. First, however, we must use the axiom, KISS - keep it super simple. We will get smarter by taking simple steps one at a time.

Also, the numbers of each LCP give general and potential information only, and while the root systems of each set give greater detail of influence and reality, there are simply too many variables and possibilities to see specifics, which is why in Chapter One it is mentioned that "we see through a glass darkly." Yes, we can see, but our vision is obscured not only by our own limited perception but also by the infinite number of possible outcomes in any given energy field.

Additionally, we must keep in mind that, like a coin, each number is intrapolar (two-sided), maintaining a positive and negative aspect within itself. The sides of the number 1 are self-centered absorption (negative) and divine union/oneness (positive); the sides of the number 2 are war (negative) and peace (positive); the number 3, overt vanity (negative) or spiritual integration (positive) and so forth. The operative question then becomes, "Which side of the coin is the person manifesting?" A little of both, perhaps? Then, too, positive people will always see the glass (whatever the glass represents) as half full while less positive individuals will see the glass as half empty. These are issues relating to the level of individual consciousness of the person. Spiritually focused people will always find the silver lining in every cloud, while those less disposed will see only doom and gloom. Therefore, our ability to forecast what the numbers in a chart represent is heavily dependent on the person's attitude for whom we are doing an analysis. Forecasting, then, becomes an act of assessing *potentials*, not certainties and learning to interpret the interaction of numerical fields, an art.

Explanation of LCP Components

Now let's look more closely at how to read a Life Cycle Pattern. Here is a 1/6 LCP, that of a 5 Expression individual.

Influence	1	2	3	4	5	6	7	8	9
Expression	(+5)	(+5)	(+5)	(+5)	(+5)	(+5)	(+5)	(+5)	(+5)
Transition Roots					10	11	12	13	14
Outcome	**6**	**7**	**8**	**9**	**1**	**2**	**3**	**4**	**5**
LCP Simplified	**1/6**	**2/7**	**3/8**	**4/9**	**5/1**	**6/2**	**7/3**	**8/4**	**9/5**

1/6 LCP

When any incoming influence is a One (1), the outgoing realities of a 5 Expression person will be in the arena of the Six (6). This incoming 1 energy could be anything governed by the number One: an authority figure, male (father, grandfather, uncle, brother, husband, male friend), calendar date, any person (regardless of gender) with a 1 Expression, Lifepath or PE; an event whose Expression is also a One; a condition of independence or leadership; a time of new beginnings, and so forth. Whatever the One entity or event is, as it merges with and filters through the 5 energy it will always manifest itself in the energy field of the heart, hearth, home, love life of the person, adjustability, community, art and beauty - i.e. the Six (6).

However, this is only true for a 5 Expression individual. A Six Expression person will see things differently because when the energies of the One (1) enter his life, the outcome energies will be manifested in the energy field of the Seven (7) and its attributes of thought, reflection, introspection, analysis, seclusion, separation, perfection, criticism, mysticism, religion, spirituality, secrecy, privacy, withdrawal and so forth, not the Six (6). Why? Because 1 (incoming energy) + 6 (Expression) = 7 (outcome energy). When the incoming One energy enters the life of a Four (4) Expression person, the outcome will be in the field of the 5 and its attributes of freedom, change, uncertainty, experience, exploration, shifts, movement, the senses and diversification. Why? Because 1 (incoming energy) + 4 (Expression) = 5 (outcome energy field). Got it?

With this understanding it is clear why we all see things differently. Hence the phrase, "we don't see things the way they are; we see things the way we (and our numbers) are." This is one reason why tolerance is so important for each of us. Each of our realities is different! When someone utters the statement, "He just doesn't get it," it's because 'he' is looking through a different set of ciphered-colored glasses. We perceive life from the inside out, not the outside in. Yes, the events of life filter in from the outside but our judgments are made from the inside based on what we perceive as true, not what is necessarily true from a higher perspective. It's therefore a wise decision in life to always cut another person some slack when making judgments. He or she may 'not get it,' as we say, but then again, we may 'not get it' either as seen from the other person's point of view.

2/7 LCP

In the cycle of life, the number One (1) is always followed sequentially of course, by the number Two (2). Therefore, in the case of the 5 Expression individual, the next 1/6 LCP segment of its cycle will be a 2/7 (2 + 5 = 7). This means that when there are incoming, influencing energies relating to issues of the Two (2) - others, the female, yin, relationship, partnership, cooperation, competition, inspiration, support, helping, sharing, balancing, money, kindness and caring, conflict, diplomacy, deception and treachery - they will translate into an outcome/reality of all that the Seven (7) represents: introspection, study, thought, teaching, analysis, patience, poise, peace, disturbance, discomfort, chaos, reflection, separation, solitude, distancing, quiet, shyness, spirituality, religion, creed, dogmas, criticism, secrecy, privacy, trouble, torment, turmoil, tumult and suffering. In this 2/7 IR (influence/reality) set the individual will have to learn to be personally balanced, patient with others, as well as being wary of their deceits, treacheries and hidden agendas. There is the potential of chaos, calamity, ignobility, and heartache under this pattern so one must be careful to exercise poise, patience, tolerance, and discernment. But again, on the up side, there is the extreme potential of total peace (2) and spiritual illumination (7). This 2/7 pattern, however, is only for 5 Expression people. A 6 Expression individual will manifest a 2/8 IR (Influence/Reality) pair in which the outcome of the 2's energies will be in the 8's energy field of commerce, business, social interaction, administration, orchestration, coordination, management and worldly success or failure.

Life Cycle Patterns are wonderful tools. They reveal much about ourselves and our destinies. But, as we've seen, each LCP is *Expression Specific*. LCPs also show us how limited each of us is in our perception of life. This should humble us, calm us down and enhance our capacity for patience, tolerance, understanding, compassion, composure, discipline and self-control. As humans, even though we intrinsically possess divine potentials, we are, nonetheless, finite beings with finite perspectives . . . and our numbers prove it.

Given these examples of how to read the Life Cycle Pattern and its IR sets, let's now proceed to each of the nine LCPs and their general interpretations. The top half of each IR set gives keywords for the *influences* at hand. The bottom half offers keywords for the *outcomes* to be experienced. Keep in mind that the Influencing cipher represents the lessons to be learned or conditions and circumstances which involve us. It does not tell us what will happen. The Outcome cipher tells us what will happen.

Table of Eighty-One
Life Cycle Patterns or IR (Influence/Reality) Sets
General Description

1/2 LCP: (1 Expression)

Influence Energy	1	2	3	4	5	6	7	8	9
Outcome Energy	2	3	4	5	6	7	8	9	1

Set	Notation	Description
1	Influencing Field of Cause; Issues and Themes: ➔	Fire sign: Symbol-Sun; Self, Ego, the Yang (Male energy), Independence, Starts, New Beginnings, Patriarch, Matriarch, Authority, Creativity, Creator, Directness, Leadership, Self-Reliance, Self-Esteem, Union, Yoga, the one who stands alone and is solitary, the maverick, lone wolf, rebel.
2	Outcome Field of Effect; Realities, Experiences, Performances: ➔	Water sign: Symbol-Scales; Others, the Yin (Female energy), Support, Helping/Helper, Relationships, Partnerships, Friendships, Opposing Issues, Competition, Cooperation, Togetherness, Division, Peace/War, Conflict, Tensions; Music, Rhythm.
2	Influencing Field of Cause; Issues and Themes: ➔	Water sign: Symbol-Scales; Others, the Yin (Female energy), Support, Helping/Helper, Relationships, Partnerships, Friendships, Opposing Issues, Competition, Cooperation, Togetherness, Division, Peace/War, Conflict, Tensions; Music, Rhythm.

3	Outcome Field of Effect; Realities, Experiences, Performances: →	Air sign: Symbol-Triangle; Self-Expression, Words, Speech, Communication, Language, Art, Health, Beauty, Disease, Trinity (Father-Son-Holy Ghost; Body-Mind-Spirit), Marriage (Husband-Wife-Marriage), Children (Father-Mother-Children), Pleasure, Enjoyment, Sexuality, Vanity, Beauty, Ease, Positivity/Negativity, Verbal use, abuse, misuse, Happiness/Unhappiness, Holiness and Unholiness, Wholeness and Incompleteness.
3	Influencing Field of Cause; Issues and Themes: →	Air sign: Symbol-Triangle; Self-Expression, Words, Speech, Communication, Language, Art, Health, Beauty, Disease, Trinity (Father-Son-Holy Ghost; Body-Mind-Spirit), Marriage (Husband-Wife-Marriage), Children (Father-Mother-Children), Pleasure, Enjoyment, Sexuality, Vanity, Beauty, Ease, Positivity/Negativity, Verbal use, abuse, misuse, Happiness/Unhappiness, Holiness and Unholiness, Wholeness and Incompleteness.
4	Outcome Field of Effect; Realities, Experiences, Performances: →	Earth sign: Symbol-Square; Construction, Destruction, Work, Effort, Security, Structures, Frameworks, Patterns, Boundaries, Limitations, Routines, Rules, Order, Organization, Devotion, Discipline, Dedication, Matter, Materials, Regularity, Convention, Constriction, Restriction, Tradition, Transformation.
4	Influencing Field of Cause; Issues and Themes: →	Earth sign: Symbol-Square; Construction, Destruction, Work, Effort, Security, Structures, Frameworks, Patterns, Boundaries, Limitations, Routines, Rules, Order, Organization, Devotion, Discipline, Dedication, Matter, Materials, Regularity, Convention, Constriction, Restriction, Tradition, Transformation.
5	Outcome Field of Effect; Realities,	Fire sign: Symbol-Broken Chains; Freedom, Slavery, Detachment, Change, Movement, Motion, Shifts,

	Experiences, Performances: ➜	Shatterings, Senses, Sensation, Sexuality, Exploration, Experience, Excitement, Fun, Friends, Letting Go, Diversity, Variety, Sampling, Uncertainty, Non-Convention, Unrestrained, Unrestricted, Irregular, Restless, Wild, Speed, Revolutionary, Visionary.
5	Influencing Field of Cause; Issues and Themes: ➜	Fire sign: Symbol-Broken Chains; Freedom, Slavery, Detachment, Change, Movement, Motion, Shifts, Shatterings, Senses, Sensation, Sexuality, Exploration, Experience, Excitement, Fun, Friends, Letting Go, Diversity, Variety, Sampling, Uncertainty, Non-Convention, Unrestrained, Unrestricted, Irregular, Restless, Wild, Speed, Revolutionary, Visionary.
6	Outcome Field of Effect; Realities, Experiences, Performances: ➜	Water sign: Symbol-Heart; personal love, romance, home, family, domicile, domesticity, nurturing, support, art, music, community, family responsibility, irresponsibility, hate, jealousy, harmony, inharmony, adjustments.
6	Influencing Field of Cause; Issues and Themes: ➜	Water sign: Symbol-Heart; personal love, romance, home, family, domicile, domesticity, nurturing, support, art, music, community, family responsibility, irresponsibility, hate, jealousy, harmony, inharmony, adjustments.
7	Outcome Field of Effect; Realities, Experiences, Performances: ➜	Air sign: Symbol-Cross; Spirituality, religion, thought, analysis, reflection, introspection, contemplation, questioning, separation, shyness, distancing, disorder, discord, chaos, patience, peace, bliss, poise, perfection, study, teaching, inward seeking; internalization.
7	Influencing Field of Cause; Issues and Themes: ➜	Air sign: Symbol-Cross; Spirituality, religion, thought, analysis, reflection, introspection, contemplation, questioning, separation, shyness, distancing, disorder, discord, chaos, patience, peace, bliss, poise, perfection, study, teaching, inward seeking, internalization.

8	Outcome Field of Effect; Realities, Experiences, Performances: ➜	Earth sign: Symbol-Lemniscate (the horizontal 8). Interaction, connection, coordination, flow, disconnection, social power, material wealth, position and status; being 'in the loop'; management, administration, marketing, efficiency, executive skill, command, generalship, judgment, externalization.
8	Influencing Field of Cause; Issues and Themes: ➜	Earth sign: Symbol-Lemniscate (the horizontal 8). Interaction, connection, disconnection, social power, material wealth, position and status; being 'in the loop'; management, administration, marketing, efficiency, flow, executive, command, generalship, judgment, externalization.
9	Outcome Field of Effect; Realities, Experiences, Performances: ➜	All signs: Symbol-Crown; universality, rulership, humanitarianism, ambition, communication, commonality, completions, endings, finalizations, the 'All', the 'Many', the Macrocosm, the great life stage, literature, art, music, theater, fame, power, drama, recognition, notoriety, impersonal love and giving, benevolence, malevolence, domination, victory.
9	Influencing Field of Cause; Issues and Themes: ➜	All signs: Symbol-Crown; universality, rulership, humanitarianism, ambition, communication, commonality, completions, endings, finalizations, the 'All', the 'Many', the Macrocosm, the great life stage, literature, art, music, theater, fame, power, drama, recognition, notoriety, impersonal love and giving, benevolence, malevolence, domination, victory.
1	Outcome Field of Effect; Realities, Experiences, Performances: ➜	Fire sign: Symbol-Sun; Self, Ego, the Yang (Male energy), Independence, Starts, New Beginnings, Patriarch, Matriarch, Authority, Creativity, Creator, Directness, Leadership, Self-Reliance, Self-Esteem, Union, Yoga, the one who stands alone and is solitary, the maverick, lone wolf, rebel.

1/2 LCP Notes: (1 Expression)

The 1/2 Life Cycle Pattern of the 1 Expression is unique in the sense that it is the only LCP which contains the three pairs of oppositional binaries in which the energies are diametrically opposed to one another. These pairs are: One/Two, Four/Five and Seven/Eight. The One is self, the Two is others (mine and theirs); the Four is convention, the Five is non-convention; the Seven is internal, the Eight is external (socially retiring vs. socially embracing).

Therefore, people who have a One Expression will be constantly engaged in working with and managing the opposing energies of these three number sets. This can be a boon or a bale, a blessing or a curse. To have an understanding of opposites can be extremely beneficial. However, to be relentlessly plagued by such opposing energies can be frustrating, to say the least. Nonetheless, every One Expression person will be confronted with these sets of opposites in their lives to one degree or another. If any of the ciphers is negatively aspected in the chart viz. a viz. being voided or in a challenge position (discussed later), any adverse effects may well be exacerbated.

1/3 LCP: (2 Expression)

Influence Energy	1	2	3	4	5	6	7	8	9
Outcome Energy	3	4	5	6	7	8	9	1	2

1	Influencing Field of Cause; Issues and Themes: ➔	Fire sign: Symbol-Sun; Self, Ego, the Yang (Male energy), Independence, Starts, New Beginnings, Patriarch, Matriarch, Authority, Creativity, Creator, Directness, Leadership, Self-Reliance, Self-Esteem, Union, Yoga, the one who stands alone and is solitary, the maverick, lone wolf, rebel.
3	Outcome Field of Effect; Realities, Experiences, Performances: ➔	Air sign: Symbol-Triangle; Self-Expression, Words, Speech, Communication, Language, Art, Health, Beauty, Disease, Trinity (Father-Son-Holy Ghost; Body-Mind-Spirit), Marriage (Husband-Wife-Marriage), Children (Father-Mother-Children), Pleasure, Enjoyment, Sexuality, Vanity, Beauty, Ease, Positivity/Negativity, Verbal use, abuse, misuse, Happiness/Unhappiness, Holiness and Unholiness, Wholeness and Incompleteness.

2	Influencing Field of Cause; Issues and Themes: ➜	Water sign: Symbol-Scales; Others, the Yin (Female energy), Support, Helping/Helper, Relationships, Partnerships, Friendships, Opposing Issues, Competition, Cooperation, Togetherness, Division, Peace/War, Conflict, Tensions; Music, Rhythm.
4	Outcome Field of Effect; Realities, Experiences, Performances: ➜	Earth sign: Symbol-Square; Construction, Destruction, Work, Effort, Security, Structures, Frameworks, Patterns, Boundaries, Limitations, Routines, Rules, Order, Organization, Devotion, Discipline, Dedication, Matter, Materials, Regularity, Convention, Constriction, Restriction, Tradition, Transformation.
3	Influencing Field of Cause; Issues and Themes: ➜	Air sign: Symbol-Triangle; Self-Expression, Words, Speech, Communication, Language, Art, Health, Beauty, Disease, Trinity (Father-Son-Holy Ghost; Body-Mind-Spirit), Marriage (Husband-Wife-Marriage), Children (Father-Mother-Children), Pleasure, Enjoyment, Sexuality, Vanity, Beauty, Ease, Positivity/Negativity, Verbal use, abuse, misuse, Happiness/Unhappiness, Holiness and Unholiness, Wholeness and Incompleteness.
5	Outcome Field of Effect; Realities, Experiences, Performances: ➜	Fire sign: Symbol-Broken Chains; Freedom, Slavery, Detachment, Change, Movement, Motion, Shifts, Shatterings, Senses, Sensation, Sexuality, Exploration, Experience, Excitement, Fun, Friends, Letting Go, Diversity, Variety, Sampling, Uncertainty, Non-Convention, Unrestrained, Unrestricted, Irregular, Restless, Wild, Speed, Revolutionary, Visionary.
4	Influencing Field of Cause; Issues and Themes: ➜	Earth sign: Symbol-Square; Construction, Destruction, Work, Effort, Security, Structures, Frameworks, Patterns, Boundaries, Limitations, Routines, Rules, Order,

King

			Organization, Devotion, Discipline, Dedication, Matter, Materials, Regularity, Convention, Constriction, Restriction, Tradition, Transformation.
6	Outcome Field of Effect; Realities, Experiences, Performances: ➜		Water sign: Symbol-Heart; personal love, romance, home, family, domicile, domesticity, nurturing, support, art, music, community, family responsibility, irresponsibility, hate, jealousy, harmony, inharmony, adjustments.
5	Influencing Field of Cause; Issues and Themes: ➜		Fire sign: Symbol-Broken Chains; Freedom, Slavery, Detachment, Change, Movement, Motion, Shifts, Shatterings, Senses, Sensation, Sexuality, Exploration, Experience, Excitement, Fun, Friends, Letting Go, Diversity, Variety, Sampling, Uncertainty, Non-Convention, Unrestrained, Unrestricted, Irregular, Restless, Wild, Speed, Revolutionary, Visionary.
7	Outcome Field of Effect; Realities, Experiences, Performances: ➜		Air sign: Symbol-Cross; Spirituality, religion, thought, analysis, reflection, introspection, contemplation, questioning, separation, shyness, distancing, disorder, discord, chaos, patience, peace, bliss, poise, perfection, study, teaching, inward seeking; internalization.
6	Influencing Field of Cause; Issues and Themes: ➜		Water sign: Symbol-Heart; personal love, romance, home, family, domicile, domesticity, nurturing, support, art, music, community, family responsibility, irresponsibility, hate, jealousy, harmony, inharmony, adjustments.
8	Outcome Field of Effect; Realities, Experiences, Performances: ➜		Earth sign: Symbol-Lemniscate (the horizontal 8). Interaction, connection, coordination, flow, disconnection, social power, material wealth, position and status; being 'in the loop'; management, administration, marketing, efficiency, executive skill, command, generalship, judgment, externalization.

The King's Book of Numerology II: Forecasting - Part 1

7	Influencing Field of Cause; Issues and Themes: ➔	Air sign: Symbol-Cross; Spirituality, religion, thought, analysis, reflection, introspection, contemplation, questioning, separation, shyness, distancing, disorder, discord, chaos, patience, peace, bliss, poise, perfection, study, teaching, inward seeking; internalization.
9	Outcome Field of Effect; Realities, Experiences, Performances: ➔	All signs: Symbol-Crown; universality, rulership, humanitarianism, ambition, communication, commonality, completions, endings, finalizations, the 'All', the 'Many', the Macrocosm, the great life stage, literature, art, music, theater, fame, power, drama, recognition, notoriety, impersonal love and giving, benevolence, malevolence, domination, victory.
8	Influencing Field of Cause; Issues and Themes: ➔	Earth sign: Symbol-Lemniscate (the horizontal 8). Interaction, connection, coordination, flow, disconnection, social power, material wealth, position and status; being 'in the loop'; management, administration, marketing, efficiency, executive skill, command, generalship, judgment, externalization.
1	Outcome Field of Effect; Realities, Experiences, Performances: ➔	Fire sign: Symbol-Sun; Self, Ego, the Yang (Male energy), Independence, Starts, New Beginnings, Patriarch, Matriarch, Authority, Creativity, Creator, Directness, Leadership, Self-Reliance, Self-Esteem, Union, Yoga, the one who stands alone and is solitary, the maverick, lone wolf, rebel.
9	Influencing Field of Cause; Issues and Themes: ➔	All signs: Symbol-Crown; universality, rulership, humanitarianism, ambition, communication, commonality, completions, endings, finalizations, the 'All', the 'Many', the Macrocosm, the great life stage, literature, art, music, theater, fame, power, drama, recognition, notoriety, impersonal love and giving, benevolence, malevolence, domination, victory.

2	Outcome Field of Effect; Realities, Experiences, Performances: ➜	Water sign: Symbol-Scales; Others, the Yin (Female energy), Support, Helping/Helper, Relationships, Partnerships, Friendships, Opposing Issues, Competition, Cooperation, Togetherness, Division, Peace/War, Conflict, Tensions; Music, Rhythm.

1/3 LCP Notes: (2 Expression)

Through observation of the 1/3 LCP sets, we can see why the Two is such a helper/relationship-oriented energy. For example, if we look at the Influencing position of the social numbers 2-4-6, we see that they play themselves out in the realm of the social 4-6-8 triad. In other words, the outcome of the 2 influence is the 4 energy of work, effort, frameworks, devotion, dedication, faithfulness, routine, structures, organization and so forth. The 4 influence energy plays itself out in the domain of the 6 outcome vibration of love, nurturing and domestic responsibility, and when the 6 energy is in the influence position, it's outcome is in the field of the 8 vibration of interaction, connection, disconnection, social power, management, coordination, circulation and general flow. Therefore, the 2 Expression is much of the time involved with other social energies, particularly the ones dealing with devotion, love and interaction. The numbers 2-4-6-8 are generally regarded as social ciphers, while the numbers 1-3-5-7-9 are principally seen as more creative and individualistic energies.

Also notice that the 9 influence energy plays itself out in the energy field of the 2. In other words, when it comes to humanity in general, the 'many' and the 'all', the 2 Expression does so by being supportive, as witnessed by the 2 in the outcome position of the 9/2 set within this 1/3 life cycle pattern. On the flip side, the negative aspects of his IR set include dissent, deceit, interference, tension, war, argumentation, antagonism and conflict.

Within the 8/1 set we see that when interaction with others is concerned, the 2 Expression person takes the leadership role as shown by the 1 Outcome position within the set. The caution here is that the 1 outcome can also spell self-centeredness.

1/4 LCP: (3 Expression)

Influence Energy	1	2	3	4	5	6	7	8	9
Outcome Energy	4	5	6	7	8	9	1	2	3

1	Influencing Field of Cause; Issues and Themes: ➜	Fire sign: Symbol-Sun; Self, Ego, the Yang (Male energy), Independence, Starts, New Beginnings, Patriarch, Matriarch, Authority, Creativity, Creator, Directness, Leadership, Self-Reliance, Self-Esteem, Union, Yoga, the one who stands alone and is solitary, the maverick, lone wolf, rebel.
4	Outcome Field of Effect; Realities, Experiences, Performances: ➜	Earth sign: Symbol-Square; Construction, Destruction, Work, Effort, Security, Structures, Frameworks, Patterns, Boundaries, Limitations, Routines, Rules, Order, Organization, Devotion, Discipline, Dedication, Matter, Materials, Regularity, Convention, Constriction, Restriction, Tradition, Transformation.
2	Influencing Field of Cause; Issues and Themes: ➜	Water sign: Symbol-Scales; Others, the Yin (Female energy), Support, Helping/Helper, Relationships, Partnerships, Friendships, Opposing Issues, Competition, Cooperation, Togetherness, Division, Peace/War, Conflict, Tensions; Music, Rhythm.
5	Outcome Field of Effect; Realities, Experiences, Performances: ➜	Fire sign: Symbol-Broken Chains; Freedom, Slavery, Detachment, Change, Movement, Motion, Shifts, Shatterings, Senses, Sensation, Sexuality, Exploration, Experience, Excitement, Fun, Friends, Letting Go, Diversity, Variety, Sampling, Uncertainty, Non-Convention, Unrestrained, Unrestricted, Irregular, Restless, Wild, Speed, Revolutionary, Visionary.
3	Influencing Field of Cause; Issues and	Air sign: Symbol-Triangle; Self-Expression, Words, Speech, Communication, Language, Art, Health, Beauty, Disease,

	Themes: ➔	Trinity (Father-Son-Holy Ghost; Body-Mind-Spirit), Marriage (Husband-Wife-Marriage), Children (Father-Mother-Children), Pleasure, Enjoyment, Sexuality, Vanity, Beauty, Ease, Positivity/Negativity, Verbal use, abuse, misuse, Happiness/Unhappiness, Holiness and Unholiness, Wholeness and Incompleteness.
6	Outcome Field of Effect; Realities, Experiences, Performances: ➔	Water sign: Symbol-Heart; personal love, romance, home, family, domicile, domesticity, nurturing, support, art, music, community, family responsibility, irresponsibility, hate, jealousy, harmony, inharmony, adjustments.
4	Influencing Field of Cause; Issues and Themes: ➔	Earth sign: Symbol-Square; Construction, Destruction, Work, Effort, Security, Structures, Frameworks, Patterns, Boundaries, Limitations, Routines, Rules, Order, Organization, Devotion, Discipline, Dedication, Matter, Materials, Regularity, Convention, Constriction, Restriction, Tradition, Transformation.
7	Outcome Field of Effect; Realities, Experiences, Performances: ➔	Air sign: Symbol-Cross; Spirituality, religion, thought, analysis, reflection, introspection, contemplation, questioning, separation, shyness, distancing, disorder, discord, chaos, patience, peace, bliss, poise, perfection, study, teaching, inward seeking; internalization.
5	Influencing Field of Cause; Issues and Themes: ➔	Fire sign: Symbol-Broken Chains; Freedom, Slavery, Detachment, Change, Movement, Motion, Shifts, Shatterings, Senses, Sensation, Sexuality, Exploration, Experience, Excitement, Fun, Friends, Letting Go, Diversity, Variety, Sampling, Uncertainty, Non-Convention, Unrestrained, Unrestricted, Irregular, Restless, Wild, Speed, Revolutionary, Visionary.
8	Outcome Field of Effect; Realities, Experiences, Performances: ➔	Earth sign: Symbol-Lemniscate (the horizontal 8). Interaction, connection, coordination, flow, disconnection, social power, material wealth, position and status; being 'in

		the loop'; management, administration, marketing, efficiency, executive skill, command, generalship, judgment, externalization.
6	Influencing Field of Cause; Issues and Themes: ➜	Water sign: Symbol-Heart; personal love, romance, home, family, domicile, domesticity, nurturing, support, art, music, community, family responsibility, irresponsibility, hate, jealousy, harmony, inharmony, adjustments.
9	Outcome Field of Effect; Realities, Experiences, Performances: ➜	All signs: Symbol-Crown; universality, rulership, humanitarianism, ambition, communication, commonality, completions, endings, finalizations, the 'All', the 'Many', the Macrocosm, the great life stage, literature, art, music, theater, fame, power, drama, recognition, notoriety, impersonal love and giving, benevolence, malevolence, domination, victory.
7	Influencing Field of Cause; Issues and Themes: ➜	Air sign: Symbol-Cross; Spirituality, religion, thought, analysis, reflection, introspection, contemplation, questioning, separation, shyness, distancing, disorder, discord, chaos, patience, peace, bliss, poise, perfection, study, teaching, inward seeking; internalization.
1	Outcome Field of Effect; Realities, Experiences, Performances: ➜	Fire sign: Symbol-Sun; Self, Ego, the Yang (Male energy), Independence, Starts, New Beginnings, Patriarch, Matriarch, Authority, Creativity, Creator, Directness, Leadership, Self-Reliance, Self-Esteem, Union, Yoga, the one who stands alone and is solitary, the maverick, lone wolf, rebel.
8	Influencing Field of Cause; Issues and Themes: ➜	Earth sign: Symbol-Lemniscate (the horizontal 8). Interaction, connection, coordination, flow, disconnection, social power, material wealth, position and status; being 'in the loop'; management, administration, marketing, efficiency, executive skill, command, generalship, judgment, externalization.

King

50

2	Outcome Field of Effect; Realities, Experiences, Performances: ➜	Water sign: Symbol-Scales; Others, the Yin (Female energy), Support, Helping/Helper, Relationships, Partnerships, Friendships, Opposing Issues, Competition, Cooperation, Togetherness, Division, Peace/War, Conflict, Tensions; Music, Rhythm.
9	Influencing Field of Cause; Issues and Themes: ➜	All signs: Symbol-Crown; universality, rulership, humanitarianism, ambition, communication, commonality, completions, endings, finalizations, the 'All', the 'Many', the Macrocosm, the great life stage, literature, art, music, theater, fame, power, drama, recognition, notoriety, impersonal love and giving, benevolence, malevolence, domination, victory.
3	Outcome Field of Effect; Realities, Experiences, Performances: ➜	Air sign: Symbol-Triangle; Self-Expression, Words, Speech, Communication, Language, Art, Health, Beauty, Disease, Trinity (Father-Son-Holy Ghost; Body-Mind-Spirit), Marriage (Husband-Wife-Marriage), Children (Father-Mother-Children), Pleasure, Enjoyment, Sexuality, Vanity, Beauty, Ease, Positivity/Negativity, Verbal use, abuse, misuse, Happiness/Unhappiness, Holiness and Unholiness, Wholeness and Incompleteness.

1/4 LCP Notes: (3 Expression)

The 3 Expression has always been associated with health, beauty, words, communication, pleasure, enjoyment, friends and good times. The 1/4 LCP sets give many reasons why this is so.

First of all, when we look at the influence position of the numbers 3-6-9, we see that they play themselves out in the respective energy fields of the 6-9-3. The 3-6-9 triad is the modality of artistry, self-expression, love, words, communication and beauty, and as is visibly clear, both the influence and outcome of the Three, Six and Nine in the 1/4 LCP are the exact components of the 3-6-9 artistic, self-expressive, communicative triad.

Specifically, when the 3 influence of words, art, communication and self-expression comes due in a 1/4 LCP life, its outcome is in the energy field of the 6 - love, romance, matters of the
The King's Book of Numerology II: Forecasting - Part 1

heart, beauty, care and nurturing. When the 6 is in the influence position, its outcome is in the 9 field of humanity, drama, the arts, the All, the Many. The influencing 9 energy manifests in a 3 outcome field. Therefore, the 1/4 LCP is extremely strong in art, beauty, love, humanity and everything universal.

Furthermore, in the 8 influencing field of social interaction, the outcome is in the 2 arena of others, support, service, helping, partnership and relationship. This is expressed in the 8/2 modality set of the 1/4 LCP with its Three Expression.

The 5 energy of freedom, fun, excitement, diversity, exploration, experimentation, experience and change also gives more understanding. In the influence position the 5's outcome is social interaction, connection, wealth, power, worldly success and comfort as manifested in the 5/8 modality set. Therefore, there will always be a variety of successful options for the 3 Expression and its 1/4 LCP. Too, the 5's outcome position is generated from the 2 influence energy - the field of others, help and support in the 2/5 pattern. Thus, it will be expected that the 3 Expression will have a diversity of relationships, especially of the Yin type because 2 rules female energy.

1/5 LCP: (4 Expression)

Influence Energy	1	2	3	4	5	6	7	8	9
Outcome Energy	5	6	7	8	9	1	2	3	4

1	Influencing Field of Cause; Issues and Themes: ➔	Fire sign: Symbol-Sun; Self, Ego, the Yang (Male energy), Independence, Starts, New Beginnings, Patriarch, Matriarch, Authority, Creativity, Creator, Directness, Leadership, Self-Reliance, Self-Esteem, Union, Yoga, the one who stands alone and is solitary, the maverick, lone wolf, rebel.
5	Outcome Field of Effect; Realities, Experiences, Performances: ➔	Fire sign: Symbol-Broken Chains; Freedom, Slavery, Detachment, Change, Movement, Motion, Shifts, Shatterings, Senses, Sensation, Sexuality, Exploration, Experience, Excitement, Fun, Friends, Letting Go, Diversity, Variety, Sampling, Uncertainty, Non-Convention, Unrestrained, Unrestricted, Irregular,

		Restless, Wild, Speed, Revolutionary, Visionary.
2	Influencing Field of Cause; Issues and Themes: ➜	Water sign: Symbol-Scales; Others, the Yin (Female energy), Support, Helping/Helper, Relationships, Partnerships, Friendships, Opposing Issues, Competition, Cooperation, Togetherness, Division, Peace/War, Conflict, Tensions; Music, Rhythm.
6	Outcome Field of Effect; Realities, Experiences, Performances: ➜	Water sign: Symbol-Heart; personal love, romance, home, family, domicile, domesticity, nurturing, support, art, music, community, family responsibility, irresponsibility, hate, jealousy, harmony, inharmony, adjustments.
3	Influencing Field of Cause; Issues and Themes: ➜	Air sign: Symbol-Triangle; Self-Expression, Words, Speech, Communication, Language, Art, Health, Beauty, Disease, Trinity (Father-Son-Holy Ghost; Body-Mind-Spirit), Marriage (Husband-Wife-Marriage), Children (Father-Mother-Children), Pleasure, Enjoyment, Sexuality, Vanity, Beauty, Ease, Positivity/Negativity, Verbal use, abuse, misuse, Happiness/Unhappiness, Holiness and Unholiness, Wholeness and Incompleteness.
7	Outcome Field of Effect; Realities, Experiences, Performances: ➜	Air sign: Symbol-Cross; Spirituality, religion, thought, analysis, reflection, introspection, contemplation, questioning, separation, shyness, distancing, disorder, discord, chaos, patience, peace, bliss, poise, perfection, study, teaching, inward seeking, internalization.
4	Influencing Field of Cause; Issues and Themes: ➜	Earth sign: Symbol-Square; Construction, Destruction, Work, Effort, Security, Structures, Frameworks, Patterns, Boundaries, Limitations, Routines, Rules, Order, Organization, Devotion, Discipline, Dedication, Matter,

		Materials, Regularity, Convention, Constriction, Restriction, Tradition, Transformation.
8	Outcome Field of Effect; Realities, Experiences, Performances: ➜	Earth sign: Symbol-Lemniscate (the horizontal 8). Interaction, connection, disconnection, social power, material wealth, position and status; being 'in the loop'; management, administration, marketing, efficiency, flow, executive, command, generalship, judgment, externalization.
5	Influencing Field of Cause; Issues and Themes: ➜	Fire sign: Symbol-Broken Chains; Freedom, Slavery, Detachment, Change, Movement, Motion, Shifts, Shatterings, Senses, Sensation, Sexuality, Exploration, Experience, Excitement, Fun, Friends, Letting Go, Diversity, Variety, Sampling, Uncertainty, Non-Convention, Unrestrained, Unrestricted, Irregular, Restless, Wild, Speed, Revolutionary, Visionary.
9	Outcome Field of Effect; Realities, Experiences, Performances: ➜	All signs: Symbol-Crown; universality, rulership, humanitarianism, ambition, communication, commonality, completions, endings, finalizations, the 'All', the 'Many', the Macrocosm, the great life stage, literature, art, music, theater, fame, power, drama, recognition, notoriety, impersonal love and giving, benevolence, malevolence, domination, victory.
6	Influencing Field of Cause; Issues and Themes: ➜	Water sign: Symbol-Heart; personal love, romance, home, family, domicile, domesticity, nurturing, support, art, music, community, family responsibility, irresponsibility, hate, jealousy, harmony, inharmony, adjustments.
1	Outcome Field of Effect; Realities, Experiences, Performances: ➜	Fire sign: Symbol-Sun; Self, Ego, the Yang (Male energy), Independence, Starts, New Beginnings, Patriarch, Matriarch, Authority, Creativity, Creator,

		Directness, Leadership, Self-Reliance, Self-Esteem, Union, Yoga, the one who stands alone and is solitary, the maverick, lone wolf, rebel.
7	Influencing Field of Cause; Issues and Themes: ➔	Air sign: Symbol-Cross; Spirituality, religion, thought, analysis, reflection, introspection, contemplation, questioning, separation, shyness, distancing, disorder, discord, chaos, patience, peace, bliss, poise, perfection, study, teaching, inward seeking, internalization.
2	Outcome Field of Effect; Realities, Experiences, Performances: ➔	Water sign: Symbol-Scales; Others, the Yin (Female energy), Support, Helping/Helper, Relationships, Partnerships, Friendships, Opposing Issues, Competition, Cooperation, Togetherness, Division, Peace/War, Conflict, Tensions; Music, Rhythm.
8	Influencing Field of Cause; Issues and Themes: ➔	Earth sign: Symbol-Lemniscate (the horizontal 8). Interaction, connection, disconnection, social power, material wealth, position and status; being 'in the loop'; management, administration, marketing, efficiency, flow, executive, command, generalship, judgment, externalization.
3	Outcome Field of Effect; Realities, Experiences, Performances: ➔	Air sign: Symbol-Triangle; Self-Expression, Words, Speech, Communication, Language, Art, Health, Beauty, Disease, Trinity (Father-Son-Holy Ghost; Body-Mind-Spirit), Marriage (Husband-Wife-Marriage), Children (Father-Mother-Children), Pleasure, Enjoyment, Sexuality, Vanity, Beauty, Ease, Positivity/Negativity, Verbal use, abuse, misuse, Happiness/Unhappiness, Holiness and Unholiness, Wholeness and Incompleteness.

9	Influencing Field of Cause; Issues and Themes: ➔	All signs: Symbol-Crown; universality, rulership, humanitarianism, ambition, communication, commonality, completions, endings, finalizations, the 'All', the 'Many', the Macrocosm, the great life stage, literature, art, music, theater, fame, power, drama, recognition, notoriety, impersonal love and giving, benevolence, malevolence, domination, victory.
4	Outcome Field of Effect; Realities, Experiences, Performances: ➔	Earth sign: Symbol-Square; Construction, Destruction, Work, Effort, Security, Structures, Frameworks, Patterns, Boundaries, Limitations, Routines, Rules, Order, Organization, Devotion, Discipline, Dedication, Matter, Materials, Regularity, Convention, Constriction, Restriction, Tradition, Transformation.

1/5 LCP Notes: (4 Expression)

The 1/5 LCP is derived from the 4 Expression. Four is the vibration of work, service, organization, structure, security, framework, discipline, dedication, loyalty, devotion, limitation, order, regimentation, rules, routines and boundaries. The first thing of note here is that when the 4 is in the influence position, the outcome is an 8, basically the 4 doubled. Thus, the worker 4 will be efficient and connective during a 4/8 energy period. This 4/8 pattern also explains why so many extremely wealthy people have dominate Four energy in their chart. This is because the Four energy translates into the Eight energy of material wealth, comfort, success, administration, social status and power.

Where do security issues of the Four originate? From the 9 (see the 9/4 set). This means that security (4) is the outcome of power, dominance, personal integration, the masses and the public stage. This also explains why the 4 Expression can be very stubborn -- duty (4) is a derivative of power (9). No number is as potentially more stubborn or unyielding as the Four.

In the matter of domestic matters, the Four usually becomes the leader, matriarch or patriarch as a result of the 6/1 modality configuration. In this IR set the 6 energy of heart, hearth, home, love, family, domesticity and nurturing plays itself out in the arena of the 1, the vibration of the leader, the one who goes first and shows the way, the doer, the independent one, the boss or head of household. Given the Four's propensity for organization and order, it is quite understandable why

King

the Four is dominate and strong in matters of structure, frame, form, rules, regulations, discipline and duty.

And what does the Four Expression do in the field of relationships and others? It serves, supports, loves and nurtures as is characterized by its 2/6 modality.

It is interesting to see how the 6 energy of love is manifested in a Four Expression. On the one hand in the 2/6 mode it is the nurturer in relationships, and when the 6 energy of nurturing expresses itself through the influence position, the Four person becomes the leader (6/1 modality).

1/6 LCP: (5 Expression)

Influence Energy	1	2	3	4	5	6	7	8	9
Outcome Energy	6	7	8	9	1	2	3	4	5

1	Influencing Field of Cause; Issues and Themes: ➜	Fire sign: Symbol-Sun; Self, Ego, the Yang (Male energy), Independence, Starts, New Beginnings, Patriarch, Matriarch, Authority, Creativity, Creator, Directness, Leadership, Self-Reliance, Self-Esteem, Union, Yoga, the one who stands alone and is solitary, the maverick, lone wolf, rebel.
6	Outcome Field of Effect; Realities, Experiences, Performances: ➜	Water sign: Symbol-Heart; personal love, romance, home, family, domicile, domesticity, nurturing, support, art, music, community, family responsibility, irresponsibility, hate, jealousy, harmony, inharmony, adjustments.
2	Influencing Field of Cause; Issues and Themes: ➜	Water sign: Symbol-Scales; Others, the Yin (Female energy), Support, Helping/Helper, Relationships, Partnerships, Friendships, Opposing Issues, Competition, Cooperation, Togetherness, Division, Peace/War, Conflict, Tensions; Music, Rhythm.
7	Outcome Field of Effect; Realities, Experiences, Performances: ➜	Air sign: Symbol-Cross; Spirituality, religion, thought, analysis, reflection, introspection, contemplation, questioning, separation, shyness, distancing, disorder,

		discord, chaos, patience, peace, bliss, poise, perfection, study, teaching, inward seeking; internalization.
3	Influencing Field of Cause; Issues and Themes: ➔	Air sign: Symbol-Triangle; Self-Expression, Words, Speech, Communication, Language, Art, Health, Beauty, Disease, Trinity (Father-Son-Holy Ghost; Body-Mind-Spirit), Marriage (Husband-Wife-Marriage), Children (Father-Mother-Children), Pleasure, Enjoyment, Sexuality, Vanity, Beauty, Ease, Positivity/Negativity, Verbal use, abuse, misuse, Happiness/Unhappiness, Holiness and Unholiness, Wholeness and Incompleteness.
8	Outcome Field of Effect; Realities, Experiences, Performances: ➔	Earth sign: Symbol-Lemniscate (the horizontal 8). Interaction, connection, coordination, flow, disconnection, social power, material wealth, position and status; being 'in the loop'; management, administration, marketing, efficiency, executive skill, command, generalship, judgment, externalization.
4	Influencing Field of Cause; Issues and Themes: ➔	Earth sign: Symbol-Square; Construction, Destruction, Work, Effort, Security, Structures, Frameworks, Patterns, Boundaries, Limitations, Routines, Rules, Order, Organization, Devotion, Discipline, Dedication, Matter, Materials, Regularity, Convention, Constriction, Restriction, Tradition, Transformation.
9	Outcome Field of Effect; Realities, Experiences, Performances: ➔	All signs: Symbol-Crown; universality, rulership, humanitarianism, ambition, communication, commonality, completions, endings, finalizations, the 'All', the 'Many', the Macrocosm, the great life stage, literature, art, music, theater, fame, power, drama, recognition, notoriety, impersonal love and giving, benevolence, malevolence, domination, victory.

King

58

5	Influencing Field of Cause; Issues and Themes: ➔	Fire sign: Symbol-Broken Chains; Freedom, Slavery, Detachment, Change, Movement, Motion, Shifts, Shatterings, Senses, Sensation, Sexuality, Exploration, Experience, Excitement, Fun, Friends, Letting Go, Diversity, Variety, Sampling, Uncertainty, Non-Convention, Unrestrained, Unrestricted, Irregular, Restless, Wild, Speed, Revolutionary, Visionary.
1	Outcome Field of Effect; Realities, Experiences, Performances: ➔	Fire sign: Symbol-Sun; Self, Ego, the Yang (Male energy), Independence, Starts, New Beginnings, Patriarch, Matriarch, Authority, Creativity, Creator, Directness, Leadership, Self-Reliance, Self-Esteem, Union, Yoga, the one who stands alone and is solitary, the maverick, lone wolf, rebel.
6	Influencing Field of Cause; Issues and Themes: ➔	Water sign: Symbol-Heart; personal love, romance, home, family, domicile, domesticity, nurturing, support, art, music, community, family responsibility, irresponsibility, hate, jealousy, harmony, inharmony, adjustments.
2	Outcome Field of Effect; Realities, Experiences, Performances: ➔	Water sign: Symbol-Scales; Others, the Yin (Female energy), Support, Helping/Helper, Relationships, Partnerships, Friendships, Opposing Issues, Competition, Cooperation, Togetherness, Division, Peace/War, Conflict, Tensions; Music, Rhythm.
7	Influencing Field of Cause; Issues and Themes: ➔	Air sign: Symbol-Cross; Spirituality, religion, thought, analysis, reflection, introspection, contemplation, questioning, separation, shyness, distancing, disorder, discord, chaos, patience, peace, bliss, poise, perfection, study, teaching, inward seeking; internalization.
3	Outcome Field of Effect; Realities, Experiences, Performances: ➔	Air sign: Symbol-Triangle; Self-Expression, Words, Speech, Communication, Language, Art, Health, Beauty, Disease, Trinity (Father-Son-Holy Ghost; Body-Mind-

The King's Book of Numerology II: Forecasting - Part 1

		Spirit), Marriage (Husband-Wife-Marriage), Children (Father-Mother-Children), Pleasure, Enjoyment, Sexuality, Vanity, Beauty, Ease, Positivity/Negativity, Verbal use, abuse, misuse, Happiness/Unhappiness, Holiness and Unholiness, Wholeness and Incompleteness.
8	Influencing Field of Cause; Issues and Themes: ➜	Earth sign: Symbol-Lemniscate (the horizontal 8). Interaction, connection, coordination, flow, disconnection, social power, material wealth, position and status; being 'in the loop'; management, administration, marketing, efficiency, executive skill, command, generalship, judgment, externalization.
4	Outcome Field of Effect; Realities, Experiences, Performances: ➜	Earth sign: Symbol-Square; Construction, Destruction, Work, Effort, Security, Structures, Frameworks, Patterns, Boundaries, Limitations, Routines, Rules, Order, Organization, Devotion, Discipline, Dedication, Matter, Materials, Regularity, Convention, Constriction, Restriction, Tradition, Transformation.
9	Influencing Field of Cause; Issues and Themes: ➜	All signs: Symbol-Crown; universality, rulership, humanitarianism, ambition, communication, commonality, completions, endings, finalizations, the 'All', the 'Many', the Macrocosm, the great life stage, literature, art, music, theater, fame, power, drama, recognition, notoriety, impersonal love and giving, benevolence, malevolence, domination, victory.
5	Outcome Field of Effect; Realities, Experiences, Performances: ➜	Fire sign: Symbol-Broken Chains; Freedom, Slavery, Detachment, Change, Movement, Motion, Shifts, Shatterings, Senses, Sensation, Sexuality, Exploration, Experience, Excitement, Fun, Friends, Letting Go, Diversity, Variety, Sampling, Uncertainty, Non-Convention, Unrestrained, Unrestricted, Irregular, Restless, Wild, Speed, Revolutionary, Visionary.

1/6 LCP Notes: (5 Expression)

In numerology the number Five is the number of freedom, exploration and change. Why is this? As we look at the 5's LCP, the answer is quite clear. When the 5 is in the influence position, it plays itself out in the realm of the 1. This means that when the energy of change, detachment and 'letting go' comes into a person's life, the outcome will always be new beginnings and the planting of new seed. Both the 5 and 1 are fire signs as well, denoting much action and heat.

Also, when the 5 is in the outcome position, it's influencing energy is the 9. This means that when endings occur in the life of a 5 Expression person, such endings will always produce movement, shift, change, loss, detachment, possible uncertainty and freedom. Nine, like the Five and One, also has a fire element within it.

Additionally, when the 4 Influence energy of structure, framework, work and form manifests itself during the 1/6 LCP, the outcome is endings, as depicted by the 9 outcome energy in the 4/9 modality.

To add another twist, when new beginnings occur, as depicted by the 1 influence energy, the result is the 6 energy of adjustment (1/6 modality). No other life cycle pattern has this combination of new beginnings, changes, adjustments and endings so dominantly intertwined as the 1/6 LCP originating from the 5 Expression.

Five Expression people walk a two-edge sword when it comes to others. It is not uncommon for them to have difficult issues with females, relationships and other people in general. This is because of the 2/7 modality. When issues and situations involving women, others, relationships and partnerships emerge (the 2 influence), they play themselves out in the arena of the 7 outcome. The 7 represents bliss and/or chaos, peace and/or disturbance. It always brings some degree of introspection, reflection, study, teaching, thought, analysis, separation, purity, perfection, isolation, concern, worry, disruption, discomfort, distress, criticism, even chaos. The purpose of the 7 energy is to take us inward, make us think, make us introspect, make us 'go deep' into our psyche wherein we will find the way out, for the way out is in. The lesson of the 7 is to be still and "know that I am God." Unfortunately, this process is usually discomforting, at least in the beginning, but the wisdom, inner vision and spiritual progress made in the ascent is well worth it. Therefore, not to despair with this energy. Just go IN. It is there where we learn to find the way out.

Ironically, the same 2/7 energy pattern which creates discomfort can also create great calm, spirituality, peace, and bliss - states which occupy the opposite side of the 7 polar coin. In the realm of others, for example, the 5 Expression person may well have their highest and best good in his heart. He may well become the teacher of spiritual matters, the one who shows others how to attain deep truths of life and move to the inner chamber of the hurricane where all is perfectly still and calm rather than being caught up in the swirling winds of its outer circle. Seven is the energy of the student, teacher, philosopher and mystic.

In its highest sense, Two rules perfect peace and balance; Seven rules purity, perfection and spirituality. Therefore, the 2/7 combination has the potential of generating great peace of the spirit. If the Two is imbalanced and the Seven reverts to imperfection, then the outcome of the 2/7 modality may well be destructive ignobility and interpersonal chaos in the realm of relationships, others and females.

1/7 LCP: (6 Expression)

Influence Energy	1	2	3	4	5	6	7	8	9
Outcome Energy	7	8	9	1	2	3	4	5	6

1	Influencing Field of Cause; Issues and Themes: ➔	Fire sign: Symbol-Sun; Self, Ego, the Yang (Male energy), Independence, Starts, New Beginnings, Patriarch, Matriarch, Authority, Creativity, Creator, Directness, Leadership, Self-Reliance, Self-Esteem, Union, Yoga, the one who stands alone and is solitary, the maverick, lone wolf, rebel.
7	Outcome Field of Effect; Realities, Experiences, Performances: ➔	Air sign: Symbol-Cross; Spirituality, religion, thought, analysis, reflection, introspection, contemplation, questioning, separation, shyness, distancing, disorder, discord, chaos, patience, peace, bliss, poise, perfection, study, teaching, inward seeking; internalization.
2	Influencing Field of Cause; Issues and Themes: ➔	Water sign: Symbol-Scales; Others, the Yin (Female energy), Support, Helping/Helper, Relationships, Partnerships, Friendships, Opposing Issues, Competition, Cooperation, Togetherness, Division, Peace/War, Conflict, Tensions; Music, Rhythm.
8	Outcome Field of Effect; Realities, Experiences, Performances: ➔	Earth sign: Symbol-Lemniscate (the horizontal 8). Interaction, connection, coordination, flow, disconnection, social power, material wealth, position and status; being 'in

King

62

		the loop'; management, administration, marketing, efficiency, executive skill, command, generalship, judgment, externalization.
3	Influencing Field of Cause; Issues and Themes: ➜	Air sign: Symbol-Triangle; Self-Expression, Words, Speech, Communication, Language, Art, Health, Beauty, Disease, Trinity (Father-Son-Holy Ghost; Body-Mind-Spirit), Marriage (Husband-Wife-Marriage), Children (Father-Mother-Children), Pleasure, Enjoyment, Sexuality, Vanity, Beauty, Ease, Positivity/Negativity, Verbal use, abuse, misuse, Happiness/Unhappiness, Holiness and Unholiness, Wholeness and Incompleteness.
9	Outcome Field of Effect; Realities, Experiences, Performances: ➜	All signs: Symbol-Crown; universality, rulership, humanitarianism, ambition, communication, commonality, completions, endings, finalizations, the 'All', the 'Many', the Macrocosm, the great life stage, literature, art, music, theater, fame, power, drama, recognition, notoriety, impersonal love and giving, benevolence, malevolence, domination, victory.
4	Influencing Field of Cause; Issues and Themes: ➜	Earth sign: Symbol-Square; Construction, Destruction, Work, Effort, Security, Structures, Frameworks, Patterns, Boundaries, Limitations, Routines, Rules, Order, Organization, Devotion, Discipline, Dedication, Matter, Materials, Regularity, Convention, Constriction, Restriction, Tradition, Transformation.
1	Outcome Field of Effect; Realities, Experiences, Performances: ➜	Fire sign: Symbol-Sun; Self, Ego, the Yang (Male energy), Independence, Starts, New Beginnings, Patriarch, Matriarch, Authority, Creativity, Creator, Directness, Leadership, Self-Reliance, Self-Esteem, Union, Yoga, the one who stands alone and is solitary, the maverick, lone wolf, rebel.

The King's Book of Numerology II: Forecasting - Part 1

5	Influencing Field of Cause; Issues and Themes: ➜	Fire sign: Symbol-Broken Chains; Freedom, Slavery, Detachment, Change, Movement, Motion, Shifts, Shatterings, Senses, Sensation, Sexuality, Exploration, Experience, Excitement, Fun, Friends, Letting Go, Diversity, Variety, Sampling, Uncertainty, Non-Convention, Unrestrained, Unrestricted, Irregular, Restless, Wild, Speed, Revolutionary, Visionary.
2	Outcome Field of Effect; Realities, Experiences, Performances: ➜	Water sign: Symbol-Scales; Others, the Yin (Female energy), Support, Helping/Helper, Relationships, Partnerships, Friendships, Opposing Issues, Competition, Cooperation, Togetherness, Division, Peace/War, Conflict, Tensions; Music, Rhythm.
6	Influencing Field of Cause; Issues and Themes: ➜	Water sign: Symbol-Heart; personal love, romance, home, family, domicile, domesticity, nurturing, support, art, music, community, family responsibility, irresponsibility, hate, jealousy, harmony, inharmony, adjustments.
3	Outcome Field of Effect; Realities, Experiences, Performances: ➜	Air sign: Symbol-Triangle; Self-Expression, Words, Speech, Communication, Language, Art, Health, Beauty, Disease, Trinity (Father-Son-Holy Ghost; Body-Mind-Spirit), Marriage (Husband-Wife-Marriage), Children (Father-Mother-Children), Pleasure, Enjoyment, Sexuality, Vanity, Beauty, Ease, Positivity/Negativity, Verbal use, abuse, misuse, Happiness/Unhappiness, Holiness and Unholiness, Wholeness and Incompleteness.
7	Influencing Field of Cause; Issues and Themes: ➜	Air sign: Symbol-Cross; Spirituality, religion, thought, analysis, reflection, introspection, contemplation, questioning, separation, shyness, distancing, disorder, discord, chaos, patience, peace, bliss, poise, perfection, study, teaching, inward seeking; internalization.
4	Outcome Field of Effect;	Earth sign: Symbol-Square; Construction, Destruction, Work,

King

	Realities, Experiences, Performances: ➔	Effort, Security, Structures, Frameworks, Patterns, Boundaries, Limitations, Routines, Rules, Order, Organization, Devotion, Discipline, Dedication, Matter, Materials, Regularity, Convention, Constriction, Restriction, Tradition, Transformation.
8	Influencing Field of Cause; Issues and Themes: ➔	Earth sign: Symbol-Lemniscate (the horizontal 8). Interaction, connection, coordination, flow, disconnection, social power, material wealth, position and status; being 'in the loop'; management, administration, marketing, efficiency, executive skill, command, generalship, judgment, externalization.
5	Outcome Field of Effect; Realities, Experiences, Performances: ➔	Fire sign: Symbol-Broken Chains; Freedom, Slavery, Detachment, Change, Movement, Motion, Shifts, Shatterings, Senses, Sensation, Sexuality, Exploration, Experience, Excitement, Fun, Friends, Letting Go, Diversity, Variety, Sampling, Uncertainty, Non-Convention, Unrestrained, Unrestricted, Irregular, Restless, Wild, Speed, Revolutionary, Visionary.
9	Influencing Field of Cause; Issues and Themes: ➔	All signs: Symbol-Crown; universality, rulership, humanitarianism, ambition, communication, commonality, completions, endings, finalizations, the 'All', the 'Many', the Macrocosm, the great life stage, literature, art, music, theater, fame, power, drama, recognition, notoriety, impersonal love and giving, benevolence, malevolence, domination, victory.
6	Outcome Field of Effect; Realities, Experiences, Performances: ➔	Water sign: Symbol-Heart; personal love, romance, home, family, domicile, domesticity, nurturing, support, art, music, community, family responsibility, irresponsibility, hate, jealousy, harmony, inharmony, adjustments.

1/7 LCP Notes: (6 Expression)

As the 5 Expression potentially has difficulties with others, relationships and females as depicted by its 2/7 LCP modality set, the 6 Expression may have difficulties with individuals, authority figures and males because of its 1/7 modality set, especially if in a chart the 1 manifests as a Challenge, Void or Voided Challenge (discussed later). Anyone with a 6 Expression will have this 1/7 modality and, subsequently, may engender potential challenges with male/yang energy, authority figures, leaders or with him/her self (because 1 rules the self and the ego).

Contrarily, this pattern is extremely beneficial for connecting with others and female energy as manifested in the 2/8 modality. Relationships, because they're ruled by the number 2, have potential for being quite connective, especially if the 2 and the 8 are not afflicted by void or challenge.

Six Expression people may well be the ones who take charge in structured environments such as the home or workplace as reflected in the 4/1 modality. They are also potentially nurturing when it comes to the masses and humanity in general because of the 9/6 IR set. No two numbers carry more love and compassion than the 6 & 9: the former being personal love and the latter being humanitarian love and service.

When it comes to self expression, communication and words, 6 Expressions can be quite forceful because the 3 energy in this pattern plays itself out in the energy field of power, exposure and domination, i.e., the 9 (3/9 set). The caution here is to make sure the communication is neither brusque nor harsh. If 9 is contained in the P/E position (meaning the individual has a 3 Lifepath [6 Expression + 3 Lifepath = 9 Performance/Experience]), power with words - positive or negative - is quite possible.

Work for the 1/7 LCP person will be perfection-oriented because of the 7/4 modality where the analysis and perfection qualities of the 7 manifest themselves in the 4 field of order, work, design, effort, organization, mechanics and all things of structure. And . . . because of the 4/1 pattern, the 6 Expression individual will be a self-starter and capable of working alone without external direction.

King

1/8 LCP: (7 Expression)

Influence Energy	1	2	3	4	5	6	7	8	9
Outcome Energy	8	9	1	2	3	4	5	6	7

1	Influencing Field of Cause; Issues and Themes: ➜	Fire sign: Symbol-Sun; Self, Ego, the Yang (Male energy), Independence, Starts, New Beginnings, Patriarch, Matriarch, Authority, Creativity, Creator, Directness, Leadership, Self-Reliance, Self-Esteem, Union, Yoga, the one who stands alone and is solitary, the maverick, lone wolf, rebel.
8	Outcome Field of Effect; Realities, Experiences, Performances: ➜	Earth sign: Symbol-Lemniscate (the horizontal 8). Interaction, connection, coordination, flow, disconnection, social power, material wealth, position and status; being 'in the loop'; management, administration, marketing, efficiency, executive skill, command, generalship, judgment, externalization.
2	Influencing Field of Cause; Issues and Themes: ➜	Water sign: Symbol-Scales; Others, the Yin (Female energy), Support, Helping/Helper, Relationships, Partnerships, Friendships, Opposing Issues, Competition, Cooperation, Togetherness, Division, Peace/War, Conflict, Tensions; Music, Rhythm.
9	Outcome Field of Effect; Realities, Experiences, Performances: ➜	All signs: Symbol-Crown; universality, rulership, humanitarianism, ambition, communication, commonality, completions, endings, finalizations, the 'All', the 'Many', the Macrocosm, the great life stage, literature, art, music, theater, fame, power, drama, recognition, notoriety, impersonal love and giving, benevolence, malevolence, domination, victory.
3	Influencing Field of Cause; Issues and Themes: ➜	Air sign: Symbol-Triangle; Self-Expression, Words, Speech, Communication, Language, Art, Health, Beauty, Disease, Trinity (Father-Son-Holy Ghost; Body-Mind-Spirit),

		Marriage (Husband-Wife-Marriage), Children (Father-Mother-Children), Pleasure, Enjoyment, Sexuality, Vanity, Beauty, Ease, Positivity/Negativity, Verbal use, abuse, misuse, Happiness/Unhappiness, Holiness and Unholiness, Wholeness and Incompleteness.
1	Outcome Field of Effect; Realities, Experiences, Performances: ➜	Fire sign: Symbol-Sun; Self, Ego, the Yang (Male energy), Independence, Starts, New Beginnings, Patriarch, Matriarch, Authority, Creativity, Creator, Directness, Leadership, Self-Reliance, Self-Esteem, Union, Yoga, the one who stands alone and is solitary, the maverick, lone wolf, rebel.
4	Influencing Field of Cause; Issues and Themes: ➜	Earth sign: Symbol-Square; Construction, Destruction, Work, Effort, Security, Structures, Frameworks, Patterns, Boundaries, Limitations, Routines, Rules, Order, Organization, Devotion, Discipline, Dedication, Matter, Materials, Regularity, Convention, Constriction, Restriction, Tradition, Transformation.
2	Outcome Field of Effect; Realities, Experiences, Performances: ➜	Water sign: Symbol-Scales; Others, the Yin (Female energy), Support, Helping/Helper, Relationships, Partnerships, Friendships, Opposing Issues, Competition, Cooperation, Togetherness, Division, Peace/War, Conflict, Tensions; Music, Rhythm.
5	Influencing Field of Cause; Issues and Themes: ➜	Fire sign: Symbol-Broken Chains; Freedom, Slavery, Detachment, Change, Movement, Motion, Shifts, Shatterings, Senses, Sensation, Sexuality, Exploration, Experience, Excitement, Fun, Friends, Letting Go, Diversity, Variety, Sampling, Uncertainty, Non-Convention, Unrestrained, Unrestricted, Irregular, Restless, Wild, Speed, Revolutionary, Visionary.
3	Outcome Field of Effect; Realities,	Air sign: Symbol-Triangle; Self-Expression, Words, Speech, Communication, Language, Art, Health, Beauty, Disease,

	Experiences, Performances: →	Trinity (Father-Son-Holy Ghost; Body-Mind-Spirit), Marriage (Husband-Wife-Marriage), Children (Father-Mother-Children), Pleasure, Enjoyment, Sexuality, Vanity, Beauty, Ease, Positivity/Negativity, Verbal use, abuse, misuse, Happiness/Unhappiness, Holiness and Unholiness, Wholeness and Incompleteness.
6	Influencing Field of Cause; Issues and Themes: →	Water sign: Symbol-Heart; personal love, romance, home, family, domicile, domesticity, nurturing, support, art, music, community, family responsibility, irresponsibility, hate, jealousy, harmony, inharmony, adjustments.
4	Outcome Field of Effect; Realities, Experiences, Performances: →	Earth sign: Symbol-Square; Construction, Destruction, Work, Effort, Security, Structures, Frameworks, Patterns, Boundaries, Limitations, Routines, Rules, Order, Organization, Devotion, Discipline, Dedication, Matter, Materials, Regularity, Convention, Constriction, Restriction, Tradition, Transformation.
7	Influencing Field of Cause; Issues and Themes: →	Air sign: Symbol-Cross; Spirituality, religion, thought, analysis, reflection, introspection, contemplation, questioning, separation, shyness, distancing, disorder, discord, chaos, patience, peace, bliss, poise, perfection, study, teaching, inward seeking; internalization.
5	Outcome Field of Effect; Realities, Experiences, Performances: →	Fire sign: Symbol-Broken Chains; Freedom, Slavery, Detachment, Change, Movement, Motion, Shifts, Shatterings, Senses, Sensation, Sexuality, Exploration, Experience, Excitement, Fun, Friends, Letting Go, Diversity, Variety, Sampling, Uncertainty, Non-Convention, Unrestrained, Unrestricted, Irregular, Restless, Wild, Speed, Revolutionary, Visionary.

8	Influencing Field of Cause; Issues and Themes: ➜	Earth sign: Symbol-Lemniscate (the horizontal 8). Interaction, connection, coordination, flow, disconnection, social power, material wealth, position and status; being 'in the loop'; management, administration, marketing, efficiency, executive skill, command, generalship, judgment, externalization.
6	Outcome Field of Effect; Realities, Experiences, Performances: ➜	Water sign: Symbol-Heart; personal love, romance, home, family, domicile, domesticity, nurturing, support, art, music, community, family responsibility, irresponsibility, hate, jealousy, harmony, inharmony, adjustments.
9	Influencing Field of Cause; Issues and Themes: ➜	All signs: Symbol-Crown; universality, rulership, humanitarianism, ambition, communication, commonality, completions, endings, finalizations, the 'All', the 'Many', the Macrocosm, the great life stage, literature, art, music, theater, fame, power, drama, recognition, notoriety, impersonal love and giving, benevolence, malevolence, domination, victory.
7	Outcome Field of Effect; Realities, Experiences, Performances: ➜	Air sign: Symbol-Cross; Spirituality, religion, thought, analysis, reflection, introspection, contemplation, questioning, separation, shyness, distancing, disorder, discord, chaos, patience, peace, bliss, poise, perfection, study, teaching, inward seeking; internalization.

1/8 LCP Notes: (7 Expression)

Seven is the energy of isolation, separation, introspection, privacy, secrecy. It is the deepest of all the basic vibrations but often gets criticism (sometimes justifiable) for being distant, cool, cold, aloof. This can be an unfair assessment. Seven is deep; it is not social. Seven seeks reclusion, separation and distance so it can think, reflect, cogitate and ponder. It does this internally, not externally.

In its LCP we gain reasons why this is so. For example, look at the 9/7 modality set. Separation (7) comes from humanity (9). Therefore, 7 seeks separation from the many. It doesn't

King

necessarily want to connect with them. Coinwise, it also receives its worldwinds turmoils from the masses. However, its thoughts and reflections are the result of taking in and absorbing many philosophies, ideologies and patterns of thought. To be sure, 7 is distant but deep. It also makes a good teacher, student, intuitive.

When we look at the 7 in the influence position we see that it plays itself out in the realm of the 5, a vibration encompassing a diversity and variety of people, circumstances, philosophies. No two numbers incorporate the masses more than the 5 and 9, and the distancing and separating qualities of the 7 are inherently a part of each (7 + 7 = 14 > 5 and 7 + 9 = 16 > 7). Ironically, although the 7 seems distant, its energy of humanitarianism (9) is derived from the Influencing 2 vibration of others, support, companionship, partnership and relationship (2 + 7 = 9). In other words, Sevens give to others and are more deeply concerned with humanity than their cool exterior suggests. In fact, they are quite broad-minded when it comes to other people. Mother Teresa, Shakespeare and Amelia Earhart, for example, maintain a 7 Expression and its characteristics in their lives are unquestionable. The dangerous caveat is that 7 Expression people must not be overly critical or demanding with others, especially subordinates. If they are so disposed, mutiny, alienation and/or abandonment may be plausible scenarios.

Additionally, the social 2-4-6 outcome energies are manifested from the social 4-6-8 influence energies, giving the 7 many relationship qualities (4 + 7 = 11 > 2; 6 + 7 = 13 > 4; 8 + 7 = 15 > 6). The result is that we cannot judge the 7 book by its cover. It may seem aloof, but in reality it is very connected, committed and concerned. It just doesn't show it as warmly or as often as do other vibrations because of its internal characteristics.

Another aspect of this LCP is that the outcome energy of self, independence and individuality (1) is derived from the 3 energy of self-expression, communication and words (7 + 3 = 10 > 1). Therefore, the 7 Expression individual finds solidarity from its own personal self-expression. It doesn't necessarily need other people, although it is quite socially aware and connected as expressed in the preceding paragraph.

1/9 LCP: (8 Expression)

Influence Energy	1	2	3	4	5	6	7	8	9
Outcome Energy	9	1	2	3	4	5	6	7	8

1	Influencing Field of Cause; Issues and Themes: ➔	Fire sign: Symbol-Sun; Self, Ego, the Yang (Male energy), Independence, Starts, New Beginnings, Patriarch, Matriarch, Authority, Creativity, Creator, Directness, Leadership, Self-Reliance, Self-Esteem, Union, Yoga, the one who stands alone and is solitary, the maverick, lone wolf, rebel.
9	Outcome Field of Effect; Realities, Experiences, Performances: ➔	All signs: Symbol-Crown; universality, rulership, humanitarianism, ambition, communication, commonality, completions, endings, finalizations, the 'All', the 'Many', the Macrocosm, the great life stage, literature, art, music, theater, fame, power, drama, recognition, notoriety, impersonal love and giving, benevolence, malevolence, domination, victory.
2	Influencing Field of Cause; Issues and Themes: ➔	Water sign: Symbol-Scales; Others, the Yin (Female energy), Support, Helping/Helper, Relationships, Partnerships, Friendships, Opposing Issues, Competition, Cooperation, Togetherness, Division, Peace/War, Conflict, Tensions; Music, Rhythm.
1	Outcome Field of Effect; Realities, Experiences, Performances: ➔	Fire sign: Symbol-Sun; Self, Ego, the Yang (Male energy), Independence, Starts, New Beginnings, Patriarch, Matriarch, Authority, Creativity, Creator, Directness, Leadership, Self-Reliance, Self-Esteem, Union, Yoga, the one who stands alone and is solitary, the maverick, lone wolf, rebel.

3	Influencing Field of Cause; Issues and Themes: ➜	Air sign: Symbol-Triangle; Self-Expression, Words, Speech, Communication, Language, Art, Health, Beauty, Disease, Trinity (Father-Son-Holy Ghost; Body-Mind-Spirit), Marriage (Husband-Wife-Marriage), Children (Father-Mother-Children), Pleasure, Enjoyment, Sexuality, Vanity, Beauty, Ease, Positivity/Negativity, Verbal use, abuse, misuse, Happiness/Unhappiness, Holiness and Unholiness, Wholeness and Incompleteness.
2	Outcome Field of Effect; Realities, Experiences, Performances: ➜	Water sign: Symbol-Scales; Others, the Yin (Female energy), Support, Helping/Helper, Relationships, Partnerships, Friendships, Opposing Issues, Competition, Cooperation, Togetherness, Division, Peace/War, Conflict, Tensions; Music, Rhythm.
4	Influencing Field of Cause; Issues and Themes: ➜	Earth sign: Symbol-Square; Construction, Destruction, Work, Effort, Security, Structures, Frameworks, Patterns, Boundaries, Limitations, Routines, Rules, Order, Organization, Devotion, Discipline, Dedication, Matter, Materials, Regularity, Convention, Constriction, Restriction, Tradition, Transformation.
3	Outcome Field of Effect; Realities, Experiences, Performances: ➜	Air sign: Symbol-Triangle; Self-Expression, Words, Speech, Communication, Language, Art, Health, Beauty, Disease, Trinity (Father-Son-Holy Ghost; Body-Mind-Spirit), Marriage (Husband-Wife-Marriage), Children (Father-Mother-Children), Pleasure, Enjoyment, Sexuality, Vanity, Beauty, Ease, Positivity/Negativity, Verbal use, abuse, misuse, Happiness/Unhappiness, Holiness and Unholiness, Wholeness and Incompleteness.

The King's Book of Numerology II: Forecasting - Part 1

5	Influencing Field of Cause; Issues and Themes: ➜	Fire sign: Symbol-Broken Chains; Freedom, Slavery, Detachment, Change, Movement, Motion, Shifts, Shatterings, Senses, Sensation, Sexuality, Exploration, Experience, Excitement, Fun, Friends, Letting Go, Diversity, Variety, Sampling, Uncertainty, Non-Convention, Unrestrained, Unrestricted, Irregular, Restless, Wild, Speed, Revolutionary, Visionary.
4	Outcome Field of Effect; Realities, Experiences, Performances: ➜	Earth sign: Symbol-Square; Construction, Destruction, Work, Effort, Security, Structures, Frameworks, Patterns, Boundaries, Limitations, Routines, Rules, Order, Organization, Devotion, Discipline, Dedication, Matter, Materials, Regularity, Convention, Constriction, Restriction, Tradition, Transformation.
6	Influencing Field of Cause; Issues and Themes: ➜	Water sign: Symbol-Heart; personal love, romance, home, family, domicile, domesticity, nurturing, support, art, music, community, family responsibility, irresponsibility, hate, jealousy, harmony, inharmony, adjustments.
5	Outcome Field of Effect; Realities, Experiences, Performances: ➜	Fire sign: Symbol-Broken Chains; Freedom, Slavery, Detachment, Change, Movement, Motion, Shifts, Shatterings, Senses, Sensation, Sexuality, Exploration, Experience, Excitement, Fun, Friends, Letting Go, Diversity, Variety, Sampling, Uncertainty, Non-Convention, Unrestrained, Unrestricted, Irregular, Restless, Wild, Speed, Revolutionary, Visionary.
7	Influencing Field of Cause; Issues and Themes: ➜	Air sign: Symbol-Cross; Spirituality, religion, thought, analysis, reflection, introspection, contemplation, questioning, separation, shyness, distancing, disorder,

		discord, chaos, patience, peace, bliss, poise, perfection, study, teaching, inward seeking; internalization.
6	Outcome Field of Effect; Realities, Experiences, Performances: ➜	Water sign: Symbol-Heart; personal love, romance, home, family, domicile, domesticity, nurturing, support, art, music, community, family responsibility, irresponsibility, hate, jealousy, harmony, inharmony, adjustments.
8	Influencing Field of Cause; Issues and Themes: ➜	Earth sign: Symbol-Lemniscate (the horizontal 8). Interaction, connection, coordination, flow, disconnection, social power, material wealth, position and status; being 'in the loop'; management, administration, marketing, efficiency, executive skill, command, generalship, judgment, externalization.
7	Outcome Field of Effect; Realities, Experiences, Performances: ➜	Air sign: Symbol-Cross; Spirituality, religion, thought, analysis, reflection, introspection, contemplation, questioning, separation, shyness, distancing, disorder, discord, chaos, patience, peace, bliss, poise, perfection, study, teaching, inward seeking; internalization.
9	Influencing Field of Cause; Issues and Themes: ➜	All signs: Symbol-Crown; universality, rulership, humanitarianism, ambition, communication, commonality, completions, endings, finalizations, the 'All', the 'Many', the Macrocosm, the great life stage, literature, art, music, theater, fame, power, drama, recognition, notoriety, impersonal love and giving, benevolence, malevolence, domination, victory.
8	Outcome Field of Effect; Realities, Experiences, Performances: ➜	Earth sign: Symbol-Lemniscate (the horizontal 8). Interaction, connection, coordination, flow, disconnection, social power, material wealth, position and status; being 'in the loop'; management, administration, marketing, efficiency, executive skill, command, generalship, judgment, externalization.

1/9 LCP Notes: (8 Expression)

Eight is the vibration of interaction and connection, commerce, business, administration, management, being 'in the loop' and liking the role of the mover and shaker. It likes power, success, achievement and recognition. As the other numbers, its LCP shows us why this is so.

First, the influence 1 energies of the self and its interests play themselves out in the realm of the All, the Many, mankind, power, dominance, domination, dominion, mass recognition, the public stage, triumph and rulership - the 9 Outcome energy field. Eights love power, money, material comfort, recognition, ambition and self-promotion.

To corroborate this understanding of the 8 Expression and its 1/9 LCP, when we look at the 9 energy and its modality set, we see that it manifests in the realm of the Eight (9/8). In other words, power is placed in the loop of interaction and interconnection. This is why it has the potential of being socially and materially successful. Eight is the highest social vibration; Nine, the most public. Eight is also the conduit through which money (ruled by the 2 energy) and power flow.

Another chief indicator is that when it comes to the realm of others (2), the Eight Expression is focused on its own self, needs, independence and creativity. This is not a judgment, just an observation of numerical fact, but it does explain why 8 people are not only successful but often self-absorbed. When they think of self they want power (1/9); when they think of power they want connection and interaction (9/8), and when they're in relationship, their primary concern is for themselves (2/1).

Furthermore, when it comes to success and interacting with others (8 energy) the 8 Expression person is quite studious, as noted by the 7 Outcome energy in the 8/7 modality set ($8 + 8 = 16 > 7$). But in can also be secretive and ruthless. Eights think deeply about how to connect and be successful, about how to make that 'deal' or create success. In other words, their minds are geared to the *manipulation* of social success, wealth, prosperity and comfort (positively or negatively) and that's what they think about the most. Hence, that's what they become. If they have a flaw, it's trying to make other people believe they can do the same thing. But such is not the case. We are what are numbers dictate and this is reflected in our fate and, of course, our numbers.

Eights take their pleasure and comfort from stability, solidity and security as manifested in the 4/3 modality set, and when the energy of pleasure enters their life cycles, it translates into the world of relationship and support of others or being cared for as witnessed by the 3/2 IR pattern.

King

1/1 LCP: (9 Expression)

Influence Energy	1	2	3	4	5	6	7	8	9
Outcome Energy	1	2	3	4	5	6	7	8	9

1	Influencing Field of Cause; Issues and Themes: ➔	Fire sign: Symbol-Sun; Self, Ego, the Yang (Male energy), Independence, Starts, New Beginnings, Patriarch, Matriarch, Authority, Creativity, Creator, Directness, Leadership, Self-Reliance, Self-Esteem, Union, Yoga, the one who stands alone and is solitary, the maverick, lone wolf, rebel.
1	Outcome Field of Effect; Realities, Experiences, Performances: ➔	Fire sign: Symbol-Sun; Self, Ego, the Yang (Male energy), Independence, Starts, New Beginnings, Patriarch, Matriarch, Authority, Creativity, Creator, Directness, Leadership, Self-Reliance, Self-Esteem, Union, Yoga, the one who stands alone and is solitary, the maverick, lone wolf, rebel.
2	Influencing Field of Cause; Issues and Themes: ➔	Water sign: Symbol-Scales; Others, the Yin (Female energy), Support, Helping/Helper, Relationships, Partnerships, Friendships, Opposing Issues, Competition, Cooperation, Togetherness, Division, Peace/War, Conflict, Tensions; Music, Rhythm.
2	Outcome Field of Effect; Realities, Experiences, Performances: ➔	Water sign: Symbol-Scales; Others, the Yin (Female energy), Support, Helping/Helper, Relationships, Partnerships, Friendships, Opposing Issues, Competition, Cooperation, Togetherness, Division, Peace/War, Conflict, Tensions; Music, Rhythm.
3	Influencing Field of Cause; Issues and Themes: ➔	Air sign: Symbol-Triangle; Self-Expression, Words, Speech, Communication, Language, Art, Health, Beauty, Disease, Trinity (Father-Son-Holy Ghost; Body-Mind-Spirit), Marriage (Husband-Wife-Marriage), Children (Father-Mother-Children), Pleasure, Enjoyment, Sexuality, Vanity,

		Beauty, Ease, Positivity/Negativity, Verbal use, abuse, misuse, Happiness/Unhappiness, Holiness and Unholiness, Wholeness and Incompleteness.
3	Outcome Field of Effect; Realities, Experiences, Performances: ➔	Air sign: Symbol-Triangle; Self-Expression, Words, Speech, Communication, Language, Art, Health, Beauty, Disease, Trinity (Father-Son-Holy Ghost; Body-Mind-Spirit), Marriage (Husband-Wife-Marriage), Children (Father-Mother-Children), Pleasure, Enjoyment, Sexuality, Vanity, Beauty, Ease, Positivity/Negativity, Verbal use, abuse, misuse, Happiness/Unhappiness, Holiness and Unholiness, Wholeness and Incompleteness.
4	Influencing Field of Cause; Issues and Themes: ➔	Earth sign: Symbol-Square; Construction, Destruction, Work, Effort, Security, Structures, Frameworks, Patterns, Boundaries, Limitations, Routines, Rules, Order, Organization, Devotion, Discipline, Dedication, Matter, Materials, Regularity, Convention, Constriction, Restriction, Tradition, Transformation.
4	Outcome Field of Effect; Realities, Experiences, Performances: ➔	Earth sign: Symbol-Square; Construction, Destruction, Work, Effort, Security, Structures, Frameworks, Patterns, Boundaries, Limitations, Routines, Rules, Order, Organization, Devotion, Discipline, Dedication, Matter, Materials, Regularity, Convention, Constriction, Restriction, Tradition, Transformation.
5	Influencing Field of Cause; Issues and Themes: ➔	Fire sign: Symbol-Broken Chains; Freedom, Slavery, Detachment, Change, Movement, Motion, Shifts, Shatterings, Senses, Sensation, Sexuality, Exploration, Experience, Excitement, Fun, Friends, Letting Go, Diversity, Variety, Sampling, Uncertainty, Non-Convention, Unrestrained, Unrestricted, Irregular, Restless, Wild, Speed, Revolutionary, Visionary.

5	Outcome Field of Effect; Realities, Experiences, Performances: ➜	Fire sign: Symbol-Broken Chains; Freedom, Slavery, Detachment, Change, Movement, Motion, Shifts, Shatterings, Senses, Sensation, Sexuality, Exploration, Experience, Excitement, Fun, Friends, Letting Go, Diversity, Variety, Sampling, Uncertainty, Non-Convention, Unrestrained, Unrestricted, Irregular, Restless, Wild, Speed, Revolutionary, Visionary.
6	Influencing Field of Cause; Issues and Themes: ➜	Water sign: Symbol-Heart; personal love, romance, home, family, domicile, domesticity, nurturing, support, art, music, community, family responsibility, irresponsibility, hate, jealousy, harmony, inharmony, adjustments.
6	Outcome Field of Effect; Realities, Experiences, Performances: ➜	Water sign: Symbol-Heart; personal love, romance, home, family, domicile, domesticity, nurturing, support, art, music, community, family responsibility, irresponsibility, hate, jealousy, harmony, inharmony, adjustments.
7	Influencing Field of Cause; Issues and Themes: ➜	Air sign: Symbol-Cross; Spirituality, religion, thought, analysis, reflection, introspection, contemplation, questioning, separation, shyness, distancing, disorder, discord, chaos, patience, peace, bliss, poise, perfection, study, teaching, inward seeking; internalization.
7	Outcome Field of Effect; Realities, Experiences, Performances: ➜	Air sign: Symbol-Cross; Spirituality, religion, thought, analysis, reflection, introspection, contemplation, questioning, separation, shyness, distancing, disorder, discord, chaos, patience, peace, bliss, poise, perfection, study, teaching, inward seeking; internalization.
8	Influencing Field of Cause; Issues and Themes: ➜	Earth sign: Symbol-Lemniscate (the horizontal 8). Interaction, connection, coordination, flow, disconnection, social power, material wealth, position and status; being 'in the loop'; management, administration, marketing,

		efficiency, executive skill, command, generalship, judgment, externalization.
8	Outcome Field of Effect; Realities, Experiences, Performances: ➔	Earth sign: Symbol-Lemniscate (the horizontal 8). Interaction, connection, coordination, flow, disconnection, social power, material wealth, position and status; being 'in the loop'; management, administration, marketing, efficiency, executive skill, command, generalship, judgment, externalization.
9	Influencing Field of Cause; Issues and Themes: ➔	All signs: Symbol-Crown; universality, rulership, humanitarianism, ambition, communication, commonality, completions, endings, finalizations, the 'All', the 'Many', the Macrocosm, the great life stage, literature, art, music, theater, fame, power, drama, recognition, notoriety, impersonal love and giving, benevolence, malevolence, domination, victory.
9	Outcome Field of Effect; Realities, Experiences, Performances: ➔	All signs: Symbol-Crown; universality, rulership, humanitarianism, ambition, communication, commonality, completions, endings, finalizations, the 'All', the 'Many', the Macrocosm, the great life stage, literature, art, music, theater, fame, power, drama, recognition, notoriety, impersonal love and giving, benevolence, malevolence, domination, victory.

1/1 LCP Notes: (9 Expression)

Nine is the most universal of all the basic numbers. Nine is the humanitarian, the universal giver and helper, the public figure, philanthropist, dramatist, theologian, musician, ruler, volunteer, world correspondent and reporter. Nine has charisma and power. Its LCP is definitively clear on this.

As we look at the 1/1 modality sets of the 9 Expression, we see that the influence energy field and the outcome energy field are identical. No other LCP maintains such an identity. This is where the Nine gets its power. Why is this and what does it mean?

Nine is the Grand Elemental. It mixes and matches with every thing and every one. When 9 is added to any number, the outcome is always that number. For example, when Nine is added to Five, the result is Five ($9 + 5 = 14$; $1 + 4 = 5$). When Nine is added to Eight, the result is Eight ($9 + 8 = 17$; $1 + 7 = 8$). So it is with all the numbers. The influence and outcome energy are identical in every set of the 9 LCP.

What this basically means is that when a 9 Expression person talks with anyone, that person will feel as though the 9 person understands him, and essentially this is correct. Nines have a broad scope of inclusion and universal understanding. They get along with just about everyone and everyone gets along with them.

This chameleon effect of the 9 accounts for its charisma, popularity, personal power, public recognition and fame. An excellent example of the 9 energy in action was the life of Elvis Presley who had a 9 Expression, a 9 Lifepath and a 9 Performance/Experience. He, his lifepath and ultimate role in life were universal. With such a saturation of 9 energy in his chart, accompanied by a Lifepath whose core was centered in One energy of the self, he could not have avoided the public stage, the masses or its consciousness. He was so popular, in fact, that after he died there was a major movement to declare a national holiday in his honor. Yet, Presley's personal life was centered primarily in himself as is reflected by the large amount of One energy in his Life Matrix.

Another characteristic of the 1/1 LCP is that when things are good, they're very good, but when they're bad, they're challenging to say the least. Why? Because the influence and outcome energies are identical. When, for example, issues of happiness or self-fulfillment enter the life stream, the outcome is happiness and self-fulfillment. But contrarily, when energies of chaos or disruption enter the life stream, there is no other energy to buffer or mitigate them. They become the outcome itself. This is additionally exacerbated if the particular number in question is void (missing in the chart), challenged (locked in a challenge position) or worse - a voided challenge wherein the challenged number is also voided in the chart. So . . . with the 9 Expression person, when it's hot, it's really hot; when it's cold, it's really cold; when it's good, it's really good, and when it's bad . . . ouch!

One of the major cautions for the 9 Expression individual is to remember that 9 has the potential to mix with anyone - good or bad, saint or sinner. Therefore, always working to one's highest and best spiritual good is critical to the health and well-being of this numerical power.

The King's Book of Numerology II: Forecasting - Part 1

Nines can fall to demonic depths as easily as they can elevate to honorable heights. Regardless of the direction they travel, they will always have charisma.

Another thing to remember is that 9 rules. It is the most dominate of the nine vibrations. It can be extremely dominating, domineering, brash, brusque, rude, crude, imperious, malefic and malevolent or, acting within its opposite polarity, extremely benefic and benevolent, generous, gracious, kind, loving, giving, selfless and sacrificing, totally committed to the good of humanity because it manifests humanitarianism with an all-encompassing and welcoming embrace. In this regard, it would be wise for the 9 person to take to heart the words of Lord Acton to Bishop Mandell Creighton (1887): "Power tends to corrupt, and absolute power corrupts absolutely. Great men are almost always bad men." Another quote from Albert Einstein bears citing here: "The highest destiny of the individual is to serve rather than to rule," and from Shakespeare: "Uneasy lies the head that wears a crown."

What's Your Life Cycle Pattern?

In order to understand ourselves in relation to the various components of our destiny and the timelines contained within its boundaries, it is imperative for each of us to know our specific Life Cycle Pattern. Since our LCP is dependent upon our Expression, we have to calculate the Expression first. A simple letter value chart is included here for our computations. More detail regarding the Expression can be found in *The King's Book of Numerology, Volume I, Foundations & Fundamentals* (www.richardking.net).

Simple Letter Value Chart

A	B	C	D	E	F	G	H	I
J	K	L	M	N	O	P	Q	R
S	T	U	V	W	X	Y	Z	
1	**2**	**3**	**4**	**5**	**6**	**7**	**8**	**9**

Using the Simple Letter Value Chart above, associate each letter of your name with its correlating number. Add left to right and reduce to a single digit. Then add this number to the number 1, the first number of any LCP set (defining it) and finish out the sequence as we've discussed.

As an example of calculating the Expression, let's use the name Richard Johnston Roe (RJ), our imaginary friend from KBN1.

R	i	c	h	a	r	d	J	o	h	n	s	t	o	n	R	o	e
9	9	3	8	1	9	4	1	6	8	5	1	2	6	5	9	6	5

These numbers, added together, equal a 97 > 16 > 7. Thus, RJ's Expression is a 7. His LCP will therefore be a 1/8 (1 + 7 = 8).

Another Perspective: What Creates My Realities?

There are nine basic thematic realities in life as manifested in the effect portion of the LCP matrices. By asking ourselves where each of these originate, we may gain a deeper insight into the cause and effect aspect of our lives. In effect, we are reverse engineering (working backward) to solve the problem of life's recurring cycles. Rather than find the cause and look for the effect, we start with the effect and look for the cause.

For example, where do we get love (6) from in our chart? What gives us a sense of independence and identity (1)? From what energy field will chaos (2 and/or 7) most likely originate? What vibration gives us happiness and fulfillment (3)? The answer lies in our own LCP matrix. Just look for the number that creates the outcome cipher.

There are, of course, only nine life cycle patterns. Each of our lives fits into one of these matrices, and by dividing the world's population by nine, we realize that 1/9th of the world shares the same pattern we possess. Like snowflakes, we're all alike, yet different. Specific factors in our charts make each one of our lives unique, but larger and more general vibrational fields make us the same. The life cycle patterns begin to define us in a general sense by placing each of us into one of the nine cause/effect LCP fields. By working backwards from the effect field of the LCP to its causal field we can help increase our understanding of life and its workings.

The Nine Basic Numerological Themes

1   Yang/ego/identity/self/independence/leadership/action/initiation/authority figures

2   Yin/others/partnership/support/balance/teamwork/competition/antagonism/war/peace

3   Fulfillment/expression/communication/pleasure/joy/beauty/art/words/health/disease

4   Security/work/effort/restriction/limitation/convention/tradition/order/control/regulation

5   Freedom/slavery/change/loss/detachment/experience/senses/movement/motion/variety

6   Love/hate/nurturing/compassion/home/hearth/romance/adjustment/community/art

7   Peace/chaos/separation/alienation/thought/analysis/review/introspection/study/teaching

8   Success/failure/socialization/interaction/flow/continuity/connection/disconnection

9   Power/expansion/acclaim/terminations/macrocosm/universality/education/notoriety/fame

Take each of the nine basic numerological themes of life listed above. Make each of them into a question. For example, "Where does my feeling of love and nurturing come from?" These are the attributes of the 6 energy. Or, "Where does my sense of happiness, joy, pleasure and fulfillment come from?" These are the attributes of the 3 energy. The I/R (influence/reality) sets of your personal LCP hold the answer. The number associated with your question will be in the bottom position of the I/R set (the Outcome aspect). The number in the top position, the Influence aspect, will supply the answer. Any number, it must be remembered, can also represent a person, an aspect of another person's Basic Matrix, a place, a situation, event or circumstance.

For example, let's answer the question, "Where does my sense of love and nurturing come from" for each of the nine basic Expressions and their accompanying LCPs. The 1 Expression (1/2 LCP) gets its love and nurturing from the 5 energy (5 + 1 = 6). In other words, a person with an Expression of 1 will always get their love from people, situations and circumstances manifesting change, motion, movement, freedom, experience, variety, diversity, exploration and the senses. This is found by looking at the 5/6 I/R set of the 1's life cycle pattern.

The 2 Expression individual (1/3 LCP) receives his love and nurturing from the energy field of the 4 vibration (4 + 2 = 6). This is reflected in the 2 Expression's 4/6 I/R set. In other words, when a 2 person has security, stability, structure, order, work, conformity and a sense of tradition in his life (4), whether that security, stability, etc., comes in the form of people, conditions, circumstances or events, he will feel loved and nurtured (6).

For the 3 Expression, love and nurturing come from the 3 energy of self-fulfillment, communication, art, friends, pleasure and good times (3 + 3 = 6). It is also true that the 3's

84

nurturing comes from himself. This is revealed in the 3/6 I/R set. This also explains in part why the 3 Expression may sometimes be vain and narcissistic. It is the only vibration whose love and nurturing spring from within its very own energy field, i.e., itself.

Partnership, relationship, togetherness, support and female energy will be the source of love and nurturing for the 4 Expression as reflected in the 2/6 I/R set of its 1/5 LCP. This is important for the 4 Expression person because the 2 and 6 are social numbers and, like the 4 itself, they are relationship oriented: the number 2 rules togetherness and the 6 governs the family and domestic environment.

The 5 Expression individual will find he receives his love and nurturing from the 1 energy. As always, any of the numbers can be people. They can also be components of another person's Basic Matrix. Therefore, that which gives love and nurturing to the 5 person may be the individual Nature of another person or even that person's 1 Lifepath or 1 Performance/Experience vibration. The love could also come from the individual's own creativity and leadership function. Most certainly it will come from the yang aspect of creation. The 5 Expression's love aspect can be found in his 1/6 I/R set.

For the 6 Expression individual, her sense of love is derived from the 9 energy of power, acclaim, art, philanthropy, recognition and the macrocosm ($9 + 6 = 15 > 6$). Therefore, she is universal in receipt of her nurturing and will embrace many people, cultures, languages and vocations. Because of this 9 energy and its broad based vibrational field, the 6 person may well have an eclectic group of friends and associates. This is visible in the 9/6 I/R set of the 6 Expression's LCP.

Love for the 7 Expression will originate from social interaction, success and power ($8 + 7 = 15 > 6$). This is interesting because 7 and 8 are exact opposites. Yet, when the interconnective, external and circulatory energies of the 8 mix with the internal, reclusive and analytical vibrations of the 7, the 6 vibration of love, nurturing, family and domesticity is the result as is expressed in the 8/6 I/R set of the 7's 1/8 LCP. This is an interesting combination and reveals one of life's conundrums - that opposite energies can generate love, nurturing and compassion. The numbers 7 & 8 are the only two pairs of opposites that do this. The other two pairs, the 1-2 and 4-5 do not generate this love energy. The 8 Expression person also gets his love from the 7 energy of reclusion, isolation and secrecy as is seen in the 7/6 I/R set of the 8's 1/9 LCP.

Finally, the 9 Expression individual gets personal love from the home and from those people who are more personally loving than himself as manifested by the 6/6 I/R set of the 1/1 LCP. The 9 vibration is the great humanitarian but its love is not personal. It is universal. Interestingly, the

The King's Book of Numerology II: Forecasting - Part 1

impersonally compassionate but universal 9 Expression receives its nurturing not from the masses, with which it identifies, but from the warmth of the personally loving and domestic 6 Expression (6 + 9 = 15 > 6). Thus, the 9 gives to everyone but takes its own love from the one who personally loves him. This is an interesting combination, like that of the 7 and 8 energies, because the 6 Expression gets its love from the 9 vibration - the exact energy which it nurtures. Six and Nine, however, are not opposites like the 7 and 8. In fact, they compose two of the three apexes of the artistic 3-6-9 triad.

And so the process goes for all the other vibrations. To discover where each energy originates in a person's chart, consult the I/R set of the LCP associated with the person's Expression. Remember, owing to the complexity of each person's chart, this method won't give exact answers, but it certainly will give general ones for all of mankind.

Limitations

When we study the basic nine life cycle patterns, we see that each of our lives is limited and finite. For example, when the energies of the 1 (the yang, males, new beginnings, independence, creation, activity and authority) are added to each of the nine different Expressions, each has its own field into which the 1 energy will manifest and such manifestation will be exclusive to that particular energy field only for the particular Expression involved and no other. In other words, a person with a 1 Expression, when associated with a 1 vibration will have outcomes and realities manifesting exclusively in the vibrational energy field of the 2 of others, yin, relationships, partnerships and support. He will never experience outcomes of the 1s new beginnings playing themselves out in the field of change, motion, movement, experience, freedom, diversity and exploration (the 5), or any other field for that matter. That privilege rests solely with the 4 Expression person who maintains a 1/5 LCP. The reverse is also true. The 1/5 LCP person will never experience what the 1/2 LCP person will experience or any of the other LCP configurations. And so it is with every single number of each LCP set. Each IR duo has its own specific energy field of manifestation given the same causal number.

King

Causal 1 LCPs

Causal energy	1	1	1	1	1	1	1	1	1
Expression	+1	+2	+3	+4	+5	+6	+7	+8	+9
Outcome/Reality	2	3	4	5	6	7	8	9	1
LCP	1/2	1/3	1/4	1/5	1/6	1/7	1/8	1/9	1/1

What does all this mean? Because each of the nine basic Expressions is limited to experiencing only one outcome from each of the nine single numbers, and since there are 81 LCP or IR sets, each of us, therefore, is limited to understanding only 1/9th of the total possibilities created by the 81 LCP modalities, leaving 8/9ths cast to the wind! How difficult is it, therefore, for a 7 Expression person to understand what a 2 Expression person is going through and vice-versa, or a 9 Expression person to understand what a 4 Expression individual is experiencing? It simply cannot be done. Each of us is limited to the scope of our own vibratory Life Cycle Pattern. Not only this, but we are limited to understanding life solely within the context of the energy fields established by our LCP. Truly, *we do not see things as they are, we see things the way we are.* How limited are we! How confined! How trapped! How impossible is it to change the world when we can't even begin to understand the experiences of 8/9ths of the rest of the world, much less ourselves? Food for thought.

Given this perception, love is the only solution to a successful life. It is cosmically impossible for any of us living in a normal human state to deeply understand most of what is going on around us at any one time in the world. We are all "perception challenged." The best we can do is to be loving, kind, tolerant, patient and as understanding as humanly possibly, given the limitations of our own LCP realities. If someone possesses the same LCP, we can understand him to some degree because his life experiences will be similar to ours as far as influence and outcome realities are concerned. But this will only be true in a general sense because the specific realities of our lives, as determined by the variances in our root structures, will be totally different, as will be the components of the Basic Matrices.

The only possible solution for any of us in understanding the totality of life is to make ourselves universal. To do this we must rise above the level of human consciousness to the level of the divine. When we have merged with our Source - the one and only power - then and only then will we be able to truly understand the whole because only then will we be universal. Hence, if we're serious and sincere in being truly universal, we have no other choice but to follow a spiritual path which will make us universal, make us connected to all things. Any other course of action is only fraught with severe limitations and incarcerating restrictions.

Summary

Life Cycle Patterns are, indeed, powerful tools for a numerologist. They explain why things are what they are in a general sense. Having a working knowledge of them is crucial to understanding people and to looking into the crystal ball of one's destiny. As one works with them, studies them and cogitates their inner relationship in conjunction with other aspects of the numerology chart (its timelines and matrices), their importance will become exceedingly clear. This chapter has simply offered a beginning observation of them. As each numerologist applies his craft, talents and consciousness to the work, the LCPs will yield wonderful meaning, exceptional truth, and increased understanding of life's intricate, perfect, divine design.

88

Chapter Three

PINNACLE/CHALLENGE TIMELINE

I t is now time to begin the actual forecasting process, looking into the crystal ball of our destiny. Please remember this gift must not be taken lightly. It demands enormous responsibility as well as the exercise of an elevated ethical character. Never do we have the right to use this privileged information for our own selfish ends and/or to the detriment of others. Under the edicts of karmic law, the penalties would be severe, far greater than what we may consider as payment for the actual infraction. Furthermore, we do not have the right to force information regarding a person's destiny upon anyone. If it is solicited, fine, but not otherwise.

True story. A numerologist, now deceased, used his understanding of numbers to manipulate other people during his life for his own personal, financial and sexual gain, deceiving ordinary people, clients and audiences alike. Eventually, this individual went blind. It is not beyond the reach of karmic sense to believe that as a result of his misuse of the great numerological vision he was given, his physical vision was taken from him. The law of karma is exact and inexorable. No one escapes it. Violations do generate punishment. Being cavalier, indifferent and blind to the feelings and lives of others, especially for personal gain or gratification, will only reap poisonous fruit for the violator. As Saint Ravidas says, "The fruit of action unfailingly overtakes the doer."

Knowledge of anyone's life is private. There will be times when, for example, during a social gathering, others may want to enter into a conversation between you and the person to whom you are speaking and revealing aspects about that person's life and destiny. If the person does not mind others being involved in the discussion because they are friends, family or whomever, or if the person's information resides in the public domain by their own choosing, then continuation of the conversation warrants no negative karmic backlash. However, if intruders are, in fact, intruding, then the discussion must terminate. For one gifted with this very special insight to allow his or her ego, insensitivities or insensibilities to prevail and disregard the privacy of the recipient, is highly questionable and unethical. Just as doctor/patient relationships are private and confidential, numerologist/client relationships are no less private and confidential. To err in such circumstances may be human, but there will be no absolution of the penalizing consequences.

That said, the knowledge gained from looking into one's destiny can be of immeasurable help and comfort as discussed in Chapter One. The caveat, however, is that the help must be requested and must not be shared if not requested. As one's numerological expertise and experience grow, the general flow of anyone's destiny will be an open book but that in no way translates to the numerologist's ability to be open with it. Think of this knowledge like nuclear power. When used responsibly, it generates great benefits but when misused, it destroys and, more importantly, destroys the user.

One last thought in this regard. As numerologists, we work with potentials, not certainties. Only God knows what is certain and it would be arrogant for us to predict specific events. When doing readings, it is therefore best to explain to the client that the energies discussed are not only potential in scope (not certain) but that every energy, every number, has a positive and negative aspect to it. Managing the analysis in this manner leaves the client free to draw his own conclusions, while still receiving professional counsel. Therefore, when we are engaged in forecasting, we must not lose sight of the fact that we are engaging in the process of assessing *potential realities*, not actualities. God's ways are infinite, as are the manifestations of His numbers. As numerologists, it would be wise to heed this advice.

Pinnacle/Challenge Timeline

The Pinnacle/Challenge Timeline is the most critical timeline for measuring, determining, and describing specific time periods contained with the Lifepath itself. Just as the Basic Matrix dealt with the individual's personal profile (*The King's Book of Numerology, Volume 1: Foundations & Fundamentals* [www.richardking.net]), the Pinnacle/Challenge timeline addresses a major portion of an individual's destiny. This P/C timeline is contained within the *Life Matrix*, the internal structure of the Lifepath.

Pinnacles are major time periods describing influences and activities comprising the fabric of our lives. Pinnacles may be viewed as those energies which pull us up and engage us in a positive manner. We can also look at them as the external activities present during specific time periods. In relation to a person's life, they are visible to the world and occupy one side of the activity coin of life. The Pinnacles are, metaphorically, what we see above the surface of the ocean.

The opposite side of the coin are the Challenges. *Challenges* work simultaneously with *Pinnacles*, occupying the exact same time period. *Challenges* represent those activities which may be regarded as negative in a polarity sense, not necessarily in an intellectual or philosophical sense. Challenges may also be viewed as representing those activities which are internal in scope, which involve us in ways not always visible to the outside world. Challenges may be regarded as those hidden issues lying beneath the surface of the ocean. They can also be likened to the weights we have to pull as we're climbing up a mountain. They may weigh us down, hinder us, and make us feel uncomfortable while at the same time making us stronger and more attentive to their energies.

Challenges are the obstacles, obstructions, hurdles, impediments, stumbling blocks, crosses we have to bear, weak links that need strengthening, and fields of difficulties presented to us in our life's journey. Challenges play an important role in our life and spiritual development. None of us goes through life without struggle of some kind or another. True, some souls struggle less than others but, to be sure, all of us struggle, all of us have problems and difficulties to overcome. *Challenges* are the representation of those struggles. Their true purpose is to make us stronger and more whole. Through them we pay off negative karmas we've created in other lives, actions in need of reactionary reconciliation.

In actuality, Challenges are quite positive . . . if we see them as benefic rather than malefic, as beneficial, not harmful. Unfortunately, this is not always the case because they do bring friction and discomfort into our lives, which is why we must remember that diamonds are made under extreme heat and pressure over an extended period of time, not by a mere and casual blowing of an intermittent wind. Diamonds don't become valuable gems without being subjected to stress and discomfort. As Winston Churchill quotes so beautifully, "Kites rise highest against the wind, not with it." Challenges are the wind which helps our kites fly and our ships sail. They may not be pleasant, but they are necessary, like night is to day; like wind is to kites.

Because *Pinnacles and Challenges* always work together, it begs the question, "Why"? Why would one particular set of obstacles be presented--as the other side of the coin--to a specific activity as expressed by its companion *Pinnacle*? Only God knows for sure. However, one guess is that the vibratory mix of each *Pinnacle/Challenge* component possesses karmic meaning from incarnations past. All actions, through exact, inviolable cosmic law, bear karmic consequences which are irrevocable except through Divine edict. Perhaps it is that the *Pinnacle/Challenge* mix in this life was generated by a similar mix in previous lives, generated within the same field of actions and consequences and, therefore, needs to be resolved within the same mix as well in this incarnation. It's an interesting thought but the fact is, is that we have them and, for better or for worse, we must make the best of them.

Pinnacle/Challenge Calculation

Just as the Lifepath is a derivative of the birthdate data - day, month and year -so also are the Pinnacles and Challenges. The first Pinnacle is discovered by adding the day and month of birth together, an *addcap*. The first Challenge is arrived at by subtracting the day from the month of birth or vice-versa, a *subcap*. The second Pinnacle is a combination of adding the month and year of birth together. The second Challenge results in a subtraction of the two. The third Pinnacle/Challenge combination--the Grand Pinnacle and Grand Challenge--is derived in the following manner: the Grand Pinnacle is the result of the addition of the first and second Pinnacles, while the Grand Challenge is discovered by subtracting the ciphers of the first and second Challenges. This third Pinnacle/Challenge pair, also called the Grand Couplet, represents the core of the life because it is the only P/C pairing which is a derivative of all the birthdate components - day, month and year. The other three P/C pairs are derivatives of only two components of the birthdate. The fourth and final Pinnacle (Crown Pinnacle) is the result of the addition of the day and year of birth. Its companion Crown Challenge is the result of the subtraction of these birthdate components.

As an example, we'll use a birthdate of 3 February 2000. The Simple Pinnacle/Challenge layout for this birthdate is below. The first Pinnacle is 5. It is discovered by adding the day of birth (3) to the month of birth (2 - February). The first Challenge is 1. It is discovered by subtracting the month (2) from the day (3). The second Pinnacle is 4, the sum of the month (2) and the year of birth (2). Its companion Challenge is zero (2 minus 2 = 0). The Third P/C combination--the Grand P/C combination (the Core of the Lifepath) is a 9-1. The 9 comes from the addition of the 5 (first Pinnacle) and the 4 (second Pinnacle). The 3rd Challenge (1) is derived from the subtraction of the 1st and 2nd Challenges (1- 0 = 1). The final Pinnacle (Crown Pinnacle) is a 5: the 3 of the day of birth added to the 2 of the year of birth. The final Challenge (Crown Challenge) is a 1: the 2 of the year of birth subtracted from the 3 of the day of birth.

The Simple Pinnacle/Challenge Matrix: 3 February 2000

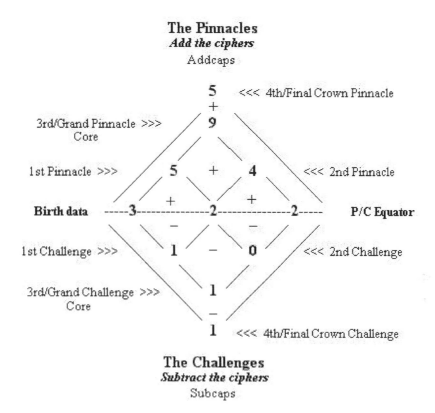

On page *one* of Volume I of *The King's Book of Numerology*, it is stated that, "God did not drop us here without a plan." Through the geometrical pattern of the *Pinnacle/Challenge Matrix* we can also say and *see* that God also did not drop us here without a design for each of our lives. This P/C Matrix clearly shows the intricate and exquisite beauty of a divine design in a form we can understand at our level. As we gaze upon this structure, we cannot help but notice the diamonds/squares formed by the Epoch-Pinnacle-Challenge trinities (Epochs are the day-month-year components of the birthdate).

In this PC Matrix, there are six squares in all. The first is formed by the 1st and 2nd Epochs (day and month) generating the 1st Pinnacle/Challenge sub-matrix. The second square is formed by the 2nd and 3rd Epochs (month and year) creating the 2nd P/C format. The third and forth squares are unique because they are the result of the interaction of all three Epochs (day, month and year) creating the third Pinnacle/Challenge design, as well as a fifth square encompassing the first four. This is why the 3rd Pinnacle and Challenge are referred to as the *Grand Pinnacle* and *Grand Challenge*--they are a composite blend of all of the Epochs and their energies. It is also why they

King

94

are considered the "Core" of the Lifepath. The sixth square is formed by the day and year Epochs (the first and third) generating the final Pinnacle and final Challenge. Throughout this work, it has been mentioned that life is a condition of vibrations within vibrations. Here we see the geometrical view of that statement, for life can also be visually depicted as a structure of squares within squares or diamonds within diamonds.

The idea of the square is important. As we know, the geometrical shape of the circle represents wholeness in a metaphysical sense. The circle contains 360 degrees. The square contains four right angles of 90 degrees each for a total of 360 degrees! In numerology, the number '36' is important because it represents the concept of *squared completion*--'9'--multiplied 4 times. *Four* represents the square of life and also the material elements of fire, water, air and earth. Therefore, within the square of matter are contained the basic ingredients of material creation! In the *Pinnacle/Challenge Matrix*, each P/C time period component is contained within the *square*. Life is, indeed, structured. It has order.

How important this is to our basic spiritual well-being and understanding. How often has any of us felt abandoned, lost, homeless? How often have we thought there is no God or that God doesn't care about us or our problems? The fact of the matter is that He is at the very root of our lives and is responsible for its very design! His universe is ordered. Even the very chaos which we perceive - internally and externally - is based on an extremely intricate organized pattern. If it were not so, the universe could not be studied; science and mathematics could not exist, nor could music fill the air with beautiful melodies because everything in existence is based on numbers - even our lives - and those numbers are the codes and ciphers depicting the vibratory fields which create the Divine Design of life for every one of us at its centermost core. Pythagoras was right: *Numbers rule the universe. Everything is arranged according to number and mathematical shape.*

As we look at the *Pinnacle/Challenge Matrix* further, we notice the shape of the triangle--the hemispheres of each square. The triangle is the symbol of perfection. It represents the Trinity, the Three-in-One construct housing the elements of Father-Son-Holy Ghost, Body-Mind-Spirit, Master-Disciple-Word, man-woman-marriage, father-mother-child. Contained within the square of life is the perfection of life. When we are structured, when we live within the confines of the Law - also the representation of the square - we will find Perfection, we will find Him.

When the 3 (representing the triangle of life) and 4 (the square of matter) are added together the result is 7, the most sacred of all numbers, for it is the synthesis of spirit and matter. Is this not one of the esoteric secrets as to why the numbers 3-4-7 are the most dominant ciphers in the Bible?

The King's Book of Numerology II: Forecasting - Part 1

Through this structure, we also notice that one apex of each triangle is pointing up; the other, down. This represents another pictorialization of the polarized nature of the universe captured so beautifully in the Yin/Yang symbol of the Tao. In this universe, there is a positive force and a negative force. It is the Way, the structure of *this* creation. The apexes of the Pinnacles point up and are the result of the positive charge. The apexes of the Challenges point down and are the result of the negative charge. Positive and negative together - both sides of the polar coin - are represented; both aspects of Nature pictorialized.

There's more. The square represents the four cosmological elements of fire, water, air, and earth. But where is the fifth, ether? It is *ether* which is responsible for man's potential greatness, for *ether* gives him his discriminating intelligence - that one factor which enables him and him alone - not animals or lesser life forms - to realize God. But *ether* is not depicted in the square. Or is it?

Ether is depicted as the elevated apex of the four-sided pyramid! The ancients knew that creation existed as a construct of fire, water, air, and earth. But they also knew that these four did not create the divinity of man. Hence, the pyramid--a four-sided construct elevating to a centermost apex, the fifth point, representing the element *ether* - man's heritage and underlying substance for his divinity! The apex of the pyramid points *up*. Up is the direction of the ascending consciousness. The apex is also elevated - it does not exist at the level of the other four elements. If man is to realize his greatness, he must look *up*! In order for him to move *up*, he must make the *Up Choice* - that choice, those collective moment-to-moment, day-to-day choices, which take him *up*, which elevate his consciousness to a level of divinity!

The Five Points of the Pyramid

<<< **The Fifth Point--Ether**

The Four points of the base:
1-fire 2-water 3-air 4-earth

Five is the *Number of Man*. It is the centerpoint, the fulcrum of the *Alpha-Numeric Spectrum* - the nine basic numbers. One through four proceed it; six through nine follow it. All men - males and females - have *five* in common more than any other number. We all have 5 senses, 5 fingers, 5 toes, 32/5 basic teeth; there are 365/14/5 days in a year, 5 rings on the Olympic flag designating the 5 Olympic continents. Additionally, *five* is the number of freedom which, in a spiritual sense, is detachment - the letting go of material creation to effectuate the process of spiritual ascension into the Inner Regions, in which *five* also has specific significance. Truly, if we desire to be free of this creation, of this bipolar construct where fire, water, air and earth combine to form a prison of material bondage, we must look *up*, move *up*, and rise *up* in our consciousness, in the direction of the Spirit. But there is a caveat relating to the *Five* and that is that its negative side is slavery, the consequence of not understanding that freedom is not a state of action without consequence but rather action taken in consideration of consequence. *Five* rules the senses, sensuality, promiscuity, hedonism, intemperance, over-indulgence - all behaviors eventually leading to enslavement.

The reason for this aside is to, once again, reiterate and bring into focus the basic underlying premise of *The King's Book of Numerology*, which is to clarify numerology as a numerical reflection depicting the intricate, yet beautiful, incarcerating framework of this dimension, thus allowing its truth to propel us to a higher truth, *the* Truth of a Divine Reality - that each of us can rise above this confining creation, become spiritually free and God-Realized. We cannot do this by studying numerology, cosmology, theology, astrology, or any other 'ology', but we can achieve such a noble goal by purifying our spirits so we can go *Within* and merge with His Spirit. *The Kingdom of God is Within. The Way Out Is In*, and the only way to get *In* is to go in, not sit on the outside thinking about, reading about or studying about what is on the inside or marvel at the structure of the outer world of phenomena, feeling as though we have arrived because we've caught a glimpse of its cosmic construction. We have not arrived at the top of the mountain until we get there. We cannot say we have crossed the finish line until the tape is broken. We cannot become God-Realized by simply being aware that we live in a restricting reality. The only way in is in, and the process of *going in* requires a lifetime of dedication to the inward journey, to the purification of the Spirit, to adjusting our behavior to correspond to His behavior. *Merging* is based on Oneness not 'twoness', not duality. To become One we must be the One. As long as we live here, we cannot make our permanent residency *There*. The *Looking Glass* is just that--a looking glass, a way of perceiving the manifestations of *this* reality. It is not the true Reality, nor can it get us *There*. Our love, devotion, dedication, determination, purification, concentration, and desire, coupled with His

Goodness and Grace, will get us There. So let's not get too caught up in *looking*. It's best to get caught up in *Doing* and, subsequently, *Being*.

Enough digression. Returning to our Pinnacle/Challenge Matrix for 3 February in the year 2000, we see that this construct is comprised of strictly single ciphers. There are no double numbers in their pure form or as a result of transition. What this tells us is that the Lifepath is a pure 7 (3 + 2 + 2 = 7). The first Epoch (3) will focus on the issues of self-expression, personal integration, communication, health, beauty, art. Its 5 First Pinnacle (3 + 2) tells us that during its reign there will be freedom, exploration, many varied experiences, a focus on the senses, people in general and movement, possibly travel and undisciplined conduct. All of this will be related to the self-expression of the individual (3 Epoch) which is further related to issues of inward searching, study, analysis, deep thinking, reflection, contemplation, spirituality, religion, philosophy, isolation, withdrawal, secrecy and mystery (the 7 Lifepath). The 1 Challenge (3 - 2) means that the main obstacle and challenge for the individual during this period will be the self, its independence, esteem, worth, value, identity and all things yang or male. When 1 appears as in a Challenge position, it is highly probable that issues involving a man or men (father, grandfather, brother, uncle, cousin, husband, friend, coach, etc.) will exist. Also included in the 1 Challenge field are authority figures or issues involving authority. Through the forces present during this time, it will be challenging for the individual to stand on his own two feet and be accounted for. This is what is mandated by this birth date, by this Lifepath, and every human being born on this date will have to deal with the same general influences during the entirety of the life journey.

The first Pinnacle/Challenge period is the most critical of the life journey. It is here that so much of the individual's character, life issues and philosophies are formulated. Of the two aspects of this P/C period, the Challenge bears the greatest weight, for herein are established the problems accompanying the individual throughout the coming years. Like a burl growing on the trunk of a new tree, problems sewn in this first P/C timeline will be with the person for life. Thus, they possess great weight and should be given appropriate attention.

The 2nd Pinnacle is ruled by the 4 vibration. Thus, it will feature activities of order, structure, work, effort, service, security, restriction and staying put, in contrast to the 5 energy of the 1st Pinnacle of freedom and movement. Because 4 and 5 are opposites, the individual will most likely experience some discomfort when the timeline shift occurs between the first and second Pinnacle because the person will be moving from an environment marked by fun, freedom and change to an environment of regimentation, order, limitation, service and certainly less freedom. A person with a 4 Soul will welcome the change because the Soul governs our needs, wants and desires and the 4

King

second Pinnacle will give the person what he wants. A 5 Soul person, however, will find the change disturbing because he will feel as though he has lost his freedom and is now suffering the bondage of shackles and chains.

The '0' Challenge in this second P/C pair shows no major obstacles during this period. Actually, there is a challenge here which will be explained in due time. It just doesn't show up in the Simple Life Matrix format.

The 3rd Pinnacle (a 9 energy) will concentrate on elevating the individual's focus to the realm of the 'many', the macrocosm, the public stage. *Nine* is artistic and philanthropic as well as inclusive of all vibrations. Therefore, the individual's thoughts and sensitivities will be cast into the arena of the macrocosm. The Challenge during this period will be the 'one', the self and its own desires, wants and needs. *Public demands* and *personal challenges* are the phrases which capture this 3rd Pinnacle/Challenge aspect of the chart.

The final Pinnacle of the 5 focuses on freedom once again. The 5, born out of the 1st Epoch 3 energy and the 3rd Epoch 2 energy, will be based on self-expression, personal integration and relationships. There will be many people, experiences and explorations during this time. These factors will all bear upon the 7 Lifepath, so much of the activity will be in the field of the mind and its thoughts. The 1 final Challenge again heralds an emphasis on the self and, to be sure, this is a lifescript where the only challenge is on the self. By the end of this life path, the individual with this Challenge format, hopefully, will have learned to be independent, to stand on his own two feet, to feel a sense of self worth, assertiveness, creation, personal integrity and self-reliance.

Pinnacle/Challenge Matrix Design: Correct and Incorrect Methods

When establishing the Pinnacle/Challenge Matrix, it is imperative that the day come first, followed by the month and then the year. This is the most accurate design for generating a numerological forecast. Placing the month first, then the day and year is incorrect. Unfortunately, this pattern has been being used in the United States for years. However, thanks to the courageous and gracious generosity of numerologist Helena Davis, the art of numerological forecasting can have a chance to grow.

As a personal note, it was Helena Davis who, early on in my career, explained to me that the forecast matrix of day, month and year was the true method of creating the Pinnacle/Challenge format. Helena had been a practicing numerologist for a quarter of a century in Los Angeles and had been placing the month first, then the day, followed by the year in keeping with the then normal practices of the times. However, late in her career, and in her eighties, she discovered the correct way of producing the PC Matrix and shared her insight with me as I was just beginning my studies, emphatically stating that the month-day-year paradigm was absolutely wrong and that the day-month-year structure totally correct. It was courageous of her to do so, for it meant acknowledging she had been incorrect in using the month, day, year design during her entire career.

Helena was a very honest human being. I believed her but still had to prove the day-month-year theory for myself. It was easy enough to prove. I simply began setting up two different charts for those people whom I knew who were old enough to have an understanding of their lives. I would establish one chart with the day-month-year design and another with the month-day-year design. Then I would simply ask the person, "Has your life been like this (explaining the chart using the day-month-year design), or like this (using the month-day-year design)? Every one confirmed it was the day, month and year design! I have been using this method since 1980 and its accuracy has never been questioned. Quite the contrary. *Therefore, when establishing a Pinnacle/Challenge Matrix, always place the day first, followed by the month and then the year.*

It is easy to see, however, how both methods can yield positive results and thereby create confusion. Why? Because in the first Pinnacle/Challenge set, even when the day and month are reversed, the resulting Pinnacle and Challenge ciphers are the same. However, the rest of the matrix will not be the same and this is where accuracies and inaccuracies are created.

Look at the following two charts. Using the birthdate of 3 February 2000, the first chart shows the correct natal forecasting configuration of day-month-year. The chart below it shows the incorrect configuration of month-day-year. Note the differences. The first PC sets are identical in both formats, but the 2nd, 3rd, and 4th sets are different . . . and inaccurate.

Accurate PC Matrix Design: Day-Month-Year

Birthdate: 3 February 2000
Layout: Day-Month-Year
Correct Configuration

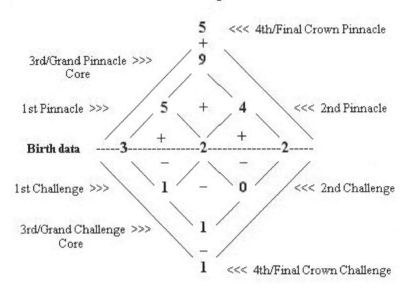

Inaccurate PC Matrix Design: Month-Day-Year

Birthdate: 3 February 2000
Layout: Month-Day-Year
Inaccurate Configuration

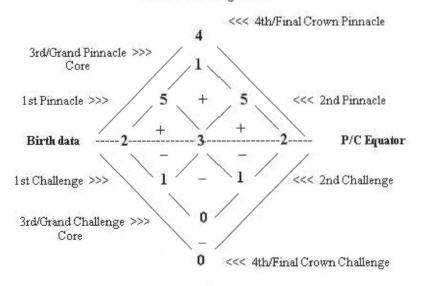

Here we see the first Pinnacle is a 5, like that in the previous chart. Too, the first Challenge Challenge is identical, a 1. But look at the rest of the Pinnacles and Challenges. They're all different. The 2nd Pinnacle is a 5, the 3rd is a 1, and the 4th is a 4. The 2nd Challenge is a 1 and the 3rd and 4th Challenges are zeros in the inaccurate version.. Giving a reading using this configuration will not only create inaccuracies but problems. Once again: do not use this month-day-year method. *When configuring the Pinnacle/Challenge Matrix, always place the day of birth first, followed by the month of birth and then the year of birth.*

The Specific Challenge

Traditionally, Pinnacles and Challenges have always been calculated using only the single numbers of the natal data reduced to a single digit. This does warrant merit, and the results do give partial truth. However, by simply and only reducing every natal component to a single digit and executing Pinnacle and Challenge calculations with the single, simple, crown cipher formats, the entire picture is not revealed, especially the Challenge picture.

In effect, reducing all natal components to a single digit before calculating the Pinnacles and Challenges is inadequate. To insure greater adequacy and accuracy, Challenges need to be generated from their original root structure in addition to being derived from the reduced, single-cipher format. With Pinnacles, the reduced format is not as critical because in the addition process the final result will always be the same. However, such is not the case with the Challenges and their calculations.

Let's take the date we've been using (3 February 2000) to explain this nuance. When each of these components is reduced to its single format, the crowns used to determine the Challenges are: 3 - 2 - 2. The 3 is a single number anyway, as is the 2. However, by reducing the year 2000 to a single digit, the full truth of the Challenge is missed.

In the chart above, which uses the birthdate of 3 February 2000, we see that the 2nd Challenge cipher is a 0. This is the result of subtracting the 2 (2000 reduced to a single digit) from the 2 cipher representing the month of February (2 - 2 = 0). However, the cipher 2000 is not a true 2. The only year in which the 2 is true was the year 2, or to show it another way, 0002. The year 2000 is not a pure 2. It is the year 2000, not 2. When we subtract 2 (the cipher for February) from 2000, the result is 1998, not zero. The quaternary root (four digit root) 1998 reduces first to 27 and then to 9. Therefore, the 2nd Challenge for the birthdate 3 February 2000 is not zero. It is 9! The only time it would be a true zero (0) would have been in the second year of recorded history, the 0002 year. See the chart below.

King

The Specific Pinnacle/Challenge Format: 3 February 2000

Birthdate: 3 February 2000
Specific 9 Challenge

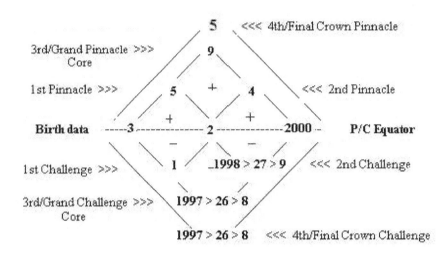

Notice also that using this *Specific Pinnacle/Challenge* format changes the 3rd and 4th Challenges as well! In the *Simple Pinnacle/Challenge* format for the date 3 February 2000, the 3rd and 4th Challenges were both 1s. Using the *Specific Pinnacle/Challenge* format the 3rd and 4th Challenges are both 8s! A truer, clearer, more accurate picture of the Challenge energies now emerges.

What does this mean? Is the *Simple Pinnacle/Challenge* format wrong? No. It simply does not give the entire picture of the Pinnacle/Challenge scenario. In effect, both the *Simple* and *Specific Pinnacle/Challenge* formats are correct, and using <u>both</u> of them yields the most accurate PC conclusions. The reality of the Challenge theory is that many birthdates have two Challenges, not just one! Some may even have three!

Therefore, the date of 3 February 2000 maintains two distinct Challenges. The *Simple* format is as follows: 1st Challenge - 1; 2nd Challenge - 0; 3rd Challenge - 1; 4th Challenge - 1. The *Specific* format is as follows: 1st Challenge - 1; 2nd Challenge - 9; 3rd Challenge - 8; 4th Challenge - 8. Both are correct; both have merit; both must be assessed to create accuracy.

As a note: adding numerical ciphers to produce Pinnacles always yields the same outcome regardless of whether the Simple or Specific format is used. Root structures, however, will be apparent using the Specific format which would not otherwise be known. Therefore, to generate an accurate analysis the Specific format should be used for the Pinnacles as well.

The admonition is: *when calculating the Pinnacles and Challenges, use both the Simple and Specific methods of calculation for greatest clarity.*

The 9 Challenge

Using the Specific method of calculating the Challenge ciphers also sheds further light on the number of zero ciphers in the Challenge matrix. As we've seen from the previous example, when the year 2000 was reduced to a single digit and the month of February, the 2 cipher, was subtracted from it, a zero was the result. In other words, the person would have no Challenges, ostensibly. However, when the year 2000 was left in tact and the 2 of February subtracted from it, the result was a 9, not a zero. Therefore, the individual with this birthdate maintains a 9 Challenge in his destiny during this particular time period, not a zero challenge. This is another reason why the *specific* format *must* be used. It reveals numbers, their corresponding energies, and challenges that would not otherwise be visible or known.

To further elucidate this concept, let's use the date: 1 October 2008. If each of the component parts of this date were first reduced to single digits and the Challenge calculations subsequently made, the result would show absolutely no Challenges whatsoever. The Simple format would reveal a 1 - 1 - 1 Epoch pattern. In the process of subtraction of these single 1 ciphers only zeros appear. See the chart below.

Simple PC Matrix: 1 October 2008

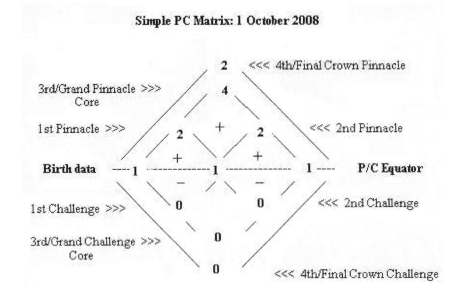

However, when the Specific format is used, the 9 appears in every position of the Challenge matrix. The Pinnacles still remain the same, however. See the following chart.

Specific PC Matrix: 1 October 2008

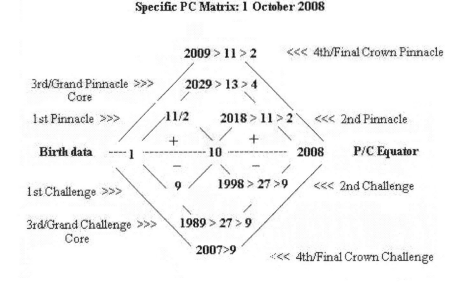

In this example we see that the subject is not devoid of any Challenges. He maintains a 9 Challenge throughout his life. Nine is the energy of power, dominance, humanity, the masses, philanthropy, higher thought, art, education, power, etc. This is quite a contrast to not having any Challenges whatsoever!

Once again, this method and these diagrams illustrate how imperative it is to use both the Simple and Specific methods of calculating the Pinnacles and Challenges. Otherwise, the timeline information will not be as accurate as it could be. This begs the question: "How are the time periods of the Pinnacle/Challenge timelines calculated?"

Timeline Calculations for the Pinnacles and Challenges

There are nine Pinnacle/Challenge Timeline Matrices - one for each of the nine basic numbers. They appear in the chart below. The first P/C Timeline is determined by subtracting the Lifepath crown (single cipher) from *thirty-six* - the binary representing the first *life square*. Thus, the first P/C Timeline will begin at birth and continue through this year. The second P/C Timeline will begin in the year following the last year of the first timeline and run for nine years. The same is true for the third P/C Timeline except, of course, it runs for nine years beginning with the first year following the end of the second P/C period. The fourth Pinnacle/Challenge Timeline begins the first year after the end of the third and continues until the end of life. To find the desired Pinnacle/Challenge Timeline Matrix, look up the Lifepath Crown in the left column of the chart below and follow the age periods to the right.

The Nine Pinnacle/Challenge Timeline Matrices

Lifepath	1st P/C Period	2nd P/C Period	3rd P/C Period	4th P/C Period
1	birth - 35 years	36 - 44	45 - 53	54 to end of life
2	birth - 34 years	35 - 43	44 - 52	53 to end of life
3	birth - 33 years	34 - 42	43 - 51	52 to end of life
4	birth - 32 years	33 - 41	42 - 50	51 to end of life
5	birth - 31 years	32 - 40	41- 49	50 to end of life
6	birth - 30 years	31 - 39	40 - 48	49 to end of life
7	birth - 29 years	30 - 38	39 - 47	48 to end of life
8	birth - 28 years	29 - 37	38 - 46	47 to end of life
9	birth - 27 years	28 - 36	37 - 45	46 to end of life

Pinnacle/Challenge Pillars

Pinnacle/Challenge Pillars are the crowns (viewed as columns for analogy sake) which support the Pinnacles and Challenges and from which the Pinnacles and Challenges take life. By analyzing these *Pinnacle/Challenge Pillars* (PC Pillars for short) we gain further insight into the substance of the crowns they generate. Returning to our basic 3-2-2 Lifepath P/C Matrix (3 February 2000), we get the following illustration.

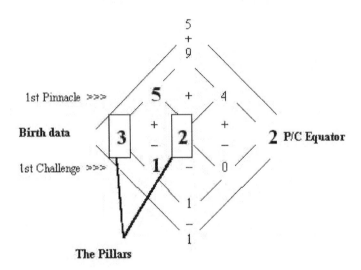

In this case, the 5 (1st Pinnacle) is a pure *five*. Its pillars are the vibrations which support it: the 3 (day of birth) and the 2 (month of birth). If the 5 were a binary such as a 14/5 or a 23/5, the 5 crown would definitely be a different color of 5 energy. These *pillars* play an important role, and therefore, in addition to determining the roots of the crown (if present), we should also look to the PC Pillars to gain additional knowledge of the crown and the story it tells.

For example, in the above illustration the pillars are 3 and 2. These represent fun, friends and relationships. This makes the 5 period of this first pinnacle filled with adventure, good times, communication, relationships, togetherness. The Challenge is a 1 - that of the male, authority figures, the self, its identity, esteem, wholeness, confidence, courage and strength. Generally, when a 1 appears in the 1st Challenge position of a chart it represents difficulties with the father or other male figures such as the grandfather, uncle and/or brothers. It can also represent self-confidence issues, a lack of feeling worthy or wanted. Authority figures or other people with 1 energy dominant in their charts may pose a problem during this energy period. In a girl's chart the 1

The King's Book of Numerology II: Forecasting - Part 1

Challenge can also manifest as being a tomboy during youth and, unfortunately, even sometimes being molested by a male figure. Whatever the specific manifestations, they will definitely be in the realm of yang energy.

However, if the pillars were both 7s, originating from the birthdate of 7 July, the Pinnacle and Challenge would be very different. First, there would be no Challenge (7 - 7 = 0). Second, 7 is the energy of study, thought, reclusion, seclusion, analysis, introspection, introversion, privacy, alienation, separation. Therefore, the resulting first Pinnacle 5 energy of freedom and exploration would be centered in nothing but 7 energy. This colors the 5 in a very different way than the five derived from the 3 and 2 energies. As is clearly visible, pinnacle pillars are important to the process of analysis and illustrate why we must look beyond single ciphers to their roots and/or pillars.

Illustrating further, if we look at the 7 Lifepath formed by the birth data of 21 November 2009, the *PC Pillars* are still different, even though the Pinnacle Crowns which they support are identical.

Pinnacle Pillars: 21 November

In this example we see that the *PC Pillars* supporting the 1st Pinnacle 32/5 Crown are 21 and 11. Not only is the 5 of a different hue (the 32 variety) but it is also fashioned from the 21 and the 11, a different pillar structure entirely from the simple 3 and 2 base of the birthdate 3 February or the 7-7 base of July 7th. This 5 Pinnacle Crown, however, could just as well have been fashioned from a birth date of 20 December. This would make the Pillars 20 and 12 in their Specific form

King

which would still give a 32/5 1st Pinnacle but, obviously, the Pillars themselves would be different, which means the 32 would be different, too. Thus, it is not enough to know the crown form, or even the root form, of any Pinnacle. In the previous examples alone, the 5 Pinnacle Crown could be formed from pillars of 3 and 2; 7 and 7; 21 and 11, or 20 and 12 - the latter two even forming the same root. The moral of this story: *when analyzing a Pinnacle Crown, look to its **roots** as well as its **pillars***. Again, we must look closely at all of the vibrations present which join to create a crown, any crown, in any position in the chart. This *Pinnacle/Challenge Pillar* theory illustrates this point and is yet another example of how numbers are mixtures of layers upon layers of vibrations and how the vibrational fabric of our lives can be so alike and yet be so different.

Grand Couplet

The Lifepath is a composite of all three of the birthdate components: day, month and year. Together, this *natal triumvirate* generates the script of our life replete with four Pinnacle/Challenge Timelines and three Epoch Timelines (to be discussed in Chapter Four). As the personal characteristics of the full name and birthdate of an individual are contained in the Basic Matrix - the subject of *The King's Book of Numerology, Volume I, Foundations & Fundamentals*, the *Life Matrix* is the name given to the structure which houses the Pinnacles, Challenges, and Epochs.

The 3rd Pinnacle and 3rd Challenge are important aspects of the Life Matrix because, as mentioned earlier, they are the only components which are derivatives (by addition or subtraction) of the natal triumvirate (day - month - year). No other Pinnacle or Challenge reflects this composition or bears this distinction. Hence, they are special; they are *grand* and are referred to collectively as the *Grand Couplet*. Separately they are referred to as the *Grand Pinnacle* and the *Grand Challenge*. In this regard, they also represent the *core* of the Life Matrix, just as the Natural Soul cipher in the Basic Matrix is the core of the person (the Expression).

Each Pinnacle and Challenge timeline exists for a limited duration. The *Grand P/C Couplet* also reigns for a specific time period of fixed years - in its case, nine years, like the second. However, because of its unique parentage - being the child of all of the *natal triumvirate* components, it carries another special distinction. The *Grand Couplet's* energy veil extends beyond its own specific nine year field, laying a blanket of energy over the pinnacles and challenges below it, as well as being the core of the Lifepath and the foundation for the Crown Pinnacle and Challenge following it. From birth onward until the end of its reign, the influence of the *Grand Couplet* can be strongly felt. It, therefore, can be regarded as the main Pinnacle and Challenge throughout life until that point in time where it is surpassed and left behind. This will occur at the beginning of the fourth Pinnacle and Challenge period, somewhere, generally speaking, between the ages of forty-six and fifty-four (see *The Nine Pinnacle/Challenge Timeline Matrices*). How much influence the Grand Couplet maintains on a person after the individual has transited its energy field of the 3rd PC position is not yet understood. However, it's power is such that it can definitely be considered as the center (the core) of the Lifepath in both the Pinnacle position (that which draws the person up and out) and the Challenge position (that which tugs at the person, forcing him to pay attention to possible stumbling blocks and hurdles along the way).

Diagram of the Grand Couplet

Simple PC Matrix: 3 February 2000

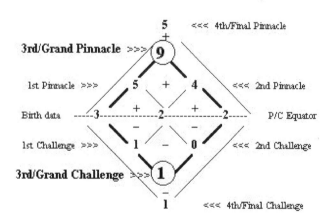

As we view the previous illustration of the Simple PC Matrix for 3 February 2000, the effect of the *Grand Couplet* is readily apparent. This 7 Lifepath configuration maintains a 9-1 Grand Couplet which will be activated during the ages of thirty-nine to forty-seven but generally activated from birth through the forty-seventh year as a result of its innate power. On the forty-eighth birthday, the Grand Couplet's energy field will be surpassed and it will no longer have a direct effect. However, all of the actions initiated during its reign, all of the seeds sown and the boomerangs thrown upon the wind, will one day return, for better or for worse, and the Grand Couplet's effect will be felt--indirectly. How important it is, therefore, to constantly mind our fields, for all crops sown in the Spring do not necessarily come to fruition in the Summer. Some seeds, sewn in Spring, are harvested in Fall when the wind may not be warm and inviting, when the fragrance and beauty of the flowers have waned and withered and when the air is filled with the quiet hush of approaching death.

The 9-1 Grand Couplet means that the individual's prime Pinnacle activity from birth to age forty-seven, will be concentrated in energies which are universal, encompassing, expansive, humanitarian, artistic, public, charismatic, all-embracing, broadcasting. The first two Pinnacles will rule directly during their allotted time but overseeing them is the Grand Rulership of the Grand Pinnacle. It is the main activity for the period of the first three Pinnacles.

So it is with the Grand Challenge. In this case, it is a 1. Hence, the fundamental obstacle during the life of the individual with this particular 3-2-2/7 Lifepath will be the self, the yang. This 9-1 Grand Couplet radiates an interesting relationship between the macro, as represented by the 9, and the micro, represented by the 1. Public and private, impersonal and personal, the many and the self - this is the primary and dominant Pinnacle/Challenge theme until age forty-eight when the new Pinnacle, the 5, comes into view. However, because of the date configuration the 4th Challenge, the 1, will remain the same.

This latter format - the 3rd and 4th Challenges being identical--is very common. In fact, it is the rule more than the exception. But there are exceptions. As we have already seen, more complex birthdates usually bear more complex results, and it is in these more involved lives and their more involved numerical patterns where the last two Challenges often vary.

But the Simple PC Matrix for the birthdate of 3 February 2000 is incomplete. As we have discovered, the Specific PC Matrix manifests a second set of Challenges, and the Grand Challenge of the Specific set is an 8. Therefore, an individual with this birthdate will have two Grand Challenges: 1 and 8.

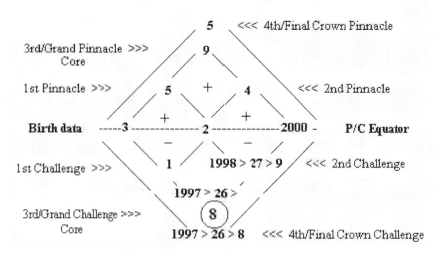

Birthdate: 3 February 2000
Specific 8 Grand Challenge

The 8 Grand Challenge will focus on areas of business, commerce, marketing, administration, social interaction, the flow of relationship, making things efficient, getting the job done, being "in the loop," experiencing financial success, wealth and power. The negative aspect of this 9 GC energy is that things can fall apart, become inefficient, uncoordinated, unprofessional, sluggish. The secret here is that one must simply "take care of business." Ignorance of this fact will create difficulties and possible failure.

Richard Johnston Roe's PC Matrix

Using both the Simple and Specific calculation methods, let's now take a look at the influences/issues/themes contained within RJ's PC Matrix. RJ's birthdate of 6 December 1999 gives him a 1 Lifepath with the Pinnacle/Challenge Timelines shown below.

Lifepath	1st PCTL	2nd PCTL	3rd PCTL	4th PCTL
1	birth - 35	36 - 44	45 - 53	54 on

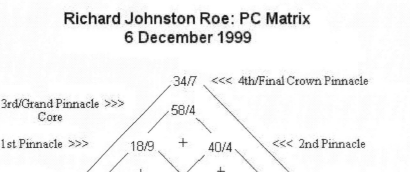

**Richard Johnston Roe: PC Matrix
6 December 1999**

From birth to age thirty-five, RJ's Pinnacle is an 18/9 so his experiences will be large. There is a good chance one of his parents is involved in an occupation dealing with the masses. He may also travel during this period. The 6 and 3 pinnacle pillars denote music or some kind of artistic endeavor and family. The 6 and 3 dual Challenges interestingly mirror the pinnacle pillars forming his first PC timeline. A lack of love or need of love within the family environment will press heavily on RJ during his formative years. This is a result of the afflicted 6 energy. His self-expression and image of himself will also be the focus of much energy as witnessed by the 3 Challenge. He could very well study writing, music, or art of some kind during this time frame as well because the number three rules words and all kinds of communication and six governs harmony and artistic beauty as well as the home life.

This theory of dual Challenges is an interesting concept and deserves more research. We know that the traditional method of only using the crown of the month, in this case a 3 from the twelve binary, is a valid theory. It has been used in numerological work of years. But we also know that December is the twelfth month and not the third month, March, so to simply address December as a three and in effect, make it March, deprives it (December) of its own identity and complexity. Hence, to identify it in Epoch terms as 12 makes logical sense. Thus, two Challenges are derived as a result of using this 12 binary as the 2nd Epoch. Furthermore, current research seems to strongly validate the validity of two Challenges. And why not? People certainly have more than one obstacle to overcome in life and this theory of dual Challenges seems to afford an appropriate explanation.

The second PC timeline shows a Pinnacle of 4 and Challenges of both 16/7 and 2. Work, career, the job, stability, security and the home life will be major themes during this time, as might also be the character traits of honesty, fidelity, effort and dependability as represented by the 4 Pinnacle. This will occur between the ages of thirty-six and forty-four. The 16/7 and 2 Challenges portend emotional dramas and difficulties with interpersonal relationships, others and females.

Challenges are basically "afflicted" energies. They cause us concern in the least and chaos in the extreme. Love problems and infidelities, separations, divorces, betrayals and other sad and sorrowful experiences usually accompany the 16/7 energy in a Challenge position. Coupled with the 2 energy which rules treachery, deceit, relationships and women, this combination does not bode well for RJ's marital or relationship happiness. Chances are good that either he or his wife will stray from the marriage, assuming he is married. If he's not married, there will still be the likelihood of betrayals of some variety with which he will have to deal. Factually, it is not uncommon for marriages to fail and divorce ensue during this 16/7 energy timeline. Nor is it uncommon for alcohol to be a problem during this period since 7 rules alcoholics and alcoholism. Without question, this will be a difficult time for RJ on a personal level. If he is spiritually aware and advanced, he will be able to buffer the storm with peace and grace, but make no doubt about it - there will be storms of spiritual testing during this phase of his life.

RJ will be working hard during this time but his love life may well undergo much stress as a result of his own incapacity to be purely loving, upright and honest. For him to be spiritually sound and whole, he will have to exhibit qualities of restraint, self-abnegation, discipline, continence and purity of behavior. This could well be a time of major ignominious conduct leading to a fall for RJ. It is a period where he is walking through an explosive mine field, and a lack of focus, especially spiritual focus, will result in his downfall, much to his chagrin. He will have to avoid indulgence in illicit love issues and dishonesty in his dealings with others, particularly women. This could be a time of financial strain and struggle and he must be careful not to turn to alcohol as a solution to his problems, problems which he could possibly create and generate through an overly imbalanced concern with himself, his desires, wants, needs and cravings. To his defense, however, the love and betrayal issues could primarily be with others. In any case, he will be experiencing them to some degree.

This is, without question, a stormy period of RJ's life and to have foreknowledge of its issues and concerns could certainly benefit him greatly. Otherwise, he will be walking ignorantly and

King

blindly into a vibrational vortex which could spell disaster for him. If he knew of his predicament beforehand, he could prepare, bolster his defenses, fight the good fight by concentrating on the positive vibrations of each cipher and, thus weather the storm successfully.

From a martial arts perspective, for example, when one fights, he is bound to get hit. No fighter who ever did a great amount of fighting ever went unscathed. But one of the keys to being a successful fighter is to avoid the big hits, to parry them, make them glance or miss their target entirely. Little blows are easier to manage than large ones, but one major impact from a blasting kick or punch could end it all suddenly and painfully. This is why excellent fighters study fighting - to acquire every advantage necessary to gain victory and keep themselves from being hit, hurt, or seriously injured. For RJ, this second life square foretells a struggle. It is unavoidable but not unmanageable. He needs to prepare properly so he can protect himself properly . . . from himself and his actions, as well as those of others within his personal environment. He also needs to be realistic about his life, its potentialities and realities.

This last statement, *being realistic about life, its potentialities and realities*, is an issue which needs addressing. Frankly, most of us are not realistic about our lives. We are so caught up in this world of illusion in which we live that everything seems to be an illusion, even ourselves. Much of our dilemma is centered in not understanding existence from a cosmic basis. It is also exacerbated by a fundamental lack of spiritual focus and substance which intensifies the effects of the maya. Our lusts, cravings, needs and banal desires further complicate the issue. We want, we want, we want, but, unfortunately, most of the time we want the wrong things. We want those things which satisfy our worldly and carnal appetites because we think they will make us happy and bring us peace. Nothing could be further from the truth.

Worldly things bring worldly rewards and satisfy the mind for a time, but the soul, which is pure Spirit, is made happy and content only by the Spirit. This is why most of us feel lost occasionally, even when things are going well from a worldly point of view. We're seeking happiness and comfort from something which cannot possibly satisfy our most primal spiritual need for fulfillment. The world will never, nor can it ever, fulfill us because it is something separate from our centermost core and its inherent needs and desires. Ultimately, we are Spirit, not flesh. This place in which we reside is more wilderness than homeland. In fact, when we travel the spiritual path for just a little distance, we find that this earthly domain is not even a good place to visit. This world in which we live is part of the nether pole of creation. It is not Home. Sooner or later we must come to grips with this fact, to the reality that we live in a nether land and we will not be happy as long as we try to make it some paradise which it can never be.

The King's Book of Numerology II: Forecasting - Part 1

Furthermore, our refusal to accept and live by the theory of sowing and reaping, cause and effect, karma, keeps us involved in a process which naturally produces pain and suffering and complicates our lives and journeys through innumerable incarnations in a myriad of bodies and forms. In any one life, we will get what is in our destiny to receive, and not one iota will be added to or subtracted from our lot. Our entire life blueprint, so say Perfect Masters, is established before we are even born, and the karmas we are to experience cannot be changed . . . by us or anyone else. To hope and pray and beseech God to give us something or take away something which is in our destiny, which He has already established by designing our blueprint for this incarnation, is being totally unrealistic. This lack of realism creates false hope, frustration, emotional imbalance, anger, worry, depression, confusion and general unhappiness.

On the other hand, if we were realistic about our lives, if we accepted what our destiny has for us and make the best of it, we can be more balanced and content. If, for example, we have a craving for candy but cannot eat it for whatever reason, why go into the candy store? Why place ourselves in a situation which is hopeless and which will only frustrate and imbalance us? Why even daydream about candy or socialize with others whose whole life is absorbed with candy? It makes no sense, and such behavior certainly creates no peace. And if we do these things, all of which frustrate us and make us unhappy, whom do we have to blame? Mommy? Daddy? The candy store owner? The candy maker? Other people who eat candy? The government for allowing candy to be sold and consumed? God for creating candy in the first place? No. We can only look to ourselves to blame for our own unhappiness, discontent, pain, suffering and hardship. As Guru Nanak says: *I blame not another, I blame my own karmas. Whatever I sowed, so did I reap. Why then put the blame on others?*

Yet, we seem to be hopelessly in love with the candy store and its wares. The basic human focus is to treat life as a candy store, a playground and quest for material acquisition and sensual indulgence rather than a divine opportunity of critical importance to the evolution and liberation of our soul. We generally seek earthly ease, not Freedom; worldly pleasure, not His Pleasure; transitory happiness, not enlightenment; all things external; few things, if any, internal. We spend our lives chained to our appetites rather than fighting to free ourselves from them. We blind ourselves to the fact that we must pay for what we do and that we must also, one day, die. For us, life is bordered by the cradle and the grave. We give no credence or consideration to the time and life before or after birth or death. We don't care from whence we came or to where we are going. Somehow, we believe that if we close our eyes to Reality, or don't question it, we can live our lives safely, free to behave and act in any manner we choose without consequence. Spiritual sight is not

King

even an issue. Worldly fame, fortune, name and pleasure are all we seek and all we seek to understand or acknowledge. For us, reality is living in the depths of the valley, not striving to climb the Mountain and discover what lies above that which we cannot see. For us, home is prison and as long as we are comfortable, we are happy, even if we are confined, constricted, restricted and chained. In fact, we love our chains and our only major concern is to upgrade them to silver and gold, showing other prisoners that we have status and merit because our chains are made of gold, not ordinary, rusty old iron or steel. Little do we think what it would be like if we had no chains, if we were free, if we revolted against the fetters of our incarceration and limitation and escaped from the prison to live beyond the realm of what we currently know.

However, as Perfect Mystics tell us, there is much more to life than we know. We *can* be free of our chains and escape from the prison. The Land beyond is sweet but remains a Home only to those with courage enough to fight for their freedom and liberation. It's the candy store or the Eternal Door. To walk through this door mandates a certain amount of spiritual maturity and a realistic perspective of life. We don't need to cry over spilt milk or suffer as a result of chasing the pot of gold at the end of the rainbow. We need to awaken to what is real and what is real for each of us as far as our own unique life path is concerned.

When we subscribe to this point of view, we will begin to gradually rise above the maya and illusion which confine us, bewilder us, blind us, entrap us and cause us untold hardship and misery. This is not running away from reality. In fact, it is running to it. Yes, it is escapism but escapism with a capital E. When we awaken to the reality of our incarceration, the only goal we should have *is* to escape, and if we choose to remain in the prison, we cannot complain about our mistreatment, our poor miserable lot, our pain, our suffering, our frustration, our nightmares, our lack of joy and happiness. As Perfect Master Maharaj Charan Singh Ji has stated so eloquently, *Just live in the creation and get out of it!* This is what we must do spiritually, and we can begin by being realistic about where we are, who we are, and what this human destiny has to offer.

Returning to RJ, we see that his 3rd PC timeline between the ages of forty-five and fifty-three shows that he is still pulled by work and career (58/4). However, by this time he has passed through the tumultuous tunnel of his life (the 2nd Challenge period) and is now confronted with issues of his own ego, self esteem, identity, worth, value, creativity and independence. The 1 Challenge always creates issues with the self to some degree. Even authority figures can come into the picture here. Because RJ's Lifepath is a 1, this period will be highlighted for sure.

Richard Johnston Roe's last PC timeline, from age fifty-four onward, includes a 7 Crown Pinnacle and dual Crown Challenges of 22/4 and 5. The 7 Pinnacle heralds the activity of
The King's Book of Numerology II: Forecasting - Part 1

internalization, introspection, reflection, study, isolation - in effect, all things internal. RJ will find himself seeking reclusion during this period. He may be asking himself the heavy questions of life: "Why am I here?" "Is there a God?" "What is life all about?" There is the chance that he will engage in activities which study the mystical and metaphysical, or he may curl up in a state of depression and isolation.

The 22/4 and 5 Challenges detail concerns with security (4) and freedom (5). The 4 and 5 together in this Crown Challenge position are not uncommon. RJ may either have great security (4) with a lot of free time on his hands (5), or he may want for security (4) while existing in a state of uncertainty (5). Both scenarios could easily play themselves out. In fact, both could be simultaneously operative. He could have great wealth (22/4) but be plagued, as many rich people are, with losing their riches; at the same time RJ could be very free and unencumbered but uncertain of his future (5). Whatever the specific manifestation is, he will definitely have to deal with security and freedom issues in some capacity during this final aspect of his life. With these varying scenarios it is clear why we must do our forecasting in the light of *potentials* rather than *certainties*.

Pinnacle/Challenge PEs

So far we've been discussing the influence/theme aspects of the energies in the Pinnacle/Challenge fields. But what happens to the individual when the P/C energies mix with the Expression energies? The answer lies in the P/Es of each Pinnacle/Challenge timeline.

The Pinnacle Challenge PE (Performance/Experience) is simply formed by adding the Expression to the influencing PC energies. This was the lesson of the Life Cycle Patterns discussed in Chapter Two.

Pinnacle (influence) **+ Expression = Pinnacle PE** (outcome)

Challenge (influence) **+ Expression = Challenge PE** (outcome)

When the Pinnacle or Challenge PE is discovered, the general outcomes to the initiating and causal energies are also discovered. Knowing these realities will give us an enormous understanding of our lifepaths and the general run of our destiny during the four major specific time periods of our lives. When we *know*, we are less prone to not knowing (i.e., being ignorant) and therefore less susceptible to making mistakes which bind us negatively in a karmic sense.

King

Knowing Pinnacle and Challenge PEs also allows us to adjust better to the ups and downs of life. Most of us intuitively know our lives anyway, and the PC complex simply confirms our intuitions. Such *knowing* illuminates our path and keeps us from being blind-sided, falling into holes and ditches, as well as being able to enjoy the sunshine days of our lives. By seeing where we're going, we can direct the energies of our being more accurately. Thus, we will not be helpless victims cast aimlessly on the ocean of life but actual participants in a very divine, special, specified journey. God's plan for us becomes clear and we, therefore, become clear. We can then work in harmony with the divine plan, not in opposition to it.

Additionally, by having awareness of the PC energies, we can see where others are having challenges, where they're going, and what their issues are. This is especially helpful in the raising of children and being more in sync with our spouse. Problems cannot be solved if the root of the problem is not known. Pinnacles and Challenges give us true knowing, true understanding, and thus allow us to be more capable of solving the problems which face us and issues presenting themselves to us as we perambulate the paths of our separate destinies.

Another major benefit to knowing the PC matrix is on the professional level. Psychologists and therapists can be of enormous assistance to their clients by knowing their clients in the deepest sense of the word, in the deepest sense of their destiny. Knowing a person's path in life and the environments he will be transiting holds untold significance for a doctor or therapist. Numerology is a science, and those professional healers who awaken to its reality will be in a position to further help those who seek their assistance. To avoid the truths numerology offers is to avoid (and deny) science and the benefits derived from it, especially for those in need of help.

To be sure, and in all truth, numerology is neither crystal ball gazing or some misguided quackery. Those who deny it, denigrate it, malign it and refuse to avail themselves of its gifts are not true scientists, regardless of their credentials; nor do they hold any real compassion for those who seek their counsel in pursuit of wellness. Ego has no place in the healing arts. The true scientist, the true healer, the true seeker, investigates and operates from a position of courage, inquisitiveness and right action. Such a professional would never leave the smallest stone unturned if that which lay beneath the stone would help other living beings under his care . . . and help them beyond the barriers of so called professional status in the hierarchy of world opinion. Knowing the lifepath of an individual and the deeper awarenesses offered by the Pinnacle/Challenge Timeline can only help. To avoid its gifts would be a sad tragedy.

Richard Johnston Roe: PC/PE Matrix

Let's now assess the Pinnacle/Challenge PE structure of RJ's Lifepath. For a less complex picture, we'll reduce all the numbers in his PC Matrix to crowns (simple ciphers). To each of the crowns we'll add RJ's Simple Expression of 7. See the PC/PE Matrix chart below.

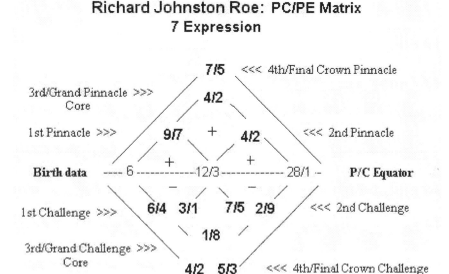

With this PC/PE Matrix we have an excellent picture of the general energy fields through which Richard Johnston Roe will be transiting during his life. The influences/issues/themes are visible in the first number of each Pinnacle/Challenge I/R set in the chart above; their outcomes, realities, performances and experiences are visible in the second number.

First Pinnacle/Challenge Set

RJ's first Pinnacle is a 9/7. The issues involved in this period are the many, the macrocosm, the public, travel, art, universality, power and dominance (9). The realties and outcomes associated with this incoming, causal energy combining with RJ's 7 Expression is a 7 effect energy field. As we recall from volume 1 of *The King's Book of Numerology*, RJ has a 7 void in his name (no G, P, or Y).

When voids appear in the PC/PE Matrix anywhere, transiting through the timeline of their energy fields will generally present difficulties. Voids are absences of specific energy. When the individual crosses fields dominated by the very energy he's lacking, problems occur. Why?

Because the person doesn't have the skills or tools needed to manage the vibration at hand. It's like being thrown into carpenter land and not having a hammer, saw, level or measuring tape. How does one manage something when he doesn't have the tools to do so? See the dilemma?

Therefore, as far as RJ's life is concerned, this opening period of his journey, which lasts from birth through age thirty-five since he has a 1 Lifepath, will constantly present him with difficulties associated with the 7 energy. Seven rules isolation, separation, heartache, suffering, sorrow, solitude, tribulation, turmoil and spiritual chastening. All of the discomfort associated at this time of his life will originate from the public at large and the store of many experiences as represented by the 9 vibration in the influence/theme position. These 7 outcome conditions may also spring from a person with a 9 Expression, Nature or PE. Numbers represent conditions, circumstances, ideals, values, specific people and the attributes present in the charts of those individuals. This is why we can see "generally" but not "specifically;" why we deal with potential realities, not actualities. There are simply too many variables to get an absolute "read" in regards to a numerology forecasting chart. Through numbers, God allows us the privilege of seeing the road map of our life's journey but not every little bump along the way.

The positive aspect of this opening 9/7 period is that 7 rules all things spiritual and mystical. RJ could easily establish a sound, spiritual foundation for the rest of his life during this opening Pinnacle period because he will be exposed to many ideas, people, circumstances, art forms and thoughts. These will deepen his understanding and breadth of knowledge.

Accompanying his 9/7 Pinnacle, RJ has two separate and distinct Challenge Sets: 6/4 and 3/1 during this opening PC timeline. The 6/4 I/R pair depicts love issues (6) in the house (4). The second 3/1 pair illustrates health issues (3) of the self (1). RJ will most likely not have an harmonious and personally fulfilling early life. There is the good possibility that he may have some physical challenge because of the 3/1 modality. To be sure, his sense of joy, fulfillment, self-expression and communicative abilities will be confronted and assaulted. From these experiences he will hopefully learn to be kind, loving, balanced, independent and whole. He will have to work on these, however. These are the lessons meant for him given by Him.

As a note, challenges, although difficult, are meant for our good. Through them we gain invaluable experiences, pay off old karmas from past lives, learn to be sensitive to the energies associated with certain vibrations, strengthen weak links and are prevented from being too complacent in life. Challenges make life exciting. They also give us the chance to become worthy and whole. No one on this earth is void of challenges. We all have them. The saving grace is that when we know what our specific Challenges are we can deal with them more efficiently and wisely, learn and grow from them, stay balanced and adjustable in life.

Second Pinnacle/Challenge Set

RJ's second Pinnacle I/R set is a 4/2. It will be active between the ages of 36 and 44. This energy pattern focuses on work (4) and relationship (2). RJ will be associated with being the supporter and helper during this phase of life. The idea of partnership is also seen in his 2/9 I/R Challenge set. Relationships (2) will expand within the macrocosm field of the many (9) and possibly create a time period where relationships, partnerships, associations (2) come to an end (9). The 7/5 modality depicts changes and movement (5) in the way he thinks (7) about life. Mentally, this will not be a static period. RJ's Expression is also a 7 so the changes could well be within himself.

Third Pinnacle/Challenge Set

This timeline period represents the Grand Pinnacle/Challenge aspect of RJ's life. It is *the* core of his destiny and influences his whole life generally but specifically between the ages of 45 to 53. Here we see a repeat of his 4/2 second Pinnacle. Therefore, the influences and themes of order, structure, work, routine, effort, discipline, devotion, loyalty, limitation and service (4) playing themselves out in the arena of relationships, females, others, support and balance (2) will dominant his life's journey in a positive sense. The main challenge of his life is the 1/8 I/R modality of self (1) in interaction (8). This energy pattern is prevalent in the charts of entrepreneurs. Eight rules business, commerce, material wealth and success. The 1 governs independence of action. Therefore, it's a good guess that RJ will be self-employed during his life, have money and experience success. The challenge will be in managing his finances and business enterprise. Remember, too, that RJ's Lifepath is a 1. This 1/8 Core/Grand Challenge intensifies the 1/8 LP/PE set of his Basic Matrix, thus creating a *stacking* of 1/8 energy and corroborating the entrepreneurial aspects of his life script.

Fourth Pinnacle/Challenge Set

This final Crown PC combination again depicts RJ's involvement with work and relationships as seen in his 4/2 Challenge. Therefore, this theme occupies a huge part of his life and its lessons. If his parents knew this when he was born, they could have focused his attention in both thought and action on the positive aspects of both the 4 and 2 energy, thus giving RJ definite tools with which to manage the situations, events and circumstances of his life's journey as they presented themselves. Knowing the road map and the things to be confronted on the journey gives untold advantages to the path traveler.

The 5/3 second Crown Challenge shows changes, motion, freedom, detachment, loss and experience playing themselves out in the realms of health, well-being, communication, self-fulfillment, personal expression, joy, pleasure, marriage and children. RJ could feel trapped by a lack or loss of his personal freedom and/or health. There is also the possible scenario of him experiencing a variety of things which bring him pleasure - a condition which would more likely than not create unwholesome results.

RJ's Crown Pinnacle I/R set is 7/5, a duplicate of one aspect of his second Challenge. The difference is that now the experiences will, with his maturity, hopefully be viewed as more positive than negative. RJ may not feel hindered or put upon by the exploration, changes, losses and movement within his mind and thoughts but welcome such things, if not seek them out himself. The other side of the coin of this 7/5 IR set is that there could potentially be losses (5) resulting from chaos and struggle (7). It's all about attitude and level of consciousness.

Summation

When working with the Pinnacle/Challenge (PC) Timeline keep these principles in mind.

1. Always format the natal data in the day-month-year pattern.

2. When calculating the Pinnacles and Challenges, use both the Simple and Specific methods of calculation to arrive at the most complete picture of the P/C Timeline.

3. Be aware of PC Pillars and root structures.

4. Remember the Grand Couplet (Grand Pinnacle and Grand Challenge) is the core of the Lifepath. It's power can neither be overlooked nor underestimated.

Chapter Four

EPOCH TIMELINE - ETL

As we have learned, the Lifepath represents the script, the dramatic screenplay of our lives. Screenplays are subdivided into acts, usually three in number. Act I establishes the characters and plot for the entire play. Act II embellishes the problem or theme of the play established in Act I and expands upon the conflict of the characters. Act III builds to a dramatic conclusion, solution and resolution of the play's theme, achieving some sort of catharsis and finalization.

Epochs are subdivisions of the Lifepath. They can be likened to the acts of the screenplay of our lives and are generated from the three parts of our birthdate: day, month and year. The day of our birth is Act I; the month represents Act II and the year of our birth equates to Act III. As we've discussed, when establishing an Epoch Timeline always place the day first, followed by the month and then the year. Never place the month first.

When we consider the Lifepath's three Acts, or Epochs, we can give them the same consideration as that of a three act screenplay. The First Epoch, Act I, sets the vibrational pattern affecting the main character. This Act will have latter consequences in generating a foundation for the rest of the life drama. This First Act is the one in which the individual will take birth and grow through adolescence to adulthood. Events, circumstances, conditions and issues occurring in Act I often involve a lifetime of resolution.

The Second Epoch, Act II, occurs during the middle years of life and generally spans the twenties, thirties, forties and sometimes fifties decades. This is the Epoch where decisions made and actions taken are done when one is in the capacity of an adult, not a child, so their consequences bear great weight in establishing core factors of responsibility, accountability, honorability, ethics and personal maturity. Normally, the physical body is at its greatest pinnacle as far as health is concerned during this stage because the body is neither painstakingly growing into adulthood or suffering the marked decline of advancing years.

The Third Epoch, Act III, generally occurs from the late forties and early fifties to the end of life. The lessons encountered and actions created earlier in life will often have their consequences felt here in this period and the life's lessons may well come to some sort of resolution and finalization should the individual live long enough.

This Third and final Epoch is critical for the soul. Bad seed sewn here will not wither and die but will come to fruition in subsequent lives. Business left undone and incomplete, unfilled desires and unresolved issues will be carried over to other incarnations. Another issue with this phase of life is that less-than-positive deeds created from birth and accumulating through life may become heavy and oppressive, making it difficult for the individual to live a relaxed, joyful and happy life. The challenge here is living with grace and poise while staying focused on preparing for the journey ahead. With these considerations, a life purely lived from birth cannot be stressed enough. This incarnation is only one phase of existence. Wise is he who looks ahead and plans his life accordingly, harmonizing his behavior with all things holy, good and pure.

Epochs as Continents

Our world has a variety of continents. As a second analogy of the Epoch picture, if our Lifepath were equated to one of nine worlds (signified by the single numbers 1-9), the three Epochs (or Acts) of one's life would be its three main continents. As actual continents possess their own distinctive geographical attributes, so the Epochs maintain their own characteristics as defined by their numerical ciphers. The first continent (first epoch) would be the land were we are born and raised. The second continent (second epoch) is the one through which we work and transit the middle part of the life journey. The third continent (third epoch) will be the energetic land mass upon which we live out the rest of our days.

Epoch Nuances

In our life each of us stars in a play (Lifepath) which is built upon three separate *Epochs*, referenced earlier as Act I, Act II and Act III. Because of the different combinations of numbers in our birthdate, there are many nuances to this play. For example, there are times when the three main acts may be duplicated within the life script itself, thus extending, repeating or reinforcing the theme of the play. A person with a 1 Lifepath could possibly have two acts within the script also governed by the number *One*. A birthdate of 1 August 2008 would create such a numeric scenario.

The King's Book of Numerology II: Forecasting - Part 1

In this case, not only would the Lifepath's major theme be centered in the 1 energy of self and yang issues, but the first and third acts of the life play would also concentrate on the 1 vibration (the birth day of 1 and the birth year of 2008, a 1 in reduction), thus intensifying the major Lifepath theme itself during different stages of the life journey. Another scenario is the birthdate 19 January 2006. The Epoch crowns of this birthdate would be 1, 1 and 8. Another possible numeric birthdate scheme would be 28 March 2004. Here the Epoch crowns would be 1, 3 and 6.

Yet, there could well be no epoch containing 1 energy and still the Lifepath would be a 1. For example, the birthdate of 5 March 2000 creates a 1 Lifepath (5 + 3 + 2 = 10 > 1) but none of its parts (Epochs) are ones. This gives a much different picture and creates a much different play than the first birthdate examples listed in the previous paragraph. In this example of a 5 March 2000 birthdate, the major theme of self, identity, independence and yang energy is the same as that of any 1 Lifepath, but the acts of the play - the continents upon which the person is to learn his lessons and act out the drama of his life - are much different. These nuances are more visually represented by the following charts.

Example #1

Lifepath
1 August 2008
1

Epoch 1	Epoch 2	Epoch 3
Day	Month	Year
1	8	2008
1	8	1

Example #2

Lifepath
19 January 2006
1

Epoch 1	Epoch 2	Epoch 3
Day	Month	Year
19	1	2006
10	1	8
1	1	8

Example #3

Lifepath
28 March 2004
1

Epoch 1	Epoch 2	Epoch 3
Day	Month	Year
28	3	2004
10	3	6
1	3	6

Example #4

Lifepath
5 March 2000
1

Epoch 1	Epoch 2	Epoch 3
Day	Month	Year
5	3	2000
5	3	2

As we can see, all of the previous birthdates generate a 1 Lifepath. However, each of these 1 Lifepaths is very different, i.e., not all 1 Lifepaths are the same and people who have a 1 Lifepath will have similar but different lives. Therefore, when analyzing a Lifepath and giving a reading, it is critical to assess the Epoch energies because they not only color the Lifepath, they create the Lifepath itself. The 1 Lifepath generated from the birthdate of 1 October 2006 is the offspring of two 1s and an 8 with roots of 2 and 6. Such a Lifepath would, therefore, be supersaturated in its early and mid-life with issues and realities of the self and its identity followed in its later years with social interaction and success (the 8 crown of 2006) which itself is derived from the energies of support, nurturing, relationship and family (2 & 6 ciphers).

A 1 LP of 5 March 2000 is the child of the 5, 3 and 2 ciphers. The first act of this life drama involves the energies of freedom, potential intemperance and lack of restraint, detachment, loss, experience, exploration, movement, motion, exuberance and possible uncertainty as marked by the 5 first Epoch (Act I). The second Epoch (Act II) is dominated by the 3 vibration of communication, self-fulfillment, self-expression, artistic pursuits, joy, pleasure, friends, health, beauty, disease, disease, vanity and entitlement, while the third Epoch (Act III) concentrates on the lessons of yin (female) energy, others, relationships, partnerships, support, caring, kindness, emotions, passivity, diplomacy, balance, conflict, interference, duplicity, contention, tension, peace and war (opposite polarities of the 2 coin). These traits are very different from the active, self-oriented, assertive, aggressive, creative, independent, isolationist, pioneering and socially interactive energies of the 1-1-8 or 1-8-1 Epoch patterns. On the surface all of the Lifepaths listed above concentrate on lessons,

King

conditions, values, circumstances and issues of the 1, but the energies beneath the surface tell a different story, an equally important story, a story that must not be overlooked, underestimated, undervalued or ignored.

This is why a person's Lifepath cannot be properly analyzed by its single cipher. Five people may all have the same Lifepath but, although there will be similarities in their lives, every one of them will experience a different journey. Since there are only nine basic numbers, 1/9th of the population of the world will have the same Lifepath. If there were nine billion people in the world, basically 1/9th (a billion people) would have a Lifepath of 1; 1/9th would have a Lifepath of 2; 1/9th, a Lifepath of 3 and so on. Yet, all of these lives would be different. Understanding Epochs, therefore, is one way to begin looking deeper into each life. Furthermore, studying the root systems of each Lifepath in both the Influence and Outcome aspects of the Life Cycle Pattern IR sets, will give tremendous clarity of the destiny involved. Add Pinnacles and Challenges to the mix and the complexity of each life begins to take shape.

Another example of Epoch nuances: a Lifepath generated by a birth date of 8 August 1997 will generate a 6 Lifepath. If we reduce each of the birthdate components to a single cipher, we see that all of the Epoch crowns are eights: 8 day + 8 month + 8 year (1997 in reduction) yields simple ciphers 8, 8 and 8 which yield a binary root of 24, generating a 6 crown. The 8 day of birth (first Epoch) is Act I; the eighth month of birth, August (second Epoch), is Act II, and Act III (third Epoch) is the year of birth 1997. Therefore, the main Lifepath themes of home, heart, family, duty, community, responsibilities and accountabilities (6 Lifepath) focus exclusively on the 8 energy of interaction, business, commerce, socialization, money, power and success for the entire lifetime. See the diagram below.

A 6 Lifepath with Identical Epoch Crowns

Lifepath
8 August 1997
6

Epoch 1	Epoch 2	Epoch 3
Day	Month	Year
8	8	26
8	8	8

However, a 6 Lifepath generated from a birthdate of 4 December 2006 will generate a completely different experience. The crowns of this birthdate are 4, 3 and 8. Here we see the First Epoch (Act I) will concentrate on the structural, security, stability and material issues of the 4 energy; the Second Epoch (Act II) will be spent within the self-fulfillment, self-expressive, friends, pleasure, joy, communicative, health, well-being and entitlement vibrational domain of the 3. The final Third Epoch (Act III) will be spent in the 8 energy field of business, commerce, social interaction and success/failure.

Lifepath
4 December 2006
6

Epoch 1	Epoch 2	Epoch 3
Day	Month	Year
4	12	8
4	3	8

More nuances. Let's take two examples: a birthdate of 6 February 2000 and another of 15 November 2009. Each of these dates generates a 1 Lifepath. Furthermore, each of the Epochs, when reduced to a single digit, mirrors the Epoch structure of the other birthdate. Both of these dates incorporate a simple Lifepath pattern of 6 - 2 - 2. However, each of the three components is different from its counterpart. The number 6 is not the number 15, even though the number 15 reduces to a 6. The number 11, although reducible to a simple 2, is not a pure 2, and the year 2009 carries an intrinsic 9 energy plus an 11 master number in its transition root format. The 15 November 2009/1 Lifepath is, therefore, more complex than the 6 February 2000/1 Lifepath.

Identical Lifepaths - Identical Epoch Crowns - Different Epoch Roots

Lifepath
6 February 2000
1

Epoch 1	Epoch 2	Epoch 3
Day	Month	Year
6	**2**	**2000**
6	2	2

Lifepath
15 November 2009
1

Epoch 1	Epoch 2	Epoch 3
Day	Month	Year
15	**11**	**2009/11**
6	2	2

Therefore, the double numbers in birth dates must be taken into account during a thorough Epoch analysis. A simple 6 Epoch focuses on pure matters of the home, hearth and heart, but a 15/6 tells a different story. Although its basic energy is of love and domesticity, it brings the dynamics of the ego, self, yang, independence, creativity, assertiveness, aggressiveness, action and leadership of the 1 into the mix along with the energies of change, exploration, experience, freedom, sensuality, detachment and diversity - attributes of the 5 energy. The subcap of the 15 cipher is a 4 challenge depicting issues to be addressed involving discipline, self-control, order, commitment, fidelity, trust, work, effort, restriction, regimentation, constriction, rules, security, service, sex and substance addictions as well as inappropriate love liaisons. Thus, the 15 energy is much more complex, and potentially more impure, than the simple 6, although both share the same 6 crown energy. How critical it is, then, to study root structures! As is visible, simple numbers (crowns) do not tell the full story of a person's destiny. Understanding the roots of numbers gives us new colors, new layers, new depths of understanding.

In these birthdates, one of the second Epochs is a pure 2; the other an 11. Again there is a huge difference between these two energies even though they, like the 15 and 6, both share the same crown (in this case a 2). The pure 2 depicted by the month of February involves all things yin - others, relationships, female issues, partnerships, teamwork, helping, supporting, intuition, interference, balance, equilibrium, negotiation, diplomacy, duplicity, passivity, indirectness. Yet, the 11, although a two in reduction, is based on the master energy of the 11 with its double 1 ciphers. Eleven is an extremely intense and active energy. While the pure 2 is predominately passive, the 11 is dynamically active and saturated in energies of the self, not of others, even though it plays itself out in the field of others as represented by its 2 crown. Eleven brings into one's life a need to balance egos - the ego of one person and the ego of a second person. Eleven is also extremely idealistic and inspiration driven. It can also represent the deceits and treacheries of others. As a master number, it has no subcap and therefore no challenge to hold it back from accomplishing its goals. It is pulled by relationship on the surface (the 2 crown) but focused in the self (the 1 energy in its 11 root structure) underneath its surface. To be sure, 11 is not 2; it is itself. It displays characteristics of the 2 but it is much more complex and intense. The simple 2 is pure water. The 11 is both fire (1) and water (2).

The same is true for the year designations of 2000 and 2009. Both exude a 2 crown, but the year 2009, as well as having an 11 transition root, also maintains a 9 focus, thus bringing the energies of the public stage, art, drama, power, dominance, melding, universality, endings, expansion, compassion, philanthropy and impersonal love into the mix. The year 2009 portends the

King

endings or global scope (9) of relationship and others (2) with an intensity of ideologies and personal involvement (the 11/2 Addcap) and concerns, trouble, recession, turmoil, suffering, examination and introspection (7 Subcap), while the year 2000 marks a period of gestation of all things yin but does not involve a global perspective with the personally intense and sorrow-laden potential of the year 2009 because it lacks the 7-9 and 11 energies inherent in the 2009 numerical pattern.

Therefore, once again, the message when reading and analyzing the Epoch Timeline is to pay strict attention to the entire Epoch cipher format in question - crowns, pillars and roots. Simply and only reducing the Epoch components to single digits minimizes the actual truth of the Epoch, the Lifepath and also the Pinnacles and Challenges. If God intended everything and everyone to be simple, He wouldn't have created double numbers to create complexities. He would have given us all birthdates between the first and ninth of every month, only had nine basic months, and only nine years of creation. Obviously this is an absurd thought, but it does underscore the critical nature of being critical in our analysis of the Epoch structure and its importance to the entire life script.

Calculating the Epoch Timelines

The calculation of the Epoch timelines has been justifiably debated within the confines of the numerology world. No definite answer has yet emerged across the board. Epochs are long periods of time and there are many factors to study in order to know *exactly* when they change. One thought is that each epoch lasts for twenty-seven years. Another theory is that the timelines for each epoch vary, the second epoch beginning in the first 1 year closest to the twenty-seventh year of birth. *The King's Numerology* system currently acknowledges both in deference to additional research. This said, in the interests of simplicity and consideration for the beginner, we'll consider each Epoch as lasting for twenty-seven years. Although definite information is not yet set in concrete as noted, it is close enough for use at this time. In later works we will address the more complex calculations of the Epoch timelines. Using a twenty-seven year period for each Epoch would give the following arrangement:

Epoch Timelines Based on Twenty-Seven Year Increments (theory)

# Epoch	Component	Age Timeline
1st	Day of Birth	Birth through 27
2nd	Month of Birth	28 through 54
3rd	Year of Birth	55 through 81

Epoch PE

Epochs, as all timelines, have PEs. The birthdate data of day, month and year generate the influences/issues/themes of the Epoch picture. The PE gives the outcomes/realities/experiences associated with the influencing energies.

To find the Epoch P/E, simply add the Simple Expression to each of the Simple Epoch Influences. Using the birthdate 14 July 2008, and an arbitrary 6 Expression, the P/Es for each Epoch would be: 1st Epoch PE: 2 (5 + 6 > 11 > 2); 2nd Epoch PE: 4 (7 + 6 = 13 > 4); 3rd Epoch PE: 7 (2008 + 6 = 2014 > 7).

Epoch/PE Calculation

		1st Epoch	2nd Epoch	3rd Epoch
Epoch Crowns		5	7	1
Expression	(+)	(6)	(6)	(6)
P/E	(=)	11/2	13/4	7
I/R Set		**5/2**	**7/4**	**1/7**

Thus, using a simple twenty-seven year timeline for each Epoch we see that Epoch 1 (5/2) will last from birth to age 27. Epoch 2 (7/4) will last from age 28 to 54. Epoch 3 will last from age 55 until death. Again, please understand this is a general timeline, not a specific timeline.

Timeline Review

Having added the Epoch timeline to our knowledge base, we have now discussed three of the nine major timelines in the King's Numerology system. The Lifepath was discussed fully in KBN1.

The Nine Major Timelines

√	1	LPTL	Lifepath Timeline
√	2	PCTL	Pinnacle/Challenge Timeline
√	3	ETL	Epoch Timeline
	4	NTL	Name Timeline
	5	LTL	Letter Timeline
	6	DTL	Decade Timeline
	7	ATL	Age Timeline
	8	UTL	Universal Timeline
	9	PTL	Personal Year Timeline

Analysis Notes

Numerology is both a science and an art. The science (forever being discovered) involves understanding the various calculations of a numerology chart. The art of numerology addresses the interrelationship of the chart's different aspects. We've now studied two timelines in this work: the Pinnacle/Challenge timeline and the Epoch timeline. How these two main timelines of the Life Matrix interact with each other is both *science* and *art*. As we gain more experience, our ability to "read" a chart will improve. This takes time and involves a lifetime of work and dedication. People and their destinies are complex, and this complexity will become apparent as we study chart after chart after chart. Yet, it is a fascinating journey and one which will totally transform our consciousness, especially when we realize there exists an infinite and indescribable power creating it all, a Power so vast and incomprehensible that we must bow in deepest humility at the scope of its power.

Before proceeding to the remaining timelines, let's take a brief respite and look more deeply into voids.

Chapter Five

VOIDS

As we learned in Chapter 13 of *The King's Book of Numerology, Volume 1: Foundations & Fundamentals,* voids represent a missing genus or group of numbers in a chart. The letters A-J-S all belong to the First Genus (that of the number 1). Each of the three numbers associated with these letters reduce to a 1 (A=1, the first letter of the alphabet; J, the tenth letter of the alphabet, is a One in reduction (10 > 1 + 0 = 1); S, the nineteenth letter of the alphabet, follows suit (19 > 1 + 9 = 10 > 1 + 0 = 1). The Second Genus (that of the number 2) consists of B-K-T; the Third Genus (the number 3) contains the letters C-L-U; the Fourth Genus: D-M-V (4); the Fifth Genus is E-N-W (5); Sixth Genus: F-O-X (6); Seventh Genus: G-P-Y (7); Eighth Genus: H-Q-Z (8); and the Ninth Genus: I-R (9).

Because numbers represent attributes, characteristics, skills, abilities and people, when they are missing in a chart they create potential problems and especially become intensified if they occupy a Challenge position in the Life Matrix. For example, if a person has no As-Js or Ss in the natal name, the individual has a One (1) void. During the life, this will translate into issues dealing with one's identity or self-esteem; problems with authority, male energy, independence, self-responsibility, creativity and leadership. If the individual has no Bs-Ks or Ts in the name, a Two (2) void exists, creating potential challenges with females, others, interpersonal relationships, diplomacy, general caring, friendship, help and support.

Most of us have a void or voids in our chart. It's normal to have them, but the more voids we have, the more potential problems and challenges we may have in life. Having voids doesn't mean we are a bad person. Many great souls have had voids. General George Patton, Princess Diana and Marilyn Monroe had a 3 void in their charts. Mother Teresa maintained a 4 void in her chart. Amelia Earhart, Charles Lindberg, Martin Luther King and William Shakespeare all had a 6 void.

King

Abraham Lincoln, Albert Einstein, Albert Schweitzer, Charles Darwin and Helen Keller had a 7 void. Having voids simply means we will have issues with those things associated with the voided number(s).

How individuals manage their voids differs from person to person. It's common to see a total neglect of the energy or a lack of caring in regards to the qualities and characteristics a voided number represents. On the other hand, it's also common that people do the opposite - try to fill the void with the exact qualities represented by the void. For example, many people with a Six (6) void spend their lives trying to find love and romance while others with a 6 void have little or no concern about a home life. In other words, people will either try to fill the hole a void creates in their life or simply ignore it all together. It's an interesting conundrum.

When voids appear in the Pinnacle/Challenge Matrix, transiting through the timeline of the void in question will, inescapably, present issues, challenges and/or difficulties for the person. Voids are absences of specific energy. When the individual crosses fields dominated by the very energy he's lacking, problems occur because he inherently lacks the skills or tools needed to manage the vibration at hand. It's like being given the job of building a house and not having a hammer, saw, level, nails or a measuring tape. How does one manage anything when he doesn't have the tools to do it? See the dilemma? It's important, therefore, that close attention be paid to voids. They are dynamic aspects of our charts and lives.

Void Chart

Void	General Description - Issues Involving:
1 **A-J-S**	the self and its worth, independence, the yang--male influence, male principles, male figures, fathers, brothers, bosses, leaders, managers, action, leadership, creativity, ego, self-esteem, taking charge, standing up for one's self, being alone, drive, ambition, direction.
2 **B-K-T**	others, relationships, the Yin--female influence, female principles, female figures, mothers, sisters, following and being the follower, supporting and being the supporter, balance, receptivity, sensitivity, tolerance, caring, helping, sharing, diplomacy, deceit, duplicity, indirectness, intuition.

3 **C-L-U**	self-expression, health, beauty, personal integration, marriage and close personal relationships, speech, friends, words, happiness, joy, ease, disease, dis-ease, communication, harshness of expression, criticism, vanity.
4 **D-M-V**	all things of structure and order, work, effort, control, roots, discipline, regimentation, details, clerical, understanding, security, service, rules, regulations, duty, devotion, fidelity, honesty, trust.
5 **E-N-W**	freedom, change, people in general, movement, experience, talents, variety, the senses, sex, crowds, activity, excitement, exploration, shifting, uncertainty, wildness, intemperate, unrestrained, undisciplined, out of control, enslavement.
6 **F-O-X**	matters of the home, heart and hearth; domesticity, family, love, sex, romance, compassion, balance, beauty, harmony, community, personal responsibility and accountability, honoring, adjustment.
7 **G-P-Y**	inner peace, spirituality, mysticism, religion, inquisition, insight, being alone; alienation, isolation, separation, privacy, reflection, poise, perfection, depth of being, thoughtfulness, concern, calm, chaos, confusion, nobility, ignobility; thoughtlessness, coldness, cruelty, ruthlessness, indifference, secretive, inconsiderate, withdrawing, receding, recession.
8 **H-Q-Z**	interaction, connection, disconnection, continuity, flow, business, commerce, worldly status, management, executive leadership, wealth, success, material power, riches, comfort, administration, manipulation, orchestration, marketing, usury, being in the loop.
9 **I-R**	universality, compassion, strength, power, rulership, respect for others, service, understanding of the 'all', the 'many', the macrocosm, impersonal love, comprehensive feeling, arrogance, dominance, being over-bearing, impudent, rude, imperious, malevolence, benevolence, broadcasting, recognition.

81 IR Dyads

There are eighty-one pairs or sets of I/R (Influence/Reality) ciphers. These are called *dyads* or *couplets*. See the following chart.

The Eight-One I/R Dyads

1/1	1/2	1/3	1/4	1/5	1/6	1/7	1/8	1/9
2/1	2/2	2/3	2/4	2/5	2/6	2/7	2/8	2/9
3/1	3/2	3/3	3/4	3/5	3/6	3/7	3/8	3/9
4/1	4/2	4/3	4/4	4/5	4/6	4/7	4/8	4/9
5/1	5/2	5/3	5/4	5/5	5/6	5/7	5/8	5/9
6/1	6/2	6/3	6/4	6/5	6/6	6/7	6/8	6/9
7/1	7/2	7/3	7/4	7/5	7/6	7/7	7/8	7/9
8/1	8/2	8/3	8/4	8/5	8/6	8/7	8/8	8/9
9/1	9/2	9/3	9/4	9/5	9/6	9/7	9/8	9/9

A void may occupy the Influence position (top number of each set), the Reality position (bottom number of each set) or both. A void in the Influence position will be notated, for example, as 3v/8; in the Reality position as 3/8v or if both 3 and 8 are void in a chart, then 3v/8v. Regardless of where the void is in the chart, it will create issues, concerns, friction, stress, difficulties and challenges in association with the attributes of the cipher(s) in question.

Types of Voids

There are multiple types of voids:

1. Basic Void: a missing genus number (1 through 9) in the Expression (natal name).

2. Grand Void: a missing genus number in the Expression and Basic Matrix

3. Voided Challenge or Pinnacle: a Void appearing in a Challenge or Pinnacle position

4. Grand Voided Challenge or Pinnacle: a Grand Void in a Challenge or Pinnacle position.

5. Voided Decade: a Void matching its decade number, e.g., a 4 void in the 40s decade.

6. Grand Voided Decade: a Grand Void matching its decade number

7. Grand Voided Challenge Decade: when a Grand Voided Challenge equals is decade.

8. Double Voided Dyad: when both numbers of an IR set are void.

9. Grand Double Voided Dyad: both IR set ciphers are Grand Voids.

1. Basic Void

This is the simplest and least intense of the voids. If the voided number(s) is present in the Basic Matrix and not aspected in a Challenge of Pinnacle position of the Life Matrix, the void will have less effect on the person's life than were it located in a Pinnacle or Challenge position. When a number is voided but appears in the Expression, Soul or Nature, the intensity of the void is mitigated.

2. Grand Void

The Grand Void is when a genus number is both missing from the Expression and the Basic Matrix. When this occurs, the issues associated with the void become more problematic because there's no buffer of the void in the Basic Matrix.

3. Voided Challenge, Pinnacle or Epoch

A voided Challenge, Pinnacle or Epoch is when a void in the name also occupies one of Challenge, Pinnacle or Epoch timelines in either an Influence or Reality position of an IR dyad (or both). Multiple voided ciphers (two or more voids appearing during the same timeline) are possible. Two are not uncommon; three are rare but possible. Any number of an IR set in a voided Challenge, Pinnacle or Epoch will pose issues. As we've learned, Challenges represent the greatest difficulties, and when the energy cipher of the Challenge is missing in the name, problems are naturally more acute. If ignored, they will create havoc in a person's life.

4. Grand Voided Challenge, Pinnacle or Epoch

Grand Voided Challenges, Pinnacles or Epochs are voids which occupy one of the Challenge, Pinnacle or Epoch timelines in either the Influence or Reality position of an IR dyad (or both). As we recall, a Grand Void is when a void is also absent from the Basic Matrix in any of its seven components: Expression, Lifepath, PE (Performance/Experience), Soul, Material Soul, Nature and Material Nature. The Grand Voided Challenge, Pinnacle or Epoch presents enormous obstacles for the individual in the field of the voided cipher and the characteristics associated with it. If a person is to manage a Grand Voided component, he must concentrate on the positive aspects of the ciphers involved. Otherwise, the outcome will be potentially disastrous, painful, sorrowful and tragic. Double Grand Voided components are not uncommon.

5. Voided Decade

A Voided Decade is when a void transits, crosses over or passes through the decade associated with it. For example, for a person with a 4 void, the Voided Decade is the Forties; for a person with a 6 void, the Voided Decade is the Sixties and so forth.

If the void does not occur in a Challenge position when it transits the Voided Decade, the energy of the decade may be a good thing for the individual because the decade energy may fulfill the missing voided energy in the individual's chart. The opposite effect could also be the case. The decade may exacerbate the void. More research needs to be conducted here but there is the possibility the outcome could be positive based on how voids work in relationships. For example, if a person has a 4 void and their significant other does not, then the former will benefit from the latter depending on how strong the 4 is in the latter's chart. The number 4 rules order and organization. A person with a 4 void, especially a 4 Grand Void, may not be well-organized. However, if that person has a significant other who has non-voided 4 energy strongly placed in their chart, especially in their Expression, PE, Soul or Nature which will make that person ordered and organized, then the person with the 4 void will be benefited from the other person's 4 energy. Therefore, in the same way corresponding decades could offer benefit to the person with the voided numerical energy. More research is needed in this field.

6. Grand Voided Decade

More research needs to be done here, too. Will the transiting decade fulfill or exacerbate the Grand Void? It could do both - fulfilling the energy but still making it challenging for the person to manage.

7. Grand Voided Challenge Decade

This is definitely problematic. Challenges create difficulties and pressures. When a Grand Voided Challenge transits its mirrored decade, its challenging aspects may well be intensified. For example, a person with a Grand Voided Challenge of 4 may have greater complications and issues in their life involving issues such as order, organization, work, security, trust, fidelity, loyalty, commitment, dedication, discipline, restraint and self-control when transiting the 40s decade because the energy of the 40s Decade could possibly magnify the missing 4 energy in the individual - for the entire ten year period beginning with the zero ciphered number 40, the year of gestation. More research is needed here, too.

8. Double Voided Dyad

When both numbers of an IR set are void it is because the filter/funnel is a 9, otherwise the top and bottom ciphers could not be the same. This is a very intense IR set. When the numbers are positive, the experience will be pleasant; if negative, it will be unpleasant.

9. Grand Double Voided Dyad

This occurs when both IR set ciphers are Grand Voids. Such a couplet can be extremely problematic, especially if the Grand Double Voided Dyad appears in a Challenge position.

Void Note

There is absolutely no question that the entire spectrum of voids and their concomitant experiences are difficult. Why people have these in their charts only God knows but rest assured, He does know and they're in our charts for a reason. One plausible theory is that voids are *karmic scales*, serving to reconcile actions committed in former lives. This would be consistent with Saint Dadu's statement: *What you have not done will never befall you. Only what you have done will befall you.* Since voids are problematic, it would make sense that the problems we experience in this life are payback from actions generated in previous lives or times. Yet, if we're to be successful in terms of living an harmonious, happy, contented, relaxed and spiritually-driven life, we must give adequate attention to our voids. It's no less important that we maintain an appropriate awareness of the voids in the charts of our loved ones. By knowing the challenges confronting them, we can help them live a more aware and meaningful life.

Knowing voids also allows us to protect ourselves from the dangers arising from the voids in the lives of others. For instance, as one example, when the 3v/8, 3/8v or 3v/8v IR dyads occupy a Challenge position, there is an extreme potential for manipulation, usury, lying, carelessness regarding health issues, anger, meanness, irascibility and open disregard for the positive flow of life and its blessings. If we're attached to a person with one of these combinations, we need to be wise and aware or we'll get used and/or played like a fiddle . . . much to our detriment and chagrin. We may care about life, joy and health but the other person may not. Obviously, this is not a good thing, and from a life partner compatibility standpoint, such antithetical ideologies cannot bode well for a long-term relationship. If one person is hell-bent on sinking his ship and his life, that's his business, but it's not incumbent on us to go down with his ship nor sacrifice our life for his or hers. We each have a responsibility to the well-being, sanctification and ascent of our own soul

142

first and foremost. We must never forget this. To do so would violate the great gift God gave each of us to elevate our soul as high as possible while we have the chance in this most precious and priceless human body. The bottom line: pay attention to voids.

Managing the Spectrum of Voids

1 Void

If we have 1 void, we need to concentrate on and work toward being whole and independent without being egocentric, arrogant and self-absorbed. A 1 voided person would be well-served in being patient with authority figures but not allowing others to dominate him or do for him. A 1 void demands we do things for ourselves, stand on our own two feet as well as standing up and being counted, being strong and courageous. It also means we must learn to be direct and forthright in our dealings with others, as well as being able to look at our faults, failings and shortcomings and not point the finger of blame on others. A 1 void can make a person very empty but dangerous. People lacking self worth often attempt to cut others down to build themselves up - a tactic that only further impacts them negatively. The 1 rules male energy and therefore male issues, and males in general will be associated with a 1 void. Ego, self and Yang issues will be exacerbated when the 1 occupies a Challenge position. Incidentally, when 1 is in any Challenge timeline whether it is voided or not, problems with the ego or males and their accompanying issues loom large, so one is cautioned to be ever vigilant if possible in keeping yang attributes in check, lest their fires run rampant, destroying them and others in the process.

2 Void

Two rules the female. Two also rules others, close interpersonal relationships, partnerships, diplomacy, tact, caring, helping, support, competition, togetherness, division, conflict, war, balance and peace. Therefore, a person with a 2 void must learn to be the helper, supporter, peace-maker, diplomat, friend, team player, partner and business associate. Women will also be a challenge, especially if the 2 occupies a Challenge timeline. This would include mothers, mothers-in-law, grandmothers, sisters, aunts, female friends and associates. A Two void could be difficult for a person with a large amount of 1 energy because the 1 focuses on himself, not others; independence, not dependence; leading not following; hoarding, not sharing.

3 Void

Three rules life, its abundance, joy, children, health, happiness, pleasure, words, speech, art, sex and self-expression. A person with a 3 void needs to focus on being positive, healthy and avoiding habits and activities that interfere with or destroy health or well-being - his own or other people's. Oftentimes, a 3 voided challenge equates to harshness and meanness in words and actions. People with a 3 void can be plagued with unhappiness, as is well-documented in the lives of Marilyn Monroe and Princess Diana, two souls who were constantly in search of finding contentment and joy in their lives. George Patton is an excellent example of a person who tried to fill the void of the 3. He was a voracious reader, but, by some accounts, vain. Because 3 rules beauty, one of the dangers is vanity and an over-exaggeration with one's self-image or in some cases, no image. Three also rules children and it's not uncommon for women with a 3 void or voided challenge to be barren or have no desire whatsoever to have children, even like them.

4 Void

Four governs order, organization, design, building, construction, destruction, structure, routines, regimens, service, matter, limitation, restriction, protection, security, loyalty, fidelity, discipline, control, mechanics, patterns, honesty and trust. Therefore, when Four is void there exist potential problems in any of these areas. When Four is a Voided Challenge or a Grand Voided Challenge, the issues become intense. Faithlessness, infidelity and dishonesty loom large, as does a person's personal security and safety. It's difficult to be organized with no organizational skills, no discipline, no self-control. Four in a Challenge position can also make one feel as though he is imprisoned. This because of the 4's propensity to confine and restrict. Other scenarios exist for this structure-oriented cipher. For example, a person with a 4v/3 may well have no code of morals or ethics to live by, engaging in pleasure, lies and unkindnesses. With this pattern, a woman may be barren of children since the 4 is besieged with a lack of structure playing itself out in the realm of children (3). Four rules matter and the material body, so when it is void it follows that there will be issues of bodily strength, security and wholeness. Finding happiness will be challenging in this 4v/3 IR set and overall health issues will be a major concern if this dyad is located in a Challenge position. Pythagoras said, "No man is free who cannot control himself," and so a lack of 4 energy could result in a loss of freedom to some extent.

5 Void

It's vary rare to have a 5 void because "E" is the most used letter in the English language and "N" is also very common. Having no 5s would affect a person's sense of movement, freedom and ability to change. If 5 is voided or challenged, drastic change, uncertainty and loss are quite possible. This is because one of the binary roots of the 5 is the 14, the cipher of loss and detachment. Five not only rules freedom but also slavery, the opposite side of its coin. Coupled with 4 energy, a person could easily find himself stuck in a rut, a ship anchored securely in place with no compunction to move, explore or be free.

6 Void

Six voids herald problems and issues with domestic matters, love, nurturing, family, heart, home and romance. It's not uncommon for famous people to have a 6 void. Einstein, Schweitzer, Shakespeare, Earhart, Lindbergh, Helen Keller and Martin Luther King, Jr. all possessed this missing cipher in their names. Yet, they were extremely successful in their fields of endeavor, leading one to surmise that perhaps if God wants a soul to dedicate itself to some line of work and not be anchored to the home, He gives it a 6 void, thus limiting its involvement in a home life and allowing for more devotion to other endeavors. It is a fact, however, that if a 6 is in a Grand Voided Challenge position, there will be extreme difficulties in the home life and in the heart. There will be a lack of love, nurturing, harmony and peace within the domicile. Adjustments and responsibilities could easily be major issues. The 6 Voided Challenge is all about love and/or the lack of it. The Six void also carries the potential concentration of its polar partners - hate, envy, jealousy, resentment. It could also be manifested in a person who has responsibility for the home as a caretaker, gardener, butler, maid, servant, attending spouse for a sick or ailing partner or family member.

7 Void

The main problem with the Seven void is depth of thought, or rather the lack of it. This can make one inconsiderate, indifferent, cold, distant, detached, even ruthless. Seven rules all things internal, especially those dealing with the mind and spirit. The perfect statuesque symbol for the Seven is Rodin's Thinker, ever posed in deep thought with his head resting on his fist, supported by his arm on his knee. Thus, no 7, no deep thinking, at least on one side of its coin. The irony is that, as we've discussed, one way voids are managed is that the person tries to fill them with the exact energy of the void. For example, Abraham Lincoln was, arguably, the greatest president in United States history and an extremely deep thinker. Yet, he maintained a 7 void, as did Helen Keller,

Albert Einstein, Albert Schweitzer, Charles Darwin, Jackie Robinson and Marilyn Monroe, although many of these people had 7s in their Basic Matrix. It's as if the lack of 7 energy drives the individual to fill himself up with it. Another issue with the 7 void is the ability to be still and calm since 7 rules peace and quiet. We know Lincoln had suffered from depression and despondency from time to time. Was this breakdown a manifestation of his 7 void? Helen Keller also had stillness issues, especially when she was young. The moral of this story, as it is with all voids - recognize that the polar differences within each number can and do manifest themselves in completely opposite ways.

8 Void

Eight rules flow and connection. It is the conduit of the numeric spectrum. When 8 is void, there is no flow, no connection, no conduit. Hence, things do not go smoothly or run efficiently. To have, for example, a person in a management or administrative position with an 8 void and no 8s in the Basic Matrix, let alone having the 8 possibly be situated as a Voided Challenge or Grand Voided Challenge in one of the P/C timelines, is tantamount to financial ruin and commercial disaster. In order for things to flow properly, one must be able to connect idea to manifestation, concept to completion, product to sale, buyer to seller. It is the 8 that allows this to happen. Worldly success has often been associated with the 8, and the reason for this is the 8's inherent capacity to connect the dots and get things done. Without an 8 in the mix, things don't get done efficiently because the energy's not there to make it happen. A person with no 8s simply can't see how to go from point A to point B. Eight is the great administrator and coordinator. Eight is also the great manipulator (remember, every number has a positive and negative aspect). Eight is equally applauded by crooks and gods alike. With 8s present in a chart, probabilities of success exist; without 8s, the outlook is slim to none that success will be a reality.

9 Void

Nine governs the public stage, theater, humanity, expansion, exposure, arts, education, fame, notoriety, endings, terminations, conclusions, resolutions, travel, respect for others, recognition and universality. Nine is the great giver, albeit an impersonal one, or the great taker, without a doubt a heartless and remorseless one. Because 9 rules the public/global stage, it is highly unusual for a person to be known by the masses without it. Nine exposes, expands, recognizes and broadcasts. Regardless of one's talents, without a 9 in the chart, notoriety will most likely never occur. This is obvious by studying the charts of famous people. Inevitably, they all have 9 somewhere in their numbers. It would be impossible to touch the public without it. The 9 void may cause people to seek the limelight or work with humanity in some manner, especially in a volunteer capacity. Nine in a pinnacle or challenge position will most likely generate travel on some level - physically, psychologically, spiritually. Without a 9 present in a chart, an individual will have a difficult time connecting with or being associated with the masses, that is unless he tries to fill his life with them.

Case Study: 7 Void

Let's now take a look at the voids in Life Matrix of Richard Johnston Roe.

R	i	c	h	a	r	d	J	o	h	n	s	t	o	n	R	o	e
9	9	3	8	1	9	4	1	6	8	5	1	2	6	5	9	6	5

Through simple observation of the numbers within his name, we see that RJR maintains a 7 void. As we recall from KBN Volume I, his Expression is a 7; Lifepath-1; P/E-8; Soul-6; Material Soul-7; Nature-1; Material Nature, a 2.

Richard Johnston Roe: PC/PE Matrix
7 Expression - 7 Material Soul - 7 Void

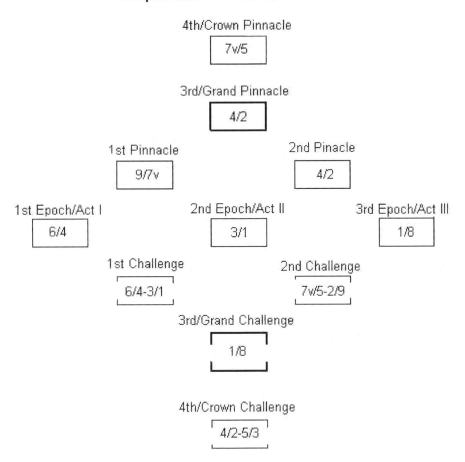

4th/Crown Pinnacle

7v/5

3rd/Grand Pinnacle

4/2

1st Pinnacle

9/7v

2nd Pinacle

4/2

1st Epoch/Act I

6/4

2nd Epoch/Act II

3/1

3rd Epoch/Act III

1/8

1st Challenge

6/4-3/1

2nd Challenge

7v/5-2/9

3rd/Grand Challenge

1/8

4th/Crown Challenge

4/2-5/3

The 7 void occupies the 9's Outcome position of the 1st Pinnacle (9/7v). It also appears in the Influence position of one of two IR sets in the 2nd Challenge as a 7v/5. This 7v/5 IR set also tops his chart in the 4th (Crown) Pinnacle position. Fortunately, RJR has a 7 Expression and a 7 Material Soul, so the conditions created by the void will not be as intense as they might otherwise be if he had no 7s in his Basic Matrix.

The 1st Pinnacle 9/7v dyad means that RJR will have trouble (7v) with the public (9) or with higher education, travel or anything represented by the Nine. Because 9 also rules endings, if they occur, they will create much stress and heartache. Nine rules distance, not just travel, and it may be that RJR will suffer the pangs of pain due to the separation of a long-distance relationship. This 1st Pinnacle will last for thirty-five years, so his discomfort will not be short. It will be a time of long suffering.

In fact, during his 2nd Challenge timeline from thirty-six to forty-four, RJR will have more trying times and they will be more intense. During this period he has two Challenges: 7v/5 and a 2/9. This couplet foretells of painful, heart-wrenching changes and losses (7v/5) and the endings of a relationship or relationships (2/9). This will definitely be the most difficult time of his life. Fortunately for him, it is only a nine year period.

Like his 2nd Challenge, RJR's 4th Pinnacle is also a 7v/5. This time period, which lasts from his early fifties until his death, should not be as difficult as his 2nd Challenge period for two reasons: first, it's not accompanied by a 2/9 IR set and second, it's in a Pinnacle position. There will still be movement, changes and losses for him, as signified in the 5 PE and these changes will be derived from his mind and thoughts, the 7 energy. In other words, he may find himself doing much thinking during this period, thinking which is diverse, mercurial and possibly liberating, or enslaving if he's working with the negative polarity of the 5 energy. It must be noted, however, that the changes originate from the 7's mental and spiritual energy fields. The changes are not associated with work (4), the home life (6) or any other energy field.

Let's now expand our understanding of the Life Matrix and its P/C (Pinnacle/Challenge) Timelines by taking a look at the Life Matrices of two famous women of the Twentieth Century - Marilyn Monroe and Princess Diana of Wales.

Chapter Six

CASE STUDIES

PRINCESS DIANA OF WALES and MARILYN MONROE

More reading

Blueprint of a Princess: Diana Frances Spencer - Queen of Hearts

The Age of the Female: A Thousand Years of Yin

The Age of the Female II: Heroines of the Shift

O ne of the best ways to learn numerology forecasting is to study the charts of famous individuals, not that famous people are more important than others, it's just that they have a known history and in researching and studying that history, much insight can be gained regarding the science of numbers and the paths of destiny.

In our study of the Life Matrix, which primarily includes the Pinnacle/Challenge Timeline, the Epoch Timeline and the Basic Matrix (KBN1), we'll first look at two very similar lives - those of Princess Diana of Wales and Marilyn Monroe. Since their lives were very much alike, if numerology has any substance, then their numbers should have similarities and, in fact, they do . . . amazingly, even hauntingly, so.

Juxtaposing the charts of these icons corroborates the validity of numerology. Both were extremely popular with the masses, icons of their age; they lived Cinderella lives (of sorts, except for the living happily ever after part); were extremely charismatic, beautiful but plagued with troubles; both were hounded relentlessly by the press and the public; both had very similar Basic Matrices; both had nineteen (19) letters in their birth names (Norma Jeane Mortenson & Diana Frances Spencer); both were born on the 1st day of the month (Monroe on 1 June 1926; Diana on 1 July 1961); both had difficult early lives and parent issues; both not only died young and at the same age of thirty-six (36) in their 2nd Pinnacle/Challenge timeline, but both also died in the month of August and both under mysterious circumstances. Both of them also had an eight (8) void. This is important because since their names had 19 letters each, the main challenge of their names (verified in the subcap of the 19 binary) is an 8, a voided cipher! Both of their Material Nature's were voided in their charts (Diana's 2 MN & 2 void; Monroe's 3 MN & 3 void).Their Epochs, Pinnacles and Challenges also clearly reveal the synchronicity of their life journeys. It's extremely fascinating. Let's look.

Basic Matrices

Here are the Basic Matrices of Princess Diana and Marilyn Monroe. Instantly we see that their Lifepaths, Expressions and Performance/Experience are identical: 7 LP, 4 Exp. and 2 PE! Also of interest is the 8 void mentioned earlier. As we'll see, there are also other similarities in their Life Matrices.

Name	LP	Exp	PE	Soul	M/S	Nat.	M/N	Voids
Princess Diana	7	4	11/2	9	7	4	2	2-8
Marilyn Monroe	7	4	11/2	8	6	5	3	3-7-8

7 Lifepath

No lifepath more potentially and potently reflects a life of mystery, chaos, betrayals, trials, tribulations, suffering, and sorrow than the Seven Lifepath. Both Princess Diana and Marilyn Monroe traveled a path of tears, their lives clear testimonies to their travails, heartaches and heartbreaks. Their broken love relationships, affairs, family tensions and divorces, early childhood parental issues of abandonment, oppressive public and media attention, emotional challenges, mysterious and tragic deaths at an early age all reflect the 7's lessons of spiritual testing and cleansing.

4 Expression

The Expression of both Norma Jeane Mortenson and Diana Frances Spencer was a Simple 4. Additionally, the General Expression of each name is an 85/13/4! Identical. Monroe also had a Master Builder 22/4 energy in her name while Diana had a 13/4. This makes perfect sense in that Monroe was more of a celebrity-driven icon than Diana. Marilyn was self-compelled to be famous. She once stated: "I want to be a big star more than anything. It's something precious." This quality is reflective of the Master Builder 22/4 energy. Diana, on the other hand, although ambitious, didn't share the same type of siren-driven fire that fueled Monroe the movie star. She did have a 22/4 in her Nature, however.

2 Performance Experience (PE)

Two rules all things female and there is no doubt these two Twentieth Century globally-renowned inamorata were all female. Relationship was important to them. They were both extremely feminine, capturing the public with equal magnetism. In fact, it's interesting to consider how their lives would have been received by the public had they lived at the same time. Perhaps it's best for history they did not. Two such powerful women living at the same time could possibly have diluted the legacy of each and their legends in life may not have become as powerful as they have become in death.

Master Numbers in the Basic Matrix

A quick study of the master numbers in the Basic Matrix of each woman reflects more truths. Monroe had a 22/4 Expression and an 11/2 PE. Diana also had an 11/2 PE while maintaining a 22/4 in her Nature. The 22/4 energy is often associated with material wealth and power. The difference between the two, and this is quite revealing, is that Marilyn had a 33/6 influence in her Material Soul. The master number 33 is a highly charged sexual and creative vibration. Since the Soul's energies define someone's needs, wants, desires, motivations and cravings, this 33/6 Material Soul energy in Monroe's chart signified her desire to be a sex kitten, which she most definitely was. However, Diana had no 33/6 energy in her Basic Matrix and was not driven, therefore, in the same way Monroe was. Diana's Soul was a 9; Material Soul, a 7. She was driven by a need to be among the masses (9) but not as a sex queen. Her 7 Material Soul reflected a need for privacy, secrecy, knowledge, wisdom, spirituality, elegance and reflection. Monroe's Material Nature was a 3, indicating a personal regard for sex, beauty, self-image, even vanity. Coupled with her 33/6 Material Soul, this combination of 3 and 6 energy intensified Monroe's sensuality, the quality for which she is most known. Diana had no 3s in her Basic Matrix and was not primarily concerned with these issues. Therefore, although the external facets of Monroe's and Diana's charts were identical, their personal internal drives were very different. Their personalities, as we know them, are clearly indicative of this distinction.

Life Matrices

Now let's study the Life Matrices of Marilyn Monroe and Princess Diana.

Marilyn Monroe: Born: Norma Jeane Mortenson - 1 June 1926; died 5 August 1962 (age 36) in her 2nd Epoch (6/1) and 2nd PC Couplet (Pinnacle: 6/1; Challenge: 3v/**88**-7v).

Basic Matrix Components

Lifepath	Expression	PE	Soul	M/S	Nature	M/N	Voids
7	**22**-4	**11**-2	8	**33**-6	5	3	3-7-8

Life Matrix Timelines

	1st Epoch	2nd Epoch	3rd Epoch
IR Sets	1/5	6/1	9/**22**-4
Timelines	birth to 29	30 to 56	57 on

Periods	1st	2nd	3rd	4th
Timelines	0 to 29	30 to 38	39 to 47	48 on
Pinnacle IRs	7v/**11**-2	6/1	**22**-4/**44**-8v	1/5
Challenge IRs	5/9	3v/**88**-7v	2/6 - 7v/**11**-2	8v/3v

<u>Life Matrix Components</u>

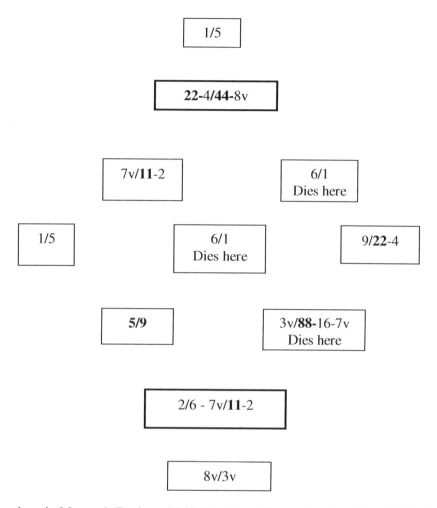

Master Numbers in Monroe's Basic and Life Matrices (General or Specific): 11-22-33-44-88

<u>Marilyn Monroe's Master Numbers</u>

When we search deeply into the root structure of Marilyn Monroe's life, we see that in her Basic and Life Matrices she possessed the master numbers 11-22-33-44-88. When we disregard (for illustration purposes) her 33 master number from her Material Soul in her Basic Matrix, her Life Matrix maintains master numbers of 11-22-44-88, a powerful group of energies representing relationship, money, power, wealth and status. It is these energies which shaped her journey through life. Of critical note in her Life Matrix is her Third Pinnacle (the core of the Lifepath and the most powerful Pinnacle/Challenge pair of any Life Matrix) which features the extremely influential 22/44 IR Set. It is this Core P/C set that dominated her life. The 22 is in the Influence

King

position; the 44 in the Outcome slot. This 22-4 and 44-8v combination is rich in worldly power, status, wealth, success and social connections. Established at birth and solidifying her fate in power and success, it was these energies that compelled her to lead the life she led, a destiny that was both immovable and unavoidable.

To understand this further: if the Life Matrix represents Monroe's world, this Grand P/C pair was the center of her world. In simple terms, the core of Marilyn Monroe's life was power, money and status. She didn't create this. Her destiny did and there was no way to avoid it, bringing to light a very important fact of life: our destiny is in our numbers. Hence, the spiritual quote from Mystic Charan Singh: *All men come into this world with a destiny of their own which goes on pushing them relentlessly on the course already marked out for them.* Wealth, power and status were marked for Monroe before she was ever born! And so are all of our destinies: they are preordained before we exit our mother's womb. This spiritual fact is corroborated by Charan Singh's master, Sawan Singh: *There is an account of every minute of a man's life. Illness, poverty, health, wealth and so on are all predestined.* So it was for Marilyn Monroe; so it is for us all.

How are Monroe's Core Pinnacle master numbers of 22 and 44 calculated? The 22 is derived from the First Pinnacle of 7 and the Second Pinnacle transition root of 15 (7 + 15 = 22). When we add Monroe's 22 transition root from her natal name, the result is 44. This 22 transition root is derived from adding the simple numbers in each of her three birth names: Norma (7); Jeane (8) and Mortenson (7). Together, 7 + 8 + 7 = 22.

This calculation illustrates why only single numbers may not tell the whole story of a person's life and why we must dig deeper in a chart to find meaningful answers. If only single numbers are used in calculations, master numbers such as those in Monroe's chart, would be missed and her life would not make total sense. Yet, it is these master numbers, derived from root systems, that clearly help define one's destiny, as is witnessed in the chart of Marilyn Monroe. The numerological moral of this story: look beneath the surface of single ciphers to decipher the truth of one's life and destiny.

"Ah," you say, "but Marilyn died in her Second P/C timeline at age 36, three years before her Grand (Core) Pinnacle/Challenge timeline was activated." True, but the Grand P/C Couplet, even though it is most intense during its primary timeline, actually rules the entire life from birth. Remember, this Third P/C set is the core of the life, the center of one's world. It's energies are always living and casting their influence throughout the entire life. They're just more acutely felt when the Grand Couplet is activated.

Monroe also maintains another 22 master number in her Third Epoch Outcome position. Again we see more power in her life's blueprint. How is this calculated? By taking the single cipher of her birth year (1926) which is a 9 and adding it to the 13 transition root of her 85 General Expression (8 + 5 = 13 plus 9 = 22). Here, again, we see the complexity of numbers and their root structures and why we must look beyond and beneath the surface of single ciphers to discover hidden truths lying deep within the numerical superstructure of one's life.

The master number Eleven occupies two places in Monroe's chart: the First Pinnacle PE (7v/11-2) and the Third Challenge PE, also a 7v/11-2. The Seven in Marilyn's chart is void, which means that the 11 will manifest a higher degree of secrecy, deceit and treachery in the realm of others and relationships than what it would have had it not originated from a voided cipher, in this case the 7 which governs things of a secretive, mental and spiritual nature. This 7v/11-2 IR set portends highly untoward events and conditions. When Challenged, it is even more severe.

What is also quite telling in Monroe's chart is her Second Challenge IR set of 3v/88-16-7v. It is in this period when she died under mysterious circumstances. The 88 is derived from her General Expression of 85 plus the 3 Influence cipher (85 + 3 = 88). Again, like the 7v/11-2, the master energy originates from a voided number, in this case the 3. Three rules life, self-expression, happiness, fortune, friends, art, communication, sex, joy, beauty, pleasure, words. Because the 3 was void in her life between the ages of 30 to 38, there is no question that Monroe was suffering and struggling mightily from personal image issues during this time period. She was very unhappy, whether the world knew it or not. A 3 void in any Challenge position most often signifies sadness, unhappiness, misfortune. The outcome of this misfortune was an 88-16-7. Both the 7 and 8 are void in her chart and, therefore, the 88-16-7 format would be more accurately written as 8v8v-16-7v. Thus the entire Second Challenge set could be written as 3v/8v8v-16-7v. Not a good indication for happiness and good fortune.

One can only shudder at the tragedy of this combination. The 88/7 in a Challenge position heralds potential great tragedy and chaos, especially when its primary ciphers are voided as reflected in its extended format of 8v8v/7v. Without question, this timeline between ages 30 and 38 was destined to be a nightmare of tragic proportions for Marilyn Monroe. Her unrestrained life of seeking and exhibiting fame, pleasure, indulgence and indiscriminate sexual trysts, often with married men, caught up with her karmically during this period. Even though she was a global icon, she was not exempt from karmic law. God's laws are holy, demand respect and sanctity and are impervious to celebrity status, human belief or mass adulation. We reap what we sow. It is the universal law of this creation and no one escapes it, not even a silver screen institution in the likes

King

of one Norma Jeane Mortenson. As Saint Ravidas declares: *The fruit of action unfailingly overtaketh the doer.* If Marilyn Monroe's legacy stands for anything of substance, let it stand for this, and let it remind us that violation of spiritual law reaps horrific harvests.

Monroe's death remains shrouded in mystery. Was she murdered? Did she commit suicide? The truth has not been publicly revealed. One can only speculate given the evidence. One thing, however, is beyond speculation. The 3v/8v8v-16-7v Second Challenge IR set portended ominous events during the nine year period of her life from ages 30 to 38. Nothing good could possibly have come out of this combination. Whether she committed suicide or was murdered is irrelevant. Something untoward was destined for her and so it was.

Had Monroe lived into her later years, they would not have been good ones. Her final Challenge was an 8v/3v. With this combination her wealth, health, beauty and success would have disintegrated. Her unhappiness would have reached deeper depths and her legend of being a sex goddess would never have materialized. Her legend was sealed by her young and tragic demise, a scenario common to many famous people. Wizened, worn and old does not convey the same image nor garner the same fascination as young, beautiful, sexy and famous. The world forgets the former, idolizes the latter.

Princess Diana: Born: Diana Frances Spencer - 1 July 1961; died 31 August 1997 (age 36).

Basic Matrix Components

Lifepath	Expression	PE	Soul	M/S	Nature	M/N	Voids
7	4	**11**-2	9	7	**22**-4	**11**-2	2-8

Life Matrix Timelines

	1st Epoch	2nd Epoch	3rd Epoch
IR Sets	1/5	7/**11**-2v	8v/3
Timelines	birth to 29	30 to 56	57 on

Periods	1st	2nd	3rd	4th
Timelines	birth to 29	30 to 38	39 to 47	48 on
Pinnacle IRs	8v/3	6/1	5/**99**-9	9/**22**-4
Challenge IRs	6/1	1/5	**22**-4/8 & 5/9	7/**11**-2v

Life Matrix Components

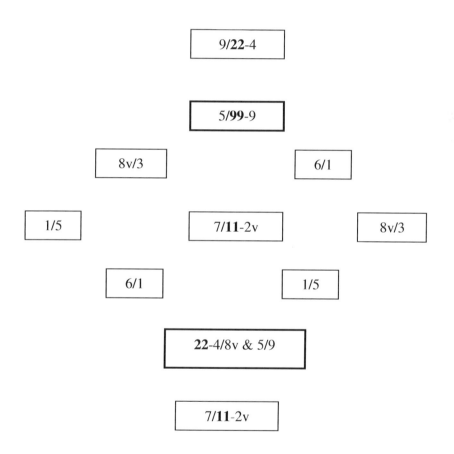

Master Numbers in Diana's Basic & Life Matrices (General or Specific): 11-22-99

Princess Diana's Master Numbers

Diana's master numbers in both her Basic and Life Matrix were 11-22-99. In contrast to Monroe, she lacked the 33/6 and therefore was not the sex kitten/symbol Marilyn was. She also did not possess the 44/8 which would have moved her into commercial circles. Rather, Diana moved in royal/rulership circles, a manifestation of the 99-9 triumvirate.

Ninety-nine (99) is the master energy of universality. It occupied the Outcome portion of her Third Pinnacle, the core of her life. And what was Diana? She was the People's Princess, the Queen of Hearts. Diana ruled . . . from her heart to the people's hearts. She didn't need a crown on her head. Her crown rested in the hearts and minds of the English masses. She was, indeed, more universal than the Queen herself. It was this 99 master energy that created her massive human appeal. In fact, when Diana died, half the world's population watched her funeral, some three billion individuals! Although she maintained a royal status for a time of her life, she was seen as a common person with common faults, sins and failings; a person whose troubled life resonated with the troubles of everyone's lives. This is one reason why she was so popular. She was loved by the people for who she was - a common human being leading an uncommon life, not for what she was - a royal Princess by marriage decree. Diana's royalty was based in her heart, not worn on her head.

And here is a great distinction between her and Monroe. Diana was the object of people's love. Monroe was the object of their lust. Diana was concerned with people's sufferings; Monroe was concerned with their pleasures. Both were icons of their time - beautiful, famous, magnetic, but it's clear who carried the banner of humanitarianism and who promoted the symbol of sex.

Like Monroe, Diana also had the 7/11-2 IR set dominate in her Life Matrix. Monroe's was in her 1st Pinnacle and 3rd Challenge; Diana's in her 2nd Epoch and 4th Challenge. Both had 11/2 PEs and Diana also had an 11/2 in her Material Nature. Unlike Monroe, Diana did not have a 7 void in her chart. Therefore, the Queen of Hearts maintained a deeper connection to people's feelings and sufferings. Both women, however, suffered from the anxiety and stress connected with the 7/11-2 energy field.

The 22 master energy was clearly dominate in Diana's chart. It ruled her Basic Nature, her Third Challenge Influence and, most importantly, it was her Crown Pinnacle PE, originating from the rulership energy of the 9! It's interesting that this 9/22-4 was in the Crown Pinnacle position of a woman who, at one time in her life, wore a crown on her head and for all of her short adult life wore a crown on her heart as well. Not to be outdone, Marilyn Monroe had a 9/22-4 in her Third Epoch! Talk about rulership!

Like Monroe, had Diana lived, she would most likely not have become the legend that she has become. Monroe had an 8v/3v in her final Challenge. Diana had an 8v/3 in her final Epoch. Things would have fallen apart for her, too. Additionally, Diana's 7/11-2v final Challenge would have generated much mental stress in the area of relationships and others. By dying tragically and young, both Princess Diana and Marilyn Monroe sealed the coffin on their legendary legacies which will live on in the perpetuity of fame, fortune and mystery.

Other similarities lend an eerie mist over both of these famous females. The IR sets of 1/5, 6/1 and 5/9 are dominate in their Life Matrices. Monroe had her 1/5 in both her 1st Epoch and Fourth Pinnacle. Diana's 1/5 was in her 1st Epoch and 2nd Challenge. This 1/5 Influence/Reality set in both their 1st Epochs tells a story of individual isolation, authority issues, male influence, change, uncertainty, loss, freedom and its opposite polarity, slavery.

The 6/1 combination of being alone in matters of family and the heart are found in Monroe's 2nd Epoch and 2nd Pinnacle and Diana's 1st Challenge and 2nd Pinnacle. Strange isn't it that both women died in their 2nd Pinnacle of 6/1. Incidentally, the 6 in this position maintains a 15 root in both of the women's charts, signifying untoward and negative energies in matters of the heart and home.

There is no doubt that Marilyn and Diana were hounded by the press and the public. This is a result of the 5/9 IR set. Monroe's 5/9 was in her 1st Challenge position. This was the period of her life when she was discovered and became famous. Princess Diana's 5/9 is more dramatic because this massively public energy combination occupies both the Pinnacle and Challenge positions of her Grand Couplet (3rd P/C set)! Diana could not escape the press. She could not escape the public. They were both her blessing and her curse. With this 5/9 Grand Couplet, Diana Frances Spencer could not have avoided the fame she came to experience. How powerful are numbers! How profound is the fact that our destiny is in our numbers! Even more profound is the Power that creates it all!

In quick review, it is uncanny, but logical, how the charts of these two legendary icons, Marilyn Monroe and Princess Diana of Wales, could be so very similar. They both had 7 Lifepaths, 4 Expressions and 11-2 PEs. The IR sets dominating their charts were 1/5, 5/9, 6/1, 7/11-2, 8/3, 9/22-4 and 22-4/8. Both had 8 voids, nineteen(19) letters in their birth names, were born on the 1st of the month, died in their 2nd Pinnacle/Challenge period at the age of thirty-six in the month of August and each death was cloaked in mysterious circumstances. They were both beautiful, famous beyond belief, suffered mentally and emotionally, were icons of their times and both left legacies for the ages to study and decipher, legacies by the way, generated by both of them having a 9/22-4 IR set in a final position: Monroe's in her 3rd Epoch and Diana's in her 4th Pinnacle.

Yet, because numerology is a science, such likeness is expected because the lives of these women were extremely parallel. There is no way their lives could have been drastically different because the numbers in their charts were not different. Their similar numbers mirrored their similar lives. Or more precisely said, their similar lives mirrored their similar numbers. How much more evidence is needed to corroborate the fact that numerology is a true and exact science? How long will it be before the professional scientific community and the world at large accept this truth? How long will it be before numerology becomes a viable tool to assist people in living a richer, fuller, wiser and more whole life?

In Summation

Before we continue this edition of *The King's Book of Numerology II: Forecasting - Part 1*, there are a few reminders for those of us who become involved professionally or even casually in numerology and divination:

1. Having a knowledge of one's destiny is sacred information. It must be managed responsibly and respectfully.

2. When counseling a client, always speak in terms of potentials, not actualities. Numbers have two sides - one positive and one negative. Encourage the positive; warn against the negative.

3. Destiny cannot be changed. The energy fields in a chart dictate the influences and outcomes an individual will experience through the course of his/her life journey. Experience will corroborate this fact of life. Counsel people to work with their energies, not against them. As numerologists, we cannot change what God has written for a person's life. What we can do is help people understand their lives and come to a place of peace with it.

4. The Law of Karma is exact and inexorable. Misuse of this sacred science of numbers generates enormous penalties to be reconciled in this life or future lives. Numerology must never be used in any way other than assisting in achieving one's highest and best Good. To

use such information in pursuits of gambling, sexual conquest, power plays or to gain a personal advantage; to deceive, manipulate, control or to engage in any other activities furthering negative and untoward advantages will generate negative consequences far beyond what will appear to be a fair repayment of the infraction. To walk this path is to walk on the edge of a cliff. It is a privilege and gift not to be misused and demands the most acute responsibility.

So far, this edition of *The King's Book of Numerology* has touched on the secrets and mysteries of destiny and creation itself relative to the Pinnacle/Challenge and Epoch timelines. Yet, there is more, much more. Let's keep studying.

King

Chapter Seven

NAME TIMELINE (NTL)

Names are identifying labels. Our birth names are the words which distinguish us from others. However, there is more to a name than meets the ear. Names give attributes, characteristics, and descriptions of us. Names also tell time, as do the letters which form them (see following chapter: *Letter Timeline*). Names also tell stories - of our lives and destinies. Names are vibratory patterns containing much of the mystery of who we are and where we're going in life. Names contain many secrets to our destiny and give us great knowledge for understanding the puzzle of life. When we understand the power and magic in names, we will make great strides in knowing ourselves and others.

Names are fascinating. We all have several. Interestingly, our names are divine appellations, personal monikers that God wanted us to have in this incarnation in order to fulfill its destiny. We think our parents name us. In effect, our parents are the conduit through which the names descend from a higher power. So often in life we make the mistake of thinking that our creativity, intelligence, knowledge, and so forth come from us. In reality, such things come through us, not from us. So it is with our parents naming us. Our birth names actually come through our parents, not from our parents. Our lives are pre-established in extensive detail before we exit our mother's womb. We have a certain name because we have a certain destiny to fulfill; we do not have a certain destiny because we have a certain name, and that name, that destiny, is created by our Creator, not by us mere mortals.

Our names, however, are not us in the deepest spiritual sense. Our names describe the parameters and actions of the character we play on the great life stage during the drama of this incarnation. In our next human birth, should we be fortunate enough to receive one (a rare gift), we will acquire another name and another birth date, but that name (and its subnames) will only be associated with that incarnation. They will describe the actor/actress taking center stage in that life play during that particular phase of the soul's existence in this dimension.

We are much deeper than our names. We are essence of God. We cannot be destroyed unless He chooses to destroy us. By being a spark of His radiance, we are as potentially infinite as He is. When we merge in His Oneness, this will be obvious. Now we are separate and finite. But, to be sure, we are not our names. We are much more than that.

Our destiny is manifested in the exact, full name at birth and the date of our birth. It is that name and date that establish the vibratory matrix of our life and destiny. All of the names within the context of the full given name must be used in generating an accurate numerology chart and . . . with their exact spelling. One wrong letter will alter the structure of the numerological blueprint. Even if a child's name was changed a few weeks after birth, experience has shown that generally the given name at the time of birth is the one from which the destiny is taken.

Does this mean that all name changes are false? No. Name changes do sometimes have validity. A good example was the name change of Joseph Stalin (see *The King's Book of Numerology, Volume I, Foundations & Fundamentals*). Generally, however, name changes have no effect on the basic blueprint of one's destiny. If there is a question as to which of two names is accurate, simply do two charts and compare the life experiences of the person involved using both names. This will give a definitive answer unless the new name has an identical vibratory matrix as the original name, which would be unusual.

Name Timeline (NTL)

Our full name at birth, the Expression, represents a span of time equal to the numerical configuration of its General root structure. For example, let's take the name Richard Johnston Roe, our friend from volume one.

R	I	C	H	A	R	D	J	O	H	N	S	T	O	N	R	O	E
9	9	3	8	1	9	4	1	6	8	5	1	2	6	5	9	6	5

General Expression = 97

RJ's General Expression is 97. Therefore, the influence of his natal name will last for ninety-seven years, at which time it will recycle beginning with the first R of his first name, Richard. When this Expression is added to his Simple 1 Lifepath , we find that his Basic Matrix P/E is an 8.

Interestingly, just as we use his full natal name to determine his P/E, so we use the same process to determine the length of time and P/E for each separate name within the full name. For example, the name "Richard" will have its own General Expression of forty-three years with an 8 P/E (same as his Basic Matrix Umbrella: Expression = 7; Lifepath = 1; P/E = 8). This means that the vibrational influence of "Richard" - a 43/7 energy - will last for forty-three years and carry a Simple Performance Experience vibration of 8 (7 Expression + 1 Lifepath = 8 P/E). When RJ is forty-four years old, he will move into the vibratory field of the name "Johnston" which has a General Expression and consequent timeline of thirty-four years. This will obviously carry an 8 P/E as well. When RJ is seventy-eight years of age (after he has transited the first two name timelines of "Richard" for forty-three years and "Johnston" for thirty-four years) he will enter the energy timeline of "Roe" for twenty years. The "Roe" timeline will carry a 3 Simple P/E (2 + 1 = 3). Should RJ live to be ninety eight, his name timeline will recycle to his first name again and run for a duration of another forty-three years.

R	I	C	H	A	R	D
9	9	3	8	1	9	4

43 Year Name Timeline
Carries a 7 Expression and an 8 P/E

J	O	H	N	S	T	O	N
1	6	8	5	1	2	6	5

34 Year Name Timeline
Also carries a 7 Expression and an 8 P/E

R	O	E
9	6	5

20 Year Name Timeline
Carries a 2 Expression with a 3 P/E

Given this information, we know that for the first seventy-seven years of his life RJ will be subjected to a 7/8 Name Timeline (NTL). Since this is identical to his Basic Matrix Umbrella, the 7/8 I/R set will be intensified as a result of stacking (simultaneous repetition of the same energy). Should RJ live beyond seventy-seven years, he will enter a 2/3 NTL energy field and remain there for twenty years.

Because RJ's first name carries a 43 General Expression and his second name timeline maintains a 34 General Expression (both 7s), the subcap challenge for the first two name timelines

King

will also be identical - a 1/2 I/R set (the 1 differential of both expression binaries plus his simple 1 Lifepath). This 1/2 pattern will involve himself and yang energy as influence (1) playing itself out in the realm of others and yin energy (2). His third name timeline (the 20 of "Roe") will generate a 2/3 subcap challenge, identical to the addcap pinnacle (addcap > 2 + 1 = 3; subcap > 2 + 1 = 3) All zero ciphers binaries (10, 20, 30, etc.) will have identical addcaps and subcaps). With this 2/3 I/R set, RJ will be involved with others and female energy (2) as it manifests in the vibrational field of the 3 of self-expression, pleasure, communication, fulfillment, friends, art, health, and well-being.

Note: when computing the Name Timeline and the Letter Timeline (to follow in the next chapter), add the Simple Lifepath cipher to each simple cipher of each separate name of the NTL or LTL (letter timeline). The P/Es of the other timelines to follow (UTL, ATL, PTL) are formed by adding the Expression to them rather than the LP cipher. It's not the same with the NTL or LTL. Adding an Expression to an Expression doesn't work in generating a reality energy. We have to add either an Expression energy to the Lifepath or a Lifepath cipher to the Expression for there to be accuracy in the analytical process.

Name Timeline-Specific Expression

As we know from KBN1, each name possesses a *Crown, General Root* and a *Specific Root*. The *General Root* determines the timeline, but the *Specific Root* adds specific coloring to the *crown*, furnishing us with additional information about each name. The specific roots of each of RJ's names are:

Richard-61; Johnston-115; Roe: 38. The 61 references family and heart issues embracing leadership, the self and independence. The 115 specific root of Johnston indicates a concentration of self, independence and freedom within the realm of the 7's energies if the mind and indwelling spirit. The 38 specific root of Roe indicates artistic and communicative connection and interaction.

Name	R	I	C	H	A	R	D	
Specific Root	18	9	3	8	1	18	4	**61**
General Root	9	9	3	8	1	9	4	43

Name	J	O	H	N	S	T	O	N	
Specific Root	10	15	8	14	19	20	15	14	**115**
General Root	1	6	8	5	1	2	6	5	34

Name	R	O	E	
Specific Root	18	15	5	**38**
General Root	9	6	5	20

Souls & Natures

Each separate name of the full natal name obviously has its own expression energy. Furthermore, each separate name also maintains its own Soul and Nature energies. RJ's Soul and Nature energies are below.

Soul Energies of each of RJ's separate names

The Soul of "Richard" is a 1

Name	R	I	C	H	A	R	D	
Specific Root		9			1			10 > 1
General Root		9			1			ditto

The Soul of "Johnston" is a 3

Name	J	O	H	N	S	T	O	N	
Specific Root		15					15		30 > 3
General Root		6					6		12 > 3

The Soul of "Roe" is a 2

Name	R	O	E	
Specific Root		15	5	20 > **2**
General Root		6	5	11 > 2

King

Nature Energies of each of RJ's separate names

The Nature of "Richard" is a 33/6

Name	R	I	C	H	A	R	D	
Specific Root	18		3	8		18	4	51 > 6
General Root	9		3	8		9	4	33 > 6

The Nature of "Johnston" is a 22/4

Name	J	O	H	N	S	T	O	N	
Specific Root	10		8	14	19	20		14	85 > 13 > 4
General Root	1		8	5	1	2		5	22 > 4

The Nature of "Roe" is a 9

Name	R	O	E	
Specific Root	18			18 > 9
General Root	9			9

Using the Expression, Soul, and Nature data of each separate name in the full natal Expression, we can construct a chart depicting the interrelationship of the components. In the chart below, "GR" stands for General Root (*The King's Book of Numerology, Volume 1: Foundations & Fundamentals*).

Matrix of Richard Johnston Roe's Single Names

Name	GR	Addcap Crown	Subcap Crown	Soul	Nature
Richard	43	7	1	1	6
Johnston	34	7	1	3	4
Roe	20	2	2	2	9
Full Natal Name	**97**	**7**	**2**	**6**	**1**

This information is revealing because through it we gain additional knowledge of the energies RJ will experience as he transits his destiny. Even if we did not have his birthdate, we could still decipher some valuable information about him as far as each of these NTLs is concerned.

Another interesting fact of note is that every "Richard" will share the same exact attributes to some degree, just as every "Johnston" or every "Roe" will have identical traits and characteristics as part of their makeup. All males named "Richard" will be analytical, reflective, thoughtful, quiet, and private to some degree (7 Crown). They will be motivated by energies of self, uniqueness, creativity (1) and possess a nurturing, loving, compassionate, artistic personality (6). Because of the 33 master number in their natures, all Richards will also be creative and lovingly expressive if one can penetrate the barrier of the 7 protective and isolationist energy field. All people named "Johnston" will also express characteristics of the 7 energy. The desires will be anchored in their own self-expression and fulfillment, pleasure, communication, friends, ease of living, health, beauty, and good times (3). Their natures will be sound, solid, security-conscious (4). Additionally, all Johnstons will be master builders and constructors of some type as their 4 nature maintains a 22 master builder root. Any "Roe" individual will be passive, helpful, supportive, diplomatic, friendly, others-oriented, sympathetic, balancing or argumentative, duplicitous, angry, competitive, interfering, high strung, and nervous (2) as negative polarities also apply to every cipher of every name. The 9 nature of Roe creates a sense of universality, commonalty, compassion, power, dominance, expansion, and exposure.

With this knowledge in mind regarding names, one can immediately strike up a conversation with anyone which is meaningful to the other person - if one does their numbers and concentrates on the keywords and concepts associated with those numbers. Below is a chart of simple keywords followed by a chart of some common first names. The latter serves as a guide to each name and also to the concept of using names to decipher attributes, qualities, personalities, desires, needs, wants and motivations attached to each name.

Simple Keyword Chart

1: Self, Independence, ego, individuality, identity, male/yang, fire, activity, creativity, new beginnings, ideas, genesis, union.

2: Others, support, female/yin, relationships, balance, cooperation, passivity, emotion, follower, kind, competition, contention, diplomacy, war and peace, balance, logic, reason.

3: Expression, communication, integration, health, beauty, disease and dis-ease, words, trinity, triads, marriage, children, fun, ease, pleasure, vanity, art, duplicity, duality, emotion.

4: Work, effort, structures, service, security, limitation, roots, earth, foundation, form, matter, order, organization, convention, constriction, tradition, stability, practicality, regularity, regimen, rules.

5: Freedom, slavery, detachment, exploration, senses, change, motion, movement, people, diversity, versatility, non-convention, non-tradition, irregularity, intemperance, uncertainty, loss, wild.

6: Personal love, hate, home, matters of the heart, adjustment, community, beauty, art, responsibility, hearth, domesticity, duties, obligations, envy, jealousy, bitterness, duty, devotion.

7: Spirit, spiritual, the great Within, intrinsic, analytical, reclusive, deep, mental, isolated, alienated, recessive, reflective, private, serene, shy, poised, calm, studious, inquisitive, concerned, worry, chaos.

8: Interaction, connection, disconnection, flow, commerce, social, business, coordination, orchestration, circulation, manipulation, worldly comfort and success, managerial, executive, administrative.

9: Macrocosm, world, public stage, all-inclusive, universal, humanitarian, service, endings, art, fame, the many, theatrical, broadcasting, dominate, domineering, expansive, charismatic, Chameleon.

18

Matrix of Some Common Single First Names
GR = General Root

Name	GR	Crown	Soul	Nature
Aaron	22	4	8	5
Abigail	32	5	2	3
Adam	10	1	2	8
Adrian	29	2	2	9
Aggie	29	2	6	5
Alex	15	6	6	9
Alexander	39	3	3	9
Alexis	25	7	6	1
Alicia	26	8	2	6
Alyssa	14	5	9	5
Amanda	16	7	3	4
Amber	21	3	6	6
Amy	12	3	8	4
Andrea	25	7	7	9
Andrew	29	2	6	5
Angela	22	4	7	6
Ann	11	2	1	1
Anna	12	3	2	1
Anne	16	7	6	1
Anthony	34	7	5	2
April	29	2	1	1
Austin	21	3	4	8
Barbara	25	7	3	4
Benjamin	32	5	6	8
Bianca	21	3	2	1
Blake	13	4	6	7
Bradley	31	4	4	9
Brandon	32	5	7	7
Brett	20	2	5	6
Brian	26	8	1	7
Brianna	32	5	2	3
Britney	39	3	3	9
Brittany	37	1	8	2
Brittney	41	5	3	2
Brooke	30	3	8	4
Caitlain	33	6	2	4
Caleb	14	5	6	8
Carlos	23	5	7	7
Casey	17	8	4	4
Cassandra	26	8	3	5
Cassie	20	2	6	5
Catherine	47	2	2	9

Cerise	32	5	1	4
Chad	16	7	1	6
Chandra	31	4	2	2
Charles	30	3	6	6
Chelsea	26	8	2	6
Cheyenne	43	7	4	3
Christa	33	6	1	5
Christian	47	2	1	1
Christina	47	2	1	1
Christine	51	6	5	1
Christopher	67	4	2	2
Cody	20	2	4	7
Cory	25	7	4	3
Courtney	40	4	3	1
Crystal	26	8	8	9
Cynthia	35	8	8	9
Dakota	16	7	8	8
Daniel	27	9	6	3
Danielle	35	8	2	6
David	22	4	1	3
Deborah	35	8	3	5
Dimitri	46	1	9	1
Dirk	24	6	9	6
Donald	23	5	7	7
Donna	21	3	7	5
Dorothy	42	6	1	5
Dudley	26	8	6	2
Edward	28	1	6	4
Elizabeth	43	7	2	5
Elvis	22	4	5	8
Emily	28	1	7	3
Erica	27	9	6	3
Erika	26	8	6	2
Erin	28	1	5	5
Ethan	21	3	6	6
Evan	15	6	6	9
Eve	14	5	1	4
Evelyn	29	2	8	3
Frances	30	3	6	6
Francis	34	7	1	6
Francisco	43	7	7	9
Frank	23	5	1	4
George	39	3	7	5
Georgiana	50	5	4	1
Gerald	29	2	6	5
Hanna	20	2	2	9
Harold	31	4	7	6

Harvey	34	7	4	3
Heather	38	2	2	9
Henry	34	7	3	4
Holly	27	9	4	5
Howard	33	6	7	8
Ian	15	6	1	5
Isabelle	29	2	2	9
Jacqueline	43	7	5	2
James	12	3	6	6
Jamie	20	2	6	5
Jared	20	2	6	5
Jasmine	26	8	6	2
Jason	14	5	7	7
Jeffrey	39	3	8	4
Jenna	17	8	6	2
Jennifer	45	9	1	8
Jessica	21	3	6	6
Jessie	22	4	1	3
Jesus	11	2	8	3
Joel	15	6	2	4
John	20	2	6	5
Jonathan	29	2	8	3
Jordan	26	8	7	1
Jorge	28	1	2	8
Jose	13	4	2	2
Joseph	28	1	2	8
Joshua	20	2	1	1
Juan	10	1	4	6
Justine	26	8	8	9
Kaitlyn	29	2	8	3
Karen	22	4	6	7
Katelyn	25	7	4	3
Katherine	46	1	2	8
Kathleen	31	4	2	2
Katie	19	1	6	4
Kayla	14	5	9	5
Kelly	20	2	3	8
Kelsey	23	5	8	6
Kevin	25	7	5	2
Kristen	33	6	5	1
Kristin	37	1	9	1
Kristina	38	2	1	1
Kristine	42	6	5	1
Kyle	17	8	3	5
Laura	17	8	5	3
Lauren	26	8	6	2
Laurie	30	3	9	3

174

Leah	17	8	6	2
Linda	22	4	1	3
Lindsay	30	3	8	4
Lindsey	34	7	3	4
Lisa	14	5	1	4
Loretta	28	1	3	7
Lori	27	9	6	3
Lorie	32	5	2	3
Luis	16	7	3	4
Madonna	26	8	8	9
Marcus	21	3	7	5
Margaret	38	2	7	4
Maria	24	6	2	4
Marissa	26	8	2	6
Marjorie	44	8	3	5
Martin	30	3	1	2
Mary	21	3	8	4
Maryann	32	5	9	5
Matthew	27	9	6	3
Megan	22	4	6	7
Michael	33	6	6	9
Michelle	40	4	1	3
Miguel	31	4	8	5
Mitchell	37	1	5	6
Molly	23	5	4	1
Monica	28	1	7	3
Natalie	26	8	7	1
Natasha	19	1	3	7
Nate	13	4	6	7
Nathan	22	4	2	2
Nathaniel	39	3	7	5
Neal	14	5	6	8
Neil	22	4	5	8
Nicholas	36	9	7	2
Oliver	36	9	2	7
Olivia	32	5	7	7
Paige	29	2	6	5
Patricia	41	5	2	3
Paul	14	5	4	1
Paula	15	6	5	1
Rachel	29	2	6	5
Rebecca	28	1	2	8
Richard	43	7	1	6
Robert	33	6	2	4
Roberta	34	7	3	4
Roy	22	4	4	9
Ryan	22	4	8	5

Sabrina	28	1	2	8
Samantha	23	5	3	2
Samuel	17	8	9	8
Sarah	20	2	2	9
Sean	12	3	6	6
Shane	20	2	6	5
Shannon	31	4	7	6
Shaun	18	9	4	5
Shawn	20	2	1	1
Sheldon	32	5	2	3
Stephanie	43	7	2	5
Stephen	33	6	1	5
Steven	22	4	1	3
Stewart	25	7	6	1
Tammy	18	9	8	1
Tara	13	4	2	2
Taylor	28	1	5	5
Teresa	23	5	2	3
Thomas	22	4	7	6
Tiffany	36	9	8	1
Timothy	38	2	4	7
Travis	26	8	1	7
Trevor	35	8	2	6
Tyler	26	8	3	5
Vanessa	18	9	7	2
Veronica	42	6	3	3
Vicky	25	7	7	9
Victor	33	6	6	9
Victoria	43	7	7	9
Vincent	33	6	5	1
Wallace	21	3	7	5
Whitney	41	5	3	2
William	34	7	1	6

Homonymous Names

Homonyms are one of two or more words that have the same sound and often the same spelling but differ in meaning. For example, the word "park" can mean an area of land set aside for public use, an athletic stadium (as in "ball park"), the position in an automatic transmission that disengages the gears, or it can mean the process of putting, placing, or leaving a vehicle in a certain location.

Names can also be homonymous, i.e., having the same sound. For example, Ann and Anne sound the same but are spelled differently. Other homonymous name sets are Britney, Brittney, and

Brittany; Catherine and Katherine; Frances and Francis; Lindsay and Lindsey; Laurie, Lorie, Lori; Sean, Shaun, and Shawn; Stephen and Steven. However, although these names sound the same, they can be quite different energetically because their letter construction is different and each letter carries its own specific vibration. Let's look at these sets a little more closely.

Set #1: Britney - Brittany -Brittney

Name	GR	Crown	Soul	Nature
Britney	39	3	3	9
Brittany	37	1	8	2
Brittney	41	5	3	2

At first glance we see that each of the Expressions are different. Britney is a 3; Brittany, a 1, and Brittney a 5. All are odd numbers so each will have a sense of creativity. The most publicly artistic will be Britney with a 39 General Root. The 3 rules art and the 9 rules exposure and universality. The subcap challenge of the 39 is 6. Therefore, Britney represents the 3-6-9 artistic triad. Not only that, but the Crown and Soul are both 3s and the Nature is a 9, making her charismatic and dominant. Without question, the energies of Britney are musical, artistic, publicly oriented, and self-expressive. Everything about the name reflects artistry, beauty, harmony, power, and exposure.

Brittany is the most independent of the three variations with her 1 Crown. She is also the most mentally creative as expressed by the 37 General Root. The 8 Soul of Brittany desires success; her personality is partnership-oriented as reflected in her 2 Nature. There may be some conflict within her, however, as her 1 Crown (yang energy) clashes with her 2 Nature (yin energy). Of the three variations, Brittany has the greatest potential to be a writer. Three rules communication and seven rules thought. Words - the tools of a writer - are nothing more than thoughts placed on paper in order to communicate. The 4 subcap challenge from the 37 General Root focuses on work, effort, structure, framework, and form. When creative thoughts and ideas take form, they often do so in the guise of words.

Brittney will be the most free-spirited and fun-loving of the three. The 5 energy makes her adventurous, exploratory, even wild and untamed. Her 3 Soul seeks pleasure and communication and her 2 Nature seeks relationship and partnership. Brittney will, like Brittany, be a helper and companion, whereas Britney will be the ruler, the one manifesting the most public power and attraction.

Set #2: Catherine - Katherine

Name	GR	Crown	Soul	Nature
Catherine	47	2	2	9
Katherine	46	1	2	8

Catherine and Katherine are a conundrum. Both have 2 Souls so both want to be the support person, the helper, the partner. Yet, while Catherine will demonstrate this 2 quality outwardly and be more like her desires, Katherine may be more high-strung and involved in personal conflict. This is for two main reasons. First, Katherine's Crown is a 1 - this is direct opposition to her 2 Soul. Second, Katherine begins with a K, the 11th letter of the alphabet. Eleven always carries high energy. Nervousness and tension are potential byproducts of the 11 vibration. The positive side for Katherine is that she has the ability to understand both men (1) and women (2) and both sides of issues because she is composed of these opposing vibrations.

Interestingly, Catherine's General Root is a 47/11/2 energy so she also has the tension generating 2 in her field. However, Catherine begins with the letter C which is the energy carrying the greatest amount of ease, pleasure, and comfort. Catherine's 9 Nature makes her more dominant than Katherine, but Katherine is more business-oriented and connective than Catherine because of her 8 Nature. Of the two, Katherine is certainly the most independent and leadership-oriented due to her 1 Expression Crown. Catherine, however, carries the most potentially domineering energy because of her 9 Nature.

Set #3: Frances - Francis

Name	GR	Crown	Soul	Nature
Frances (female)	30	3	6	6
Francis (male)	34	7	1	6

"Frances" is generally regarded as the spelling of the female form of this name while "Francis" is its male counterpart. Examples are Diana Frances Spencer (Princess Diana) and Sir Francis Drake (European explorer of the 16th Century).

Both Frances and Francis have loving, compassionate, nurturing dispositions and personalities as reflected in their 6 Natures, but Frances also has a 6 Soul, making her driven to be compassionate, loving, and domestic. Frances is certainly the more expressive of the two as is witnessed by her 3 Crown and 30 General Root. Francis seeks independence and self identity and is

King

quite reflective, analytical, reclusive, private, quiet, and withdrawn as depicted in his 7 Crown. With his accompanying 1 Soul, which harmonizes with its 7 Crown (1 and 7 together create the most isolated and solo cipher set), Francis is certainly prone to being a loner, pioneer, explorer, to being sensitive, courageous, and in need of space and quiet. Francis is the more distant and cool of the two, but he is also the deepest and most spiritually acclimated. Isn't it interesting that both these names harmonize with their gender: Frances, the female, the softer, more domestic and loving; Francis, the male, more courageous and daring. How perfectly is nature reflected even through our names!

Set #4: Lindsay - Lindsey

Name	GR	Crown	Soul	Nature
Lindsay	30	3	8	4
Lindsey	34	7	3	4

Here we see Lindsay being fun-loving, social, pleasure-oriented and communicative - energies of the 3 and 8, and Lindsey being inwardly focused, analytical, reclusive, quiet, poised, and given to much internalization - all attributes of the 7, while at the same time having the desire and need for what Lindsay is expressing externally - the 3 energy. Lindsay is the social butterfly; Lindsey is the thinker, student and inquisitor.

Set #5: Laurie - Lori - Lorie

Name	GR	Crown	Soul	Nature
Laurie	30	3	9	3
Lori	27	9	6	3
Lorie	32	5	2	3

This trio is all communicative, fun-loving, seeks pleasure, fulfillment, friends, and good times. This is evident by their 3 Nature and the letter "L" which is a 3 vibration. Both Laurie and Lori are quite artistic and like to mingle with the masses because of their 9 energy. Lorie seeks relationship and tends to be driven by a sense of freedom, change, excitement, experience, motion, movement and the senses.

Set #6: Neal - Neil

Name	GR	Crown	Soul	Nature
Neal	14	5	6	8
Neil	22	4	5	8

Neil is the builder (22/4), the one who likes to construct things - from actual structures to portfolios to works of art of all kinds. He thrives on, and in fact needs, the variety of stimulation (5 Soul). Neal is changeable, versatile, active, and always on the move. He's motivated by love and family - the 6 vibration. Both Neal and Neil are highly interactive socially, like money, success, and power (8 Nature).

Set #7: Sean - Shaun - Shawn

Name	GR	Crown	Soul	Nature
Sean	12	3	6	6
Shaun	18	9	4	5
Shawn	20	2	1	1

This trio is highly diverse. Sean is communicative, artistic, romantic, and loving as witnessed by his 3 Crown, 6 Nature, and 6 Soul. Shaun seeks stability and security (4 Soul) but is changeable and unpredictable (5 Nature). This 4 vs. 5 pattern creates a natural conflict in him between convention (4) and non-convention (5); security (4) and freedom (5); reservation (4) and spontaneity (5). However, he is the most universal of the three because of his 9 Expression Crown and 5 Nature. No two numbers involve the masses more than the 5 and 9. Shawn, although relationship and others oriented on the surface (2), is driven by a sense of self, personal identity, and independence (1). He is, ironically, the most passive and yet independent of the three because of the 1 vs. 2 conjunction.

Set #8: Stephen - Steven

Name	GR	Crown	Soul	Nature
Stephen	33	6	1	5
Steven	22	4	1	3

This twosome reveals a motivation of self, leadership, and independence (1 Soul). Stephen is lovingly expressive, highly artistic, and communicative (33/6 Expression); Steven, the builder and

King

worker (22/4 Expression). Stephen is changeable, versatile, and exploratory (5 Nature), while Steven is artistic, self-expressive, approachable, and friendly (3 Nature).

Matrix Twins

Other than homonymous names, there are those which sound different, are spelled differently, but which have the same matrix. These are called *matrix twins*. For example, "Kathleen" and "Jose" don't seem alike as far as their sound is concerned, but their Crowns, Souls, and Natures are identical. Both have a 4 Crown, 2 Soul, and 2 Nature. Each is driven by relationship (2). Each is the helper by nature (2) and each is a worker (4).

Name	GR	Crown	Soul	Nature
Kathleen	31	4	2	2
Jose	13	4	2	2

"Jason" and "Olivia" are also *matrix twins*. Each possesses a 5 Crown of freedom, adventure, motion, movement, versatility, and the senses; a 7 Soul and 7 Nature which make them very aloof, internal, solitude-seeking and perfection thinking. Each is active externally, but each really does seek solace. Such a juxtaposition of numbers can be tricky to read because on the outside these two like action and motion (5 Expression Crown), but on the inside they love quiet and seek time alone (7 Soul and 7 Nature). If there is a difference between the two, it is in the General Root structure. Olivia's 32/5 will cause her to be more gregarious and friendly than Jason who's 14/5 cipher will make him more freedom oriented and detaching.

Name	GR	Crown	Soul	Nature
Jason	14	5	7	7
Olivia	32	5	7	7

"Marissa" and "Danielle" possess energies of relationship (2), love and family (6), and interaction (8). They will be very social, warm, companionship oriented. They will also like money, power, and material comforts (8). If negatively disposed, they could be highly manipulative (8) and deceptive (2).

Name	GR	Crown	Soul	Nature
Marissa	26	8	2	6
Danielle	35	8	2	6

Master Names

Master Names are another interesting variant of names in general. Master names possess a master number in their General Root structure. The following list is comprised of names and words carrying a 22 master builder vibration. Each of these names will be involved somehow with structures - be they financial, material, artistic, literary. The reality of the 22 energy is that it loves to build, form, formulate, work, design, organize, and serve. It does so in the field of relationship as is witnessed by its double two root of 22. Interestingly, and as a side note, Elvis Aaron Presley's first two names, Elvis and Aaron, are both 22 master builder vibrations. What other notable people come to mind who have this powerful master builder energy in their numerology charts? Hank *Aaron* (famous baseball player), *David* Brinkley (famous newscaster), *Neil* Armstrong (famous astronaut), *Thomas* Jefferson (famous American statesman) . . . ad infinitum. Also of interest are words such as *food*, *water*, *corn* and *master*.

22 - *Master Builder* Names

Name/Word	GR	Crown	Soul	Nature
Aaron	22	4	8	5
Angela	22	4	7	6
Born	22	4	6	7
David	22	4	1	3
Elvis	22	4	5	8
Food	22	4	3	1
Jessie	22	4	1	3
Karen	22	4	6	7
Linda	22	4	1	3
Lord	22	4	6	7
Master	22	4	6	7
Megan	22	4	6	7
Nathan	22	4	2	2
Neil	22	4	5	8
Roy	22	4	4	9
Ryan	22	4	8	5
Steven	22	4	1	3
Thomas	22	4	7	6
Water	22	4	6	7

Twenty-two is not the only master number. All identical double number roots are master numbers: 11 - 22 - 33 - 44 - 55 - 66 - 77 - 88 - 99. Below is a partial chart of names maintaining a 33 vibration - the master Imaginator/Communicator. For more information on *master numbers*, refer to *The King's Book of Numerology, Volume I, Foundations & Fundamentals*. Recognize any famous people with this 33 master vibration in their charts? *Michael* Jordan (basketball), *Howard* Cosell (broadcaster), *Stephen* King (writer), *Robert* E. Lee (Civil War General), *Vincent* Price (actor), and . . . ad infinitum as well.

33: *Master Imaginator/Communicator* Names

Name	GR	Crown	Soul	Nature
Caitlain	33	6	2	4
Christa	33	6	1	5
Howard	33	6	7	8
Kristen	33	6	5	1
Michael	33	6	6	9
Robert	33	6	2	4
Stephen	33	6	1	5
Victor	33	6	6	9
Vincent	33	6	5	1

Name Waves

As cosmic energy travels in waves, just like the ocean, so do names. What is popular at one time in history may be totally unpopular at another time. Courtesy of the Social Security Administration is a list of the ten most popular names during the year 1900 and 1990. Notice the changes.

Top Ten Most Popular Names of 1900
Male - Female Rank

Male	Female
John	Mary
William	Helen
James	Margaret
George	Anna
Joseph	Ruth
Charles	Elizabeth
Robert	Dorothy
Frank	Marie
Edward	Mildred
Henry	Alice

Top Ten Most Popular Names of the 1990s

Male	Female
Michael	Ashley
Christopher	Jessica
Matthew	Emily
Joshua	Sarah
Jacob	Samantha
Andrew	Brittany
Daniel	Amanda
Nicholas	Elizabeth
Tyler	Taylor
Joseph	Megan

The only male name still in the top ten after 90 years is "Joseph." The only female name still in the top ten after 90 years is "Elizabeth." What will the most popular names be in the year 2500 - Korton, Monka, Sarea, Varium, or will Joseph and Elizabeth still be around? Hmmm. Something to ponder in one's idle time (very idle time).

King

Chapter Eight

LETTER TIMELINE (LTL)

The next major timeline is the *Letter Timeline* or LTL. Like each of the names of the Name Timeline, the individual letters within each name of the Letter Timeline also indicate time periods, activities and their outcomes. In effect, the Letter Timeline is a timeline within a timeline.

Each of the letters is part of a *group* or *genus*. The name of each group is determined by the single value of the letter crowns which comprise it. For example, the letters A, J, and S all carry 1 crowns and compose group 1. The letters B, K, and T form group 2; the letters C, L and U form group 3 and so forth. There are nine groups of letters. Eight of the groups are composed of three letters each. The ninth group is composed of only two letters: I and R.

Additionally, the crowns of each group determine the length of time the influence of the letter will have effect. The timeline of the letters in Group 1 (A-J-S) will last for one year. The timeline of the letters in Group 2 (B-K-T) will last for two years and so forth.

Letter/Timeline Chart
(timeline is in years)

Group	Timeline
A-J-S	1
B-K-T	2
C-L-U	3
D-M-V	4
E-N-W	5
F-O-X	6
G-P-Y	7
H-Q-Z	8
I -R	9

The numerical ciphers of each letter not only represent the length of time each letter will transit (move through or across) a chart, they also represent those qualities and attributes associated with them. For example, the letter A will transit a chart for one year. It's energy will, therefore, generate issues, influences, and themes associated with the 1 vibration of the yang: ego, self, identity, pioneering, independence, action, new beginnings, creativity, leadership, going it alone, being solo. The letter B will transit a person's chart for two years and involve the individual in yin issues relating to females, relationship, partnership, involvement with others, support, help, balance, togetherness, competition, confliction and so forth. See the Letter/Timeline/Attribute chart following.

Letter/Timeline/Attribute Chart

Letters	Timeline	Basic Issues & Attributes
A-J-S	1	yang, self, new beginnings, action, creativity, independence, identity
B-K-T	2	yin, others, support, balance, opposition, duplicity, war/peace
C-L-U	3	trinity, self-expression, art, words, communication, health, disease
D-M-V	4	structures, security, work, effort, service, roots, rules, routines, order
E-N-W	5	freedom, slavery, detachment, shifts, exploration, senses, motion
F-O-X	6	family, the domicile, love, heart, duties, adjustments, art, hate, envy
G-P-Y	7	isolation, reflection, chaos/bliss, thought, study, analysis, withdrawal
H-Q-Z	8	social interaction, success, circulation, administration, orchestration
I -R	9	expansion, art, spotlight, humanitarianism, travel, power, public stage

Let's now apply this Letter Timeline theory to Richard Johnston Roe. We can do this in two ways: by separate name and by full name, although each method will ultimately give the same result. Using two methods will simply help establish clarity of the Letter Timeline theory.

The name "Richard" maintains a Name Timeline of forty-three years as we learned in the last chapter - this as a result of its 43 General Expression.

43 Year Name Timeline of "Richard" matches the General Expression

R	I	C	H	A	R	D	
9	9	3	8	1	9	4	> 43

This means that for forty-three years, any "Richard" will be influenced by a 7 energy with a 43 General Root. (43 > 4 + 3 = 7)

The individual letters of the name "Richard" also have their own personal timeline; hence, a timeline within a timeline, layers within layers, colors within colors, veils within veils. "R" maintains a letter value of 9. It begins at the time of birth, lasts through the ninth year and incorporates the attributes and characteristics of the 9 energy. The "I" begins at age ten and runs its course also for a period of nine years. Therefore, its timeline is from age ten to eighteen (not nineteen). Note: age ten is part of the nine year "I" period. If we add nine to ten we would get nineteen, but this would be inaccurate because it is actually a ten year period. The reason for this is because we "added to" the ten rather than "including" the ten in the calculation. Simple arithmetic will bear this out.

Age 10 to 18: a Nine Year Period

Chronological Age	10	11	12	13	14	15	16	17	18
Simple Numbers/Years	1	2	3	4	5	6	7	8	9

Age 10 to 19: a Ten Year Period

Chronological Age	10	11	12	13	14	15	16	17	18	19
Simple Numbers/Years	1	2	3	4	5	6	7	8	9	10

The "C" is a three year period and its timeline is from 19 to 21 years. The "H" runs from age 22 through 29, an eight year period. The "A" lasts for one year at age 30. The second "R" of Richard begins at age 31 and ends after the 39th year. The "D" begins at age 40 and ends when Richard's forty-third year ends. This can be depicted in the following manner.

Letter Timeline for "Richard" (as a first name)

Letter	R	I	C	H	A	R	D
Term	9	9	3	8	1	9	4
Timeline	0-9	10-18	19-21	22-29	30	31-39	40-43

We can rearrange the same data in a vertical chart, thus allowing for the issues, influences and themes of each period to be visibly brought into the equation.

Ltr.	Timeline	Term	Term Issues, Influences and Themes
R	0-9	9	travel, expansion, spotlight, public stage, endings
I	10-18	9	travel, expansion, spotlight, public stage, endings
C	19-21	3	self-fulfillment, words, joy, pleasure, friends, fun
H	22-29	8	commerce, social interaction, circulation, management
A	30	1	new beginnings, initiations, self, yang focus, ego
R	31-39	9	travel, expansion, spotlight, public stage, endings
D	40-43	4	work, effort, stability, security, routine, rules, service

Any person whose first name is "Richard" will follow this general pattern. Will all individuals named "Richard" have identical experiences? Of course not. The Letter Timeline is only one of the major timelines, not to mention the many other factors in a numerology chart creating the complexities within each "Richard," especially when the Lifepath is added to the equation. But this does give a general view of the influences and themes any Richard will experience during the Letter Timeline phases of the Name Timeline itself. To this extent, an important part of the life blueprint emerges.

Letter Timeline P/E

Because there are nine major Lifepath ciphers, when the P/E is generated for each letter by adding the specific letter and Lifepath together, discrepancies will begin to emerge between the lives of all "Richards" because each "Richard" will now experience a different reality as a direct result of having a different Lifepath. This creates the "snowflake" uniqueness within the human design process.

As in every case, the P/E gives the outcomes, realities, results, performances and experiences generated by the influencing causal energies - in this case the individual letters. The Letter Timeline Performance/Experience formula is:

Simple Letter Timeline P/E

Simple Letter + Simple Lifepath = Simple LTL P/E

Assuming we have nine "Richards" and each "Richard" has one of the nine basic Lifepaths, when we add the Lifepath cipher to each letter of the name "Richard," we create an outcome (PE) for that letter. In this case there would be a different outcome for the letters which form the name "Richard:" the R, I, C, H, A and D [R is duplicated].

As an example, let's take the P/E Outcome for the letter "C" as it relates to each of the nine Lifepath ciphers 1 - 9. The "C" energy, a 3 cipher, will generate a three year period where the issues, influences, and themes involve one's self- image, joy, health, happiness, self-expression, self-fulfillment, communication, pleasure, art, fun, friends, integrated relationship, children, and general welfare. However, when each of the different nine Lifepath ciphers is added to the 3 vibration of the "C" energy, the outcome is different for each "C" influence energy. Therefore, each of the nine "Richards" will experience something different when they transit the "C" of their names.

P/E Outcomes for the letter "C" of "Richard" with the Nine Major Lifepath Ciphers

Ltr.	Term	LP	PE	LTL PE: Outcomes, Realities, Performances
C	3	1	4	work, effort, stability, security, routine, rules, service
C	3	2	5	freedom, slavery, change, detachment, loss, experience, loss
C	3	3	6	love, family, nurturing, adjustments, responsibilities
C	3	4	7	reflection, analysis, review, peace/chaos, solitude, isolation
C	3	5	8	commerce, social interaction, circulation, management
C	3	6	9	travel, expansion, spotlight, public stage, philanthropy, theater
C	3	7	1	starts, action, new beginnings, initiations, self, yang focus, ego
C	3	8	2	females, others, partnership, relationship, support, conflict
C	3	9	3	self-fulfillment, words, joy, pleasure, friends, health, disease

And so it is with each letter of each name. The letters create the influence, term, and timeline, and the Lifepath (when added to the letter in question) determines the outcome or Performance/Experience.

We can now add the Lifepath cipher to the Letter Timeline chart of Richard (Roe) to create a P/E, thus generating a fuller understanding of the experiences he will encounter as he transits each letter of his first name. As we recall, Richard Johnston Roe's Lifepath is a 1. To arrive at the "outcome" we add the numbers of the "term" and "lifepath."

PE for the first name of "Richard" with a 1 Lifepath

PE-Outcome	1	1	4	9	2	1	5
Transition	10	10	-	-	-	10	-
Lifepath	+1	+1	+1	+1	+1	+1	+1
Term/ Letter Crown	9	9	3	8	1	9	4
Letter	R	I	C	H	A	R	D
Term	9	9	3	8	1	9	4
Age Timeline	0-9	10-18	19-21	22-29	30	31-39	40-43

Placing this information in a different format, we can add the PE [outcome] explanations.

Letter Timeline for the name "Richard" of Richard Johnston Roe

Ltr.	Term	LP	PE	LTL PE: Outcomes, Realities, Performances
R	9	+1	= 1	new beginnings, initiations, self, yang focus
I	9	+1	= 1	new beginnings, initiations, self, yang focus
C	3	+1	= 4	work, effort, stability, security, routine, service
H	8	+1	= 9	travel, expansion, spotlight, public stage, philanthropy
A	1	+1	= 2	females, others, partnership, relationship, support
R	9	+1	= 1	new beginnings, initiations, self, yang focus
D	4	+1	= 5	freedom, change, detachment, loss, experience

When we review the outcome energies of the LTL PE we need to keep in mind, as we do with all I/R modalities, that the PE is the result of a causal energy, the influencing vibration, whether that influencing energy is a letter, name, age, or calendar date as it moves through a filter or funnel. In this case with the Letter Timeline, as it is with the Name Timeline, the filter/funnel is the 1 Lifepath cipher.

Richard Johnston Roe's Letter Timeline

Let's now apply this Letter Timeline theory to Richard Johnston Roe's second and third names.

Letter Timeline for "Johnston" of Richard Johnston Roe

Outcome	2	7	9	6	2	3	7	6
Lifepath	+1	+1	+1	+1	+1	+1	+1	+1
Term/Crown	1	6	8	5	1	2	6	5
Letter	J	O	H	N	S	T	O	N
Term	1	6	8	5	1	2	6	5
Age Timeline	44	45-50	51-58	59-63	64	65-66	67-72	73-77

Letter Timeline for "Roe" of Richard Johnston Roe.

Outcome	1	7	6
Lifepath	+1	+1	+1
Term/Crown	9	6	5
Letter	R	O	E
Term	9	6	5
Age Timeline	78-86	87-92	93-97

RJ's Letter Timeline data can be reformatted into a vertical chart. The numbers in the "term" column do two things: 1. they refer to the number of years the letter's energy will be active; 2. they describe the influences and themes during those years. In other words, they occupy the Influence position of the I/R sets. The LTL PE (the Reality position of the I/R sets) is formed (in this case) by adding the "Term" cipher to the "LP" cipher which acts as the filter/funnel.

The Letter Timeline is read like any other I/R set. To recall: in the Letter Timeline, "Term" = influence/issues/themes, and PE = outcomes/realities/experiences. Richard Johnston Roe's full Letter Timeline follows.

Richard Johnston Roe
Letter Timeline

Letter	Timeline	LP		Term		PE
R	Birth to 9	1	+	9	=	1
I	10-18	1	+	9	=	1
C	19-21	1	+	3	=	4
H	22-29	1	+	8	=	9
A	30	1	+	1	=	2
R	31-39	1	+	9	=	1
D	40-43	1	+	4	=	5
J	44	1	+	1	=	2
O	45-50	1	+	6	=	7
H	51-58	1	+	8	=	9
N	59-63	1	+	5	=	6
S	64	1	+	1	=	2
T	65-66	1	+	2	=	3
O	67-72	1	+	6	=	7
N	73-77	1	+	5	=	6
R	78-86	1	+	9	=	1
O	87-92	1	+	6	=	7
E	93-97	1	+	5	=	6

Letter Timeline Analysis for Richard Johnston Roe

Let's now take this numerical information in RJ's LTL and give it some life through words. We'll assume RJ lives long enough for him to transit every letter of his natal name.

R [9/1]

This letter's energy field begins at birth and continues until age nine. During this letter timeline period the general activity will revolve around a wide view of the world, perhaps travel, but certainly the macrocosm will be highlighted. It is a period of wide scope, universal appeal, artistic expression, and impersonal love. Nine is the number of inclusion, for it holds all numbers within it's bosom. The number 9 is the Grand Elemental. Specifically, the energy field is around the individual making connections and being in the social loop as witnessed by the *specific value* of the letter R which is 18, as it is the eighteenth letter of the alphabet. The outcome of this individual's letter energy field mixing with his Lifepath will result in an interest of the self, creativity, personal independence, activity and focus. Relationships could terminate during this nine year period and there will definitely be a sense of being separate, solo, alone or the loner. There will also be an emphasis on creativity with a mental focus (7 subcap of the number 18). Dramatic changes and new beginnings are in store for RJ. It is a time of expansion in which he will experience the emergence of his own personal power.

I [9/1]

This second letter period will run from ages ten to eighteen. There will not be as much movement within the field of the 'many' since this is a pure '9', devoid of the '18' root of the previous period. Again, the self is the highlight, as is its independence and isolation. With the juxtaposition of the 1 and 9 energies, endings and new beginnings are still a part of this timeline energy field. This first eighteen years is a dynamic time of RJ's young life. He's having to learn to be independent and on his own (1 PE) at a very young age while existing in the most expansive of all energy fields - that of the 9 Letter Timeline influence.

C [3/4]

The third letter period, which will last for three years, begins at age nineteen and continues through age twenty-one. The emphasis is on self-expression, personal integration, enjoyment of life, and good times with friends. This will be a time when structures are formed and realized as a result of the 4 cipher. Because of the 3 energy, RJ could get married here or experience some sort of integrated relationship. Work will also be enjoyable, whether it is artistic, vocational, educational, or recreational.

H [8/9]

This period, a timeline of eight years from age twenty-two through twenty-nine, will be one focusing on business, commerce, social interaction, connection, and disconnection. It will surely be an expansive time because the 9 P/E crown elevates the commercial vibration of the 8 Influence to a public level. Work will be good and filled with people, variety, change, travel and experience.

The King's Book of Numerology II: Forecasting - Part 1

This is a time for RJ to be moving about in the business world, making connections, working with people and enjoying the freedom of his work.

A [1/2]

Age thirty brings new beginnings for RJ which will result in relationship. Here is a year where the yang is juxtaposed with the yin. The 2 foretells a year of others, support, cooperation, balance, partnership. This will, most likely, be a year to remember as the 'A' always brings new beginnings. Because its timeline is only one year, its impact is dynamic and not easily forgotten. This is an interesting year, too, because it is the only year when RJ will experience the energy of a transiting 'A', for he has no other 'As' in his name. All the more reason that it will be a year to remember.

R [9/1]

This nine year period from ages 31 to 39 will be a repeat of the first nine years of RJ's life except that now he is much older and more experienced and . . . less innocent and childlike. There will also be changes in other timelines which effect him so this will not be an exact duplicate of his early years, but the issues and results will be similar. Again, the outcome centers around himself and his independence in many ways. There could also be travel. Furthermore, the spotlight of the 9 energy is shining on his 1 Lifepath, so it is definitely a time of self, action, creativity, and independence.

D [4/5]

The 'D' period will be the only '4' period of RJ's life and it occurs within the forties decade in which the focus is on structures, work, limitation, effort, restriction, security, stability, and service. This 4 "D" energy occurring in the forties decade is an example of stacking. The outcome of this will be movement, motion, change, or loss in the house or work environment as a result of the 5 PE. This is one of those periods where the 4 and the 5 bump up against each other. RJ needs to accept change. It is inevitable. Clinging to old, outworn, established routines, patterns, or frameworks of any kind will only create hardship. The 5 will definitely bring some kind of change, and because of this 4 vs. 5 juxtaposition, there could well be some pulling, pushing, tugging, and clashing going on in his life. It could also simply be that his work will generate a sense of freedom for him, or he could become detached from his work. In such case as this, a careful look at other timelines will be very helpful in determining what the outcome may be.

King

Here is another powerful annual cycle for RJ. It is a year of 1 influence. Furthermore, RJ's ATL is a 44/8. Things will either come together or collapse for him. The result of the letter J transiting his Lifepath will generate an outcome involving the 2 vibration of others, relationships, possibly the end of a relationship of some kind. Partnership issues in business are very likely because of the 44/8 Age Timeline he's also experiencing. All in all, it is definitely going to be a year involving others, his issues and interactions with them, as well as commercial or contractual involvements. The energy between himself, people, and as his work will be extremely high. It will be a good year for practicing discipline, restraint, self-control, patience, and dealing with the powerful dimensions of the *forty-four* and its energy of administration, execution, coordination, management, success, failure, circulation, flow, and personal command.

O [6/7]

This particular six year period, especially since it follows the previous year's high energy focus on himself and others during his 44/8 ATL, may not be the happiest for RJ. Last year's energies involved issues and, most likely, tensions between people in relationship. This year begins a six year period of 6 energy manifesting itself in a 7 outcome. Definitely, issues of love, domesticity, family, and community will generate some degree of introspection and reflection for RJ. In order for the 7 to do its magic, some hardship, tragedy, concern, or sorrow must place him in a state of reflection. When things are going well, we generally don't reflect on them. We enjoy them. It's only when things go wrong or create pain and sorrow in our lives that we begin to think, reflect, introspect, and suffer. In other words, turn inward. RJ's heartache is stemming from love and family issues. One possibility is separation; another is divorce; yet another is an estrangement of some kind; still another may be the death of a loved one. Regardless of the specifics, the general 7 energy in the PE position will force him to be reflective, if not isolated and alone. There could well be tears. All in all, it is an excellent time for RJ to delve deeply into life and its meaning, thus gaining a sense of substance and sensitivity.

This will be a time of deep internalization and adjustment. If RJ sees this difficulty early on in his life and prepares for it--and the two identical periods to follow later when he is in his sixties and eighties--by purifying himself and developing his spiritual consciousness, this period will not bear the sting it may well otherwise have. This 6/7 energy field presents a storm within matters of the heart. It is not a vacation. Preparation is the key to success in all things, and failure to prepare, prepares us to fail. But the bright side of all this is that if RJ understands his life and its energies, he can make great spiritual strides during these turbulent tides of his life. Great stress creates great calm for those who perceive, understand, and adjust. For those who do not adjust, regret and sadness may well be the result.

H [8/9]

This is a duplicate of the eight year period RJ experienced in his mid-twenties. However, now he is in his fifties. This period will run from ages 51 to 58. It is a time of business, commerce, and the public stage, quite a contrast to the personal struggle of the previous 'O' timeline period. There will be endings in the arenas of relationship, work and career as a result of the 9 PE. RJ may retire here or change professions. He could also expand (9) his business (8) enterprise.

N [5/6]

This period of change is not a pure '5' energy field for the 'N' is the fourteenth letter of the alphabet and '14' is the number which forces us to lose that which we have in order to truly understand the meaning of freedom - that attachment is the root of all suffering, and when we become detached, voluntarily or involuntarily, we become free, unless we remain constantly attached to a higher power or energy whose attachment generates bliss, joy, and true freedom in us. Not only will RJ experience freedom during this five year period (59-63), he will constantly be engaged in the process of adjustment in his relationships, his heart, and his home life. Changes, motion, movement and experience in personal love are a certainty during this time, and RJ will do well to learn and express love in its purest form and from the deepest place of his heart.

S [1/2]

At sixty-four, RJ undergoes another year of new beginnings which address his sense of personal power and integration. The result places him in the field of the yin, of others, and relationships. Because this is his 64th year, new beginnings pertaining to domestic structures are prevalent. The 64 binary carries a 1 crown and a 2 subcap, and with this added to the 1 energy of the S, the 1 energy of self, identity, and independence will prevail strongly in his life during this year, and the 2 will bring added emphasis in relationships.

T [2/3]

Finally, at age sixty-five RJ receives a needed break from the previous twenty year's experience. This crown 2 timeline period brings an influence of support and caring into his life.

King

196

The result involves ease and enjoyment of living, self-expression, loving communication, and pleasurable work as witnessed by the 3 PE during this period. RJ needs to savor this time. There are more storms ahead.

O [6/7]

It was twenty-two years earlier when RJ experienced this same transiting energy field. It will be twenty years hence when he will experience it again. Now, at age sixty-seven, however, he may not be as strong as he was when the same energy field encompassed him from age forty-five to fifty, which may make this time period from sixty-seven to seventy-two more problematic. Again, the influencing 15/6 energy field of the O generates a 16/7 PE outcome. RJ would be well served if he had understood his life from the outset. His foreknowledge would have prepared him for these times of his destiny. The first part of his life (up to age forty-four) was spent relatively comfortably, but from mid-life on, it has been a struggle and will continue to be so. However, struggle is what makes souls great. It is also struggle which causes us to seek other avenues of comfort than simply those offered by the maya-stricken world of external phenomena and all of its ephemeral and superficial fanfare. RJ is a good candidate for the spiritual life at this point in his life, and he would do well to turn inward and seek alternative answers to his quest for personal happiness.

N [5/6]

Again, during this 14/5 period there is the potential of more loss, change, detachment, and adjustment for RJ. This was the same field he traversed fourteen years earlier from ages fifty-nine to sixty-three. Now RJ must embrace this energy again. It has been quite a trip thus far for RJ, especially during the last thirty-four years. This 'N' period lasts from ages 73-77.

R [9/1]

With 'Roe', RJ enters the name timeline of the 2, a much less stress filled vibratory field than the seven, for no numerical vibration is as potentially deep, isolating, or heart-wrenching as the 7. The 2 is certainly more tender, albeit not as deep. RJ will enter this new name timeline period at age seventy-eight. Within the context of the Letter Timeline, he will stay here for nine years until he is 86. This 9/1 Influence/Reality set is not unusual to RJ. He has experienced it three previous times during his life. The influence of the 9 energy will, once again, create expansion, travel, and

196

interaction with the masses as it focuses on the 1 energy of the self and its identity. Perhaps RJ will become a humanitarian of some sort, a philanthropist, a volunteer, or educator.

O [6/7]

RJ will certainly be familiar with the transiting 15/6 energy field of the O. He's lived through it twice before - from ages forty-five to fifty and from sixty-seven to seventy-one. This time he will transit the 6/7 I/R modality from eighty-seven to ninety-two.

E [5/6]

We've come to the end of our Letter Timeline Analysis and the end of Richard Johnston Roe's adventure through the Letter Timeline of his General Expression. This last five year period will involve RJ's life between ages ninety-three to ninety-seven. Although this energy field generates a 5/6 I/R pattern, it is not one of loss like those of the letter N and its 14/5 energy, but it is still one of change and motion within matters of the heart and family. If RJ lives on past his ninety-seventh year, his Letter Timeline will cycle back to the beginning of his natal name. Therefore, the "R" of Richard will once again come into play and begin the adventure all over again.

Letter Groups and their Specific Vibrations

In the previous description of Richard Johnston Roe's life, there was partial mention of the *specific values* of some letters - namely those of the N (14/5) and O (15/6). Below is a Group Letter Chart of Specific Vibrations which will be of help in deepening one's understanding of letters and their vibrations.

For example, the three letters comprising Group 1 (A-J-S) all have 1 crowns. Yet, the only pure 1 is the letter A. Specifically, the letter J is the tenth letter of the alphabet and S is the nineteenth. Therefore, they possess added vibrations which can be taken into account when performing a Letter Timeline analysis.

Group Letter Chart of Specific Vibrations

1 Group

Letter	GV	SV	Activity/Description
A	1	1	the yang; pure beginnings; creation/genesis; action; independence; the self.
J	1	10	the self in gestation of new beginnings and personal completeness.
S	1	19	personal empowerment; karmic balancing; self on the public stage.

2 Group

Letter	GV	SV	Activity/Description
B	2	2	the yin; relationships, others, support; equalizing; balancing; money.
K	2	11	personal attainment; self vs. self or other selves; inspiration; high energy.
T	2	20	service and support regarding others; compromise; gentleness/sweetness.

3 Group

Letter	GV	SV	Activity/Description
C	3	3	personal expression/integration; marriage; pleasure; words; fun; health.
L	3	12	yang encompassing the yin; self in relationship; beginnings with others.
U	3	21	yin encompassing the yang; others in new beginnings; balancing of the self.

4 Group

Letter	GV	SV	Activity/Description
D	4	4	structures; foundations; security; work; effort; service; restriction; toil.
M	4	13	transformations; death; restructuring; reconstruction; structural changes.
V	4	22	construction/destruction; power/wealth; manifestation of idealization.

5 Group

Letter	GV	SV	Activity/Description
E	5	5	change; freedom; movement; senses; variety; people; talents; exploration.
N	5	14	loss; new structures, forms and work places; detachment; revolution.
W	5	23	others and relationships encompassing expression, pleasure, fun and words.

6 Group

Letter	GV	SV	Activity/Description
F	6	6	personal love, romance, matters of heart/home; adjustments/responsibilities.
O	6	15	yang/action/self encompassing the senses, freedom, experience, people.
X	6	24	yin encompassing structures and forms; loving balance and devotion.

7 Group

Letter	GV	SV	Activity/Description
G	7	7	internal activity; withdrawal; isolation; analysis; spirit; thought; reflection.
P	7	16	yang/action/self encompassing love, adjustments, duty, responsibility, home.
Y	7	25	balance, equilibrium and relationship encompassing people, movement.

8 Group

Letter	GV	SV	Activity/Description
H	8	8	connection/disconnection; commerce; interaction; worldly success; flow.
Q	8	17	yang encompassing the mind and spirit to generate connections.
Z	8	26	money and love in the connecting/disconnecting loop; yin and the heart.

9 Group

Letter	GV	SV	Activity/Description
I	9	9	completion; universality; impersonal love; expansion; the world; rulership.
R	9	18	yang encompassing the 'flow'; self in interaction on the great stage of life.

Richard Johnston Roe: Letter Timeline - Specific Roots

When the *specific* letter values are added to the Letter Timeline, we can obtain a deeper insight of each letter's influence. In the following chart the specific value of each letter is placed to the right of each letter's crown in the "Term" column. Crowns are still used to generate the PE for simplicity.

King

Richard Johnston Roe

Letter Timeline
Specific Roots

Letter	Timeline	LP		Crown & Specific Root		PE
R	Birth to 9	1	+	9 [18]	=	1
I	10-18	1	+	9 [9]	=	1
C	19-21	1	+	3 [3]	=	4
H	22-29	1	+	8 [8]	=	9
A	30	1	+	1 [1]	=	2
R	31-39	1	+	9 [18]	=	1
D	40-43	1	+	4 [4]	=	5
J	44	1	+	1 [10]	=	2
O	45-50	1	+	6 [15]	=	7
H	51-58	1	+	8 [8]	=	9
N	59-63	1	+	5 [14]	=	6
S	64	1	+	1 [19]	=	2
T	65-66	1	+	2 [20]	=	3
O	67-72	1	+	6 [15]	=	7
N	73-77	1	+	5 [14]	=	6
R	78-86	1	+	9 [18]	=	1
O	87-92	1	+	6 [15]	=	7
E	93-97	1	+	5 [5]	=	6

As we can see, assessing the specific values of the letters adds more information. For example, of the four 9s in RJ's name, three [the Rs] have specific roots of 18; only one, the "I" is a pure 9. Of his three 1s, each has a different value. The A is a 1, the J is a 10 and the S is a 19. Yet, his three 6s are all 15s [Os], and of his three 5s, two are 14s [Ns] and one is a 5 [E]. All of these specific values color the crown and add more comprehensive data to the chart analysis. The bottom line, assess specific values of each letter for greater detail. Let's now move on to the Decade Timeline.

Chapter Nine

DECADE TIMELINE (DTL)

Decades are ten year periods beginning with a year whose last digit is a zero. The Alpha Stage [first decade] begins at birth and its first year is marked by a zero. This initial year may be seen as the gestation of the life journey of the following nine years. Sequentially, the Alpha Stage proceeds from birth through ages one, two, three, four, five, six, seven, eight and nine, thus activating each of these ciphers and their attributes. When age ten is reached, the individual begins the Teen's Decade, i.e., age ten is the gestation period for the nine year life cycle of the basic numbers within its transition period. The first year of each decade is always the gestation period of its decade. Therefore, ages 10, 20, 30, 40, 50, 60, 70, 80 and 90 are all gestation periods for their decades.

The decades are marked by attributes and characteristics intrinsic to those of the parent number. During the Alpha Stage/Decade, the child transits each of the basic ten ciphers (0 is one of the ten ciphers) in their purest form. This period is all about activation of the basic ciphers and their attributes. When the Teen Decade arrives, the individual begins a period of self-discovery, each year bringing a new energy to bear upon the self and the ego, the 1 (see the Teens Decade section). When the individual moves into the Twenties Decade, a shift occurs from the energy of the self, the 1, to the energy of others and relationship, the 2. The Thirties Decade brings communication, potential enjoyment, vibrancy and self-expression. The Forties bring work and service; the Fifties focus on change, motion, movement, detachment; the Sixties exude family, adjustments, home, hearth, community, nurturing; the Seventies offer a time of reflection, withdrawal, examination of the life; the Eighties manifest connections (perhaps to a higher power if not already integrated into the life) and disconnections; the Nineties express endings, conclusions, recognition and expanded understanding.

King

After the Alpha Stage, each decade also houses its own master number, thus adding power to the timeline in question. When considering each decade's master energy, be sure to take note of its crown. It will not have a subcap, as no master number does. See the following table.

The Ten Decades

[Master Number in Bold]

Alpha Stage (Activation of the nine basic energies)										
Alpha Decade	birth	1	2	3	4	5	6	7	8	9
(Self/Yang/Ego/Identity - Emergence of Master Numbers)										
Teens Decade	10	**11**	12	13	14	15	16	17	18	19
Twenties (Others/Yin/Relationship)										
Twenties Decade	20	21	**22**	23	24	25	26	27	28	29
(Expression/Integration/Friends/Enjoyment)										
Thirties Decade	30	31	32	**33**	34	35	36	37	38	39
(Work/Service/Planning/Plodding)										
Forties Decade	40	41	42	43	**44**	45	46	47	48	49
(Change/Movement/Detachment/Loss)										
Fifties Decade	50	51	52	53	54	**55**	56	57	58	59
(Adjustment/Heart/Community/Nurturing)										
Sixties Decade	60	61	62	63	64	65	**66**	67	68	69
(Analysis/Life Examination/Withdrawal/Spirit)										
Seventies Decade	70	71	72	73	74	75	76	**77**	78	79
(Connection/Disconnection)										
Eighties Decade	80	81	82	83	84	85	86	87	**88**	89
(Recognition/Conclusions/Expansions)										
Nineties Decade	90	91	92	93	94	95	96	97	98	**99**

The Teen Years

Arguably, there is no time period in the life of a human being more difficult or trying than the teenage years. Oh, my, the exasperation of it all! These years and their intrinsic energies affect not only the teenager but all of those people attached to and existing within the teenager's

The King's Book of Numerology II: Forecasting - Part 1

environment. During these years, teens are often filled with confusion, defiance, insensitivity, egomania and a whole host of other behaviors all too common to parents, teachers and other adults.

Certainly, the normal biological cycle of life development can be regarded as a major scientific cause of the difficulties teenagers face. Puberty, of course, sets in around twelve or thirteen, bringing a whole host of physical and emotional changes in the life of the maturing person. But are there any other avenues we can pursue to find answers and explanations as to why the teen years are so pressing, challenging and difficult? Can numerology shed any light on this subject? The answer is 'yes.' Numerology gives a clear reason and explanation for these often turbulent years.

If we look at the following chart, we begin to see an obvious pattern explaining this teenage challenge. Can you see what it is?

10	11	12	13	14	15	16	17	18	19

If you surmised the recurrence of the number 1 as the reason, you were right. During the teen years, every human being passes through a ten year period where the 1 energy is extremely active. At no other time in life is this ten year energy pattern repeated, unless, of course, someone were to live from 110 to 119 years of age. To place this in further perspective, we could format the previous chart in the following manner by highlighting the number 1 in bold and increasing its font size, a manner more accurately depicting the dilemma and difficulty of the teenage time period.

10	**1**1	**1**2	**1**3	**1**4	**1**5	**1**6	**1**7	**1**8	**1**9

Notice the intent and intensity of the '1' vibration now? Fairly obvious, isn't it? But what is it that makes the recurrence of the number '1' significant? We know the number '1' is the energy of the *self,* the *ego, action, independence, assertiveness* (*aggression* if extreme)*, dominance, stubbornness, uniqueness.* '1' is the energy of the *sun,* the *yang* of the Chinese Tao, the *male* energy. During the teen years, every year for ten years is dominated by an energy of *emergence, initial growth* and *survival of individual being* and *identity* . Furthermore, the '1' energy can easily slip into its unfortunate and non-positive aspects (its negative polarity) of being overly *self-centered, self-absorbed, self-motivating, self-proclaiming* and sometimes *self-defeating.* Negative '1' energy regards only itself to the exclusion of all others. Such self-centeredness is, of course,

King

deleterious to positive socialization and future success in life. Please notice the emphasis on the word 'self,' for '1' is the vibration of the self.

Additionally, as we look at the previous grids, we see that every year for the emerging teenage soul is confronted with, and attached to, a different number [hence, its numerical energy] and a whole new set of circumstances, issues, conditions, situations, lessons, challenges and problems for the emerging child to manage. In other words, not only are the teen years saturated with ego-filled and ego-driven energies, they are juxtaposed every twelve months with new and challenging issues.

At first, '1' is juxtaposed with '0'. The '1' is in gestation. Then, in the following year, it is confronted with itself in the 11th year, the master energy of the Teens Decade. Next the '1', bumps up against the reality of others and the concept of relationship (the 12th year). Then comes the change and transformation of the self and its structures at age 13. At 14, the soul begins to seek its freedom (14=5, the energy of freedom). At 15 it becomes more sexually aware. 16 brings emotional difficulties, more sexual issues and feelings of isolation, privacy, secrecy, know-it-allness. At 17 we find a concentration of independent, creative, ego-driven energy (the '1') focused on the mind and its processes. Teens can often become too belligerent and 'mouthy,' utilizing their mental skills (to their chagrin and detriment, unfortunately) to assume they are all-knowing. At age 18 the teen experience begins to end its cycle in more sobering thought, interaction and expanding awareness. Finally, at 19, the process concludes and reaches finality with concomitant new beginnings.

Not all teens, of course, go through the same degree or type of experiences. Loving and positive parenting skills can allay much of the difficulties and challenges inherent during these formative and often challenging teen years, especially if the parents are wise enough to foresee and prepare their offspring for the challenging '1' energy which will unfailingly befall and encompass them. However, the troubles enveloping teens are difficult, to say the least, especially in this day in age where basic values of respect, discipline, patience, courtesy and ethics are taking a back seat to worldly achievement, personal and instant gratification, power expansion, ego-saturation and money accumulation - the traditional plagues of mankind.

Obviously, the teen years and their energies create an extremely difficult time for everyone. The challenge during this time is to not allow the '1' energy to become self-centered but rather God centered. The '1' vibration in its most elevated expression represents the Deity, God, Spirit, Source - whole and non-separate. '1' is Union, i.e. Yoga.

Unfortunately, emerging souls mistake this reality (as do many adults) and assume they are the center of the universe, just as Aristotle believed the earth was the center of the universe. Then

The King's Book of Numerology II: Forecasting - Part 1

along came Copernicus who taught that our solar system was heliocentric, that is, that the earth revolved around the sun, not vice-versa. Likewise, spiritual maturation requires every soul in ascent mode to acquire and manifest the consciousness that God (or our Creator) is the center of life (ours and everyone else's) and we rotate around Him. He does not rotate around us. Nor does the world or life rotate around us. Unfortunately, it is difficult for a young people to acquire this understanding unless they receive some wise counseling in their early years, counseling which will help them mature through the tough teen times, i.e., the '1' years, with grace, dignity, respect and maturity.

The Decade PE (Performance/Experience) Theory

Decades represent the influential energies of their crowns which are intrinsically comprised of attributes and characteristics (see keywords, page 147). When combined with the Expression energies of an individual they generate a PE, a performance, experience, role, outcome.

Decade [influence] + **Expression** = **Performance/Experience** [outcome]

The PE, as any PE, has multiple layers associated with the roots of the Expression which creates complexity in the life. Let's study this principle using the Expression of our friend, Richard Johnston Roe, whose Expression is a 7 with roots of 16, 97 and 214.

Richard Johnston Roe: Expression

Expression	Roots
Simple	7
General	97
Specific	214
Transition	16

By adding each of these Expression numbers to each decade, we obtain an understanding of the multiple energies RJR will be experiencing during each decade.

Richard Johnston Roe: Decade PE Grid

Decade	Roots				
	Simple	**Transition**	**General**	**Specific**	**Simple PE**
	7	**16**	**97**	**214**	
10s	17-8	26-8	107-8	224-8	**8**
20s	27-9	36-9	117-9	234-9	**9**
30s	37-1	46-1	127-1	244-1	**1**
40s	47-2	56-2	137-2	254-2	**2**
50s	57-3	66-3	147-3	264-3	**3**
60s	67-4	76-4	157-4	274-4	**4**
70s	77-5	86-5	167-5	284-5	**5**
80s	87-6	96-6	177-6	294-6	**6**
90s	97-7	106-7	187-7	304-7	**7**

Through this Decade Timeline we get a snapshot of the issues, concerns, activities, experiences and performances RJR will give during each ten year period of his life through the numbers of the root structure of his Expression. Note the Decade in the far left column and its Simple PE in the far right column. We can simplify this further with the following grid in which only the 7 crown is used.

Richard Johnston Roe: Simple Decade PE Grid

Decade	Expression	Simple PE	Outcome Attributes & Issues: Keywords
	7	(decade)	
10s	17 >	**8**	Socialization, circulation, power, comfort, interaction
20s	27 >	**9**	Travel, public, art, expansion, universality, endings
30s	37 > 10	**1**	Self, new beginnings, independence, solitary, action
40s	47> 11 >	**2**	Others, females, relationship, partnership, association
50s	57 > 12 >	**3**	Self-expression, words, joy, friends, health/disease
60s	67-4	**4**	Work, service, security, order, structure/restructure
70s	77-5	**5**	Changes, movement, motion, detachment, freedom
80s	87-6	**6**	Family, adjustments, love, home, community, caring
90s	97-7	**7**	Introspection, reflection, recession, withdrawal

The King's Book of Numerology II: Forecasting - Part 1

In a general sense, everyone with a 7 Expression, like our friend RJR, will experience the same things during each decade. The same will be true for each of the other eight simple Expressions. This decade timeline is one thread of life's blueprint. Remember, our destinies are beautifully interwoven tapestries of threads of cosmic vibration manifested as numbers. Each of the timelines discussed in this book is a thread of the life blueprint fabric. The art of numerology is to understand how these threads intertwine to create the exquisite tapestry that is the destiny. Life is not simple. Life is complex. These timelines illustrate the complexity of life and explain why we are all so much alike yet different. Furthermore, they reveal the truth behind the statement of Twentieth Century Saint, Charan Singh: *We don't see things the way they are. We see things the way we are.* No truer words were ever spoken. Each of us sees life through a multilayered and variegated prism of ciphered colors specific to our own life blueprint. None of us sees things exactly the same. It's impossible. When we say someone doesn't "get it," they're no doubt thinking or saying the exact same thing about us. Perceptions are personally specific to each person. Understanding this should help us understand others and gain a sense of peace, balance and harmony as we traverse the paths of our lives.

208

Chapter Ten

AGE TIMELINE (ATL)

The first of the three major annual timelines involved in the forecasting process is the *Age Timeline* or ATL, also known as the Chronological Timeline (CTL). The other two are the Universal Timeline (UTL) and the Personal Year Timeline (PTL). These will be discussed in subsequent chapters.

The ATL is simply the age of the person and is noted in a chart as the current age in association with its single digit crown. For example, if a person is sixteen years of age, his ATL is 16/7. A thirty-three year old individual will have an ATL of 33/6. If a person is fifty-eight, his ATL is 58/4 (5 + 8 = 13 > 1 + 3 = 4).This is the simplest, most universal and most personal timeline. The Age Timeline begins annually on the individual's birthday of the current calendar year and proceeds to his next birthday in the subsequent calendar year.

The age of a person gives information as to the type of influences, issues, and themes dominant during the current chronological year. During the *alpha stage*, the individual moves through successive, pure, simple energy fields (1 through 9). Each new birthday brings a new, pure energy represented by a new whole number. When we're one year old, the concentration is on the self and its emergence into the life of this incarnation. When we're two, the attention is on that of relationships and others as we begin to experience those around us and with whom we are connected. This is the age of the "terrible twos" when children begin to exercise their own ego [developed in year 1] with the egos of others. The number two can certainly bring competition and clashing. Our third birthday brings self-expression into focus and marks the completion of the first triad of our lives--self, others and integrated relationship. Age four registers our advent into the realm of structure and completes the first major square of life solidifying our initial identity, having transited the four major cosmic elements of fire (1), water (2), air (3) and earth (4). Our fifth year ushers in change, experience, and movement away from the house, as well as an expanded interaction with people. Most of us begin our formal education at this age as we begin kindergarten. Age six brings adjustments in the home and community life and a realization of responsibility to others in the home. Seven marks the age where major mental development, concentration, and focus begin to take shape and form. From a teaching perspective there is a huge mental shift between ages seven and eight. Age eight brings issues of social connection, interaction, integration and expansion. Age nine ushers in the end of the innocence experienced during the *alpha stage* with a broadening understanding of life.

The *teens decade* moves beyond the innocence, purity, peace, and simplicity of the *alpha stage* and initiates the *self* into the mainstream of social life. Beginning with the zero cipher of gestation at age 10, the self then proceeds to transit each of the basic numbers 1 through 9. Here we see the complexity of life beginning, for now the self becomes engaged in dual ciphers, double numbers, compound vibrations and mixed energies in juxtaposition. Up to this point the vibrations were singular, pure, and simple, generating a certain amount of peace in the formative years of the alpha stage. But now, no more. The *teens decade*, because of the 1's juxtaposed relationship with other numbers, brings the advent of comparison, contrast and conflict into our lives, for now the *self*, the pure *one*, the ego, the heretofore separate identity, must deal with other numbers, other vibrations, other identities and other issues for the remainder of its life. The number 1 also signifies authority figures, especially parents, so it's logical and openly obvious, that teens often rebel against their parents, against authority figures (1) telling them, the teen and his 1 ego, what to do, giving orders, laying down family law and so forth.

A note: in any multiple number such as a binary (two digit number), a triad (three digit number), etc., the first number can be seen as encompassing, encircling, and focusing on the following number. In a binary the first number carries the dominate vibration and the second number becomes the object of its attention, i.e., the focus. In a triad, the first number encircles the second and the second encircles the third. Numerical dominance moves from left to right as each vibration encompasses and embraces the one following it. In the teens decade, for example, the energy of the 1 (the self and ego) embraces, encircles, encompasses and focuses its energies sequentially on each of the nine basic numbers as the 1 makes its journey through the teens decade from age 10 to 19.

As we all know, the teen years are potentially hard and difficult for parents and children alike. All of us are quite challenged during these years as we grow. This is not difficult to understand when we realize that each of us, with each new year cycle beginning on our birthday during the teen years, must challenge a totally new vibration and, incidentally, a new vibration with a different polarity from the year preceding it. After the gestation period of the teens decade during our tenth year, at age eleven (11) each (1) of us is placed within a natural vibratory field where we must deal with other *ones*, other beings, other egos, as well as with our own self and its ego - the second 1 cipher of the eleven binary. Thus, at age eleven the person (1) begins a new journey of self-awareness in relation to other ones (1s).

Age eleven (11) can be seen as representing the self (1) in relationship with itself (1) or with its own survival and independence (the second '1' of the 11 cipher), as well as representing the self (1) in relationship with other *ones*, with other selves, other singular egos and identities as previously stated. This concept of relationship is represented by the number 2 crown which, of course, the 11 is in reduction (1 + 1 = 2). This is a challenging time for the emerging identity. Age eleven represents a powerful moment of conflict in life - the ego (1) juxtaposed with other egos (1). This can create peace if both are moving in the same direction and share the same values, ideals, and understandings. However, it can also create tension through a challenging of wills if each of the 1s (the separate individuals) is moving in an opposing direction. Thus, a virtual tug-o-war ensues. If both ones are highly saturated with themselves and their ideals, they may clash, banging and butting heads together like two rams in conflict. This tug-o-war and clashing aspect of the 11 cipher is where tension is created. Age Eleven also manifests the first *master vibration* of the life journey. Master numbers have no subcap, no anchor to balance the 2 addcap crown so the energies are intense.

During our eleventh year, the individual must now not only confront other singular ones but negotiate the vibratory field of the *two* energy - the yin, others, relationship, passivity and support. This is represented by the 2 crown of the number eleven. It is also during this age that the individual's energies are juxtaposed with another polarity. *One* maintains a positive polarity; *two*, a negative polarity. Therefore, since polarities change by sequential order beginning with a positive polarity at age 1 and moving to a negative polarity at age 2, positive at age 3, negative at age 4 and so forth, when the individual changes age on each successive birthday, he not only moves into another energy field with a totally different set of characteristics associated with each numerical vibration, but one with an opposing polarity and, thus, he is caught swinging involuntarily back and forth to the ceaseless rhythm of the great cosmic pendulum, a condition which will be prevalent for the remainder of life. Within this construct of constant swinging, there is constant change, change especially difficult to manage for a young soul emerging from the alpha stage and beginning a transit of the teen years. This yearly transition of the emerging self through the fields of the nine basic numbers (1 to 2, 1 to 3, 1 to 4, etc.), combined with the new experience of the constant movement of the pendulum from polarity to polarity, creates a natural cosmic conflict within the individual. This is why the teen years are difficult. Every year of a teenager's life is saturated with the self in transition and exploration of some new and unknown energy. The teen years take the individual out of a singular world and force him to navigate a world of duality and all the complexities associated with it, and it all is awash with pure ego.

This state of conflictive energies reflected in the *teens decade* can be mild to severe as we all know. Not all teens have terrible experiences; quite to the contrary unless the individual chart is afflicted negatively. However, the *teens decade* is still a time period of extreme self-absorption and identity involvement because of the conjunct construction of the *one*, the self, with every other single cipher in transit on a yearly basis from age 11 to 19. This is where the teenage era finds its challenge. The ego of self (the 1) is constantly challenged by other vibrations and the ideas and realities they represent. During its alpha stage the self was the sole object of attention, i.e., its own. Now during the teen years the self is forced to expand its awareness to the macrocosm - a tough, tension-filled and exasperating shift for an emerging soul.

This concept is visually depicted by the following chart. Notice the saturation of 1 energy during the teen years. This 1 energy of self and ego has the tendency to make the individual self-absorbed, for better or worse, as it transits a timeline in which every new year brings a different energy into its budding realm of maturation. The *crown* energy can be viewed as the positive pull and the *challenge* energy as the negative pull.

Teen Years: The Self in Transit

Crown-addcap	1	2	3	4	5	6	7	8	9	1
Age	10	11	12	13	14	15	16	17	18	19
Challenge-subcap	1	0	1	2	3	4	5	6	7	8

One may argue that every decade has conflict within its binaries and this is truly accurate. However, the *teens decade* is the first decade where the conflict begins, where single ciphers find themselves in juxtaposition with other single ciphers and, because this conflictive vibratory construct is new to the emerging consciousness (the self moving out of the *alpha stage* into the arena of others), it is more difficult to traverse and manage than those of the following decades. The reason for this conflict is complexity. During the alpha stage, the individual only had to deal with himself. There existed no dual ciphers representing other energies and no *challenges* were present. However, with the onset of the teen years, dual energies and their intrinsic challenges became manifest. Life became complex. Singularity had passed into duplicity.

We can see the complexity more clearly if we place this thought in tabular form [following page]. "Ch" represents the binary *challenge* and "1 jx" means the individual (1) juxtaposed with those energies in the 'contrasting energies' column.

Teens Decade: Challenge Contrasts

Age	ch	jx	The Contrasting Energies
10/1	1	1 jx	in gestation (0)
11/2	0	1 jx	*itself* (1) generating high energy in relationship (2). No subcap anchor
12/3	1	1 jx	*others* (2) generating social interaction/fun/pleasure (3). 1 subcap.
13/4	2	1 jx	*expression* (3) generating transformation/puberty (4). 2 subcap.
14/5	3	1 jx	*structure* (4) generating change, exploration, freedom (5). 3 subcap.
15/6	4	1 jx	*senses* and *freedom* (5) generating sexual awareness (6). 4 subcap.
16/7	5	1 jx	*adjustment/ responsibility* (6) generating internal stress (7). 5 subcap.
17/8	6	1 jx	*internal awareness* (7) generating social connections (8). 6 subcap.
18/9	7	1 jx	*interaction* (8) generating completions/expansion, endings (9). 7 subcap.
19/1	8	1 jx	*the macro* (9) generating independent power, beginnings (10/1). 8 subcap.

With this view it is impossible not to comprehend the difficulty of the *teens decade*. The self (ego) is the first vibration at issue in every year - the dominant characteristic of each binary within this time period, and its self-absorption and saturation are clearly apparent. As difficult as this phase of life is for many of us, it is an unavoidable fact of life for, indeed, it is a natural state of cosmic design.

The number *One* also represents the characteristics of independence, action, reason and ego. This is the time of life when the individual is constantly testing his ability to assert himself or herself, to walk alone, to 'do it my way', to stand apart, be unique and acclaim a sense of personal identity to the world. In effect, the ego is announcing itself. Because *One* is generally driven, rigid, unbending and unconcerned with others, the *One* usually sees the world revolving around itself. It is full of ego and it would not be unrealistic to subname the *teens decade* the *ego decade*.

At age eleven, the *one* tests itself in relationship(11/2); at twelve, the individual (1) focuses on others (2), being pulled by the 3 energy (the crown) of friends, good times, communication and self-expression while at the same time being challenged by itself (the 1 challenge of the 12 cipher). At age thirteen (13), one focuses on self-expression (3), being pulled by its 4 transformative crown and challenged by the 2 energy of relationship and others. It is no coincidence that puberty generally occurs at age thirteen. Rules, regulations, order and all things of structure (4) become the main involvement of the individual at age 14 as he feels the pull of freedom and exploration (5 crown) while being challenged by his own self-expression, fulfillment and identity (3 challenge). At age fifteen the individual concentrates his attention on the 5 energies of freedom, sensual exploration, experimentation, rebellion and detachment as he is pulled by the 6 energies of love and romance but challenged by the discipline, restriction and regulatory energies of the 4. Age sixteen brings a focus of adjustments, domestic responsibilities and budding sexuality as the 1 encompasses the 6 energy of personal love, challenged by the 5 energy of excitement, experimentation, exploration, the senses and personal freedom while being pulled into the confusing, disturbing, reflective and potentially chaotic energy field of the 7. Age sixteen is probably the most critical time for a teenager. It is potentially fraught with temptations and disruptions where chaos and confusion are at their height. Seventeen expresses a concentration of mental power (7), is pulled by social interaction (8) and challenged by energies of love and responsibility (6). Age eighteen begins the waning phrase of the teen years as the individual focuses on his involvement (8) with endings and conclusions (9 crown), challenged with thoughts and uncertainties (7). This is the age when most teens graduate from high school and move into the interactive domain of adulthood. Age nineteen finds the individual in definite transition as the 1 energy of new beginnings focuses on the 9 energy of endings which create new beginnings (1 crown) which are simultaneously challenged by the 8 energy of disconnections in the basic flow of life.

In reflection of the teens decade, *One* rules reason and linear thinking. It is during the *teens decade* that the self is 'taken to school', figuratively and literally, to formulate its reasoning capacities. The individual is learning, constantly, that which is acceptable and that which is not acceptable from personal, familial and social points of view. Obviously, most of us acquire our formal education during this time, encasing levels of grade school, high school and early college. Hopefully, by the time the *teens decade* runs its course, the individual has learned to think and reason well enough to become responsible, independent and self-reliant--the main lessons to be acquired from this period of life.

The King's Book of Numerology II: Forecasting - Part 1

It would be helpful during the teen years for the individual to be taught early on that the world does not revolve around him, that there are other people in the world (other 1s) who also have individual rights and separate points of view worthy of merit. This will help mitigate the negative aspects generated as a result of the emerging ego transiting the extremely ego-saturated region of the teens decade. Self-respect, respect for and honoring of others, discipline, social manners and self-control should also be taught and, if need be, enforced. The greatest damage that can be done to a teenage child is to lead him to erroneously believe through thought and action that he is the center of the universe and that life and everyone else in the world revolve around him and are created solely for the pampering and embellishment of his ego, wants, desires needs and pleasures. Such thought only reinforces an illusion of egocentricity, promotes a problematic false sense of entitlement, and does nothing to prepare the individual for the journey ahead because once he exits the teens decade, he will from then on be involved in a world of others to some capacity. If he is not prepared for this moment, he will have a rude awakening, and the waters of his life, rather than being glassy and smooth, will be agitated, rough and possibly storm-tossed.

At twenty (20), as with all 'zero-ciphered binaries', the individual is granted a year of incubation into the approaching energy field in order to prepare itself for the coming nine year cycle of new energy as the great cosmic pendulum sways into a different vibrational domain and a whole new polarity--in this case, the domain of the *Two*. The *Twenties Decade* is the realm of the yin, the female aspect of nature. It is here the self must learn to recognize others, realize that the world does not revolve around itself and that the self, if it is going to succeed and survive, must learn to cooperate, support, share, balance, equalize and help. No longer can the *One* selfishly indulge itself because now its well-being demands a more expansive focus in the world of interpersonal relationships. The *One* must learn that there are other *Ones* (others) in this world and relationships with them are part of the life process. The 1 must also learn to let go of its extreme self-assertion that it demonstrated during the teen years and adapt a consciousness less absorbed in itself. The 2 vibration is more outwardly passive than the 1, more diplomatic, sympathetic, receptive, sensitive and concerned with others, relationships and balance - principles directly opposite to those of the teens decade with its 1 energetic focus.

It is more common than not that marital relationships are formed within this decade. The 1 energy of drive and self-awareness merges with and is softened by the 2 and its curves, its natural ability to bend, shape and support. Cooperation becomes a key principle of life. The 1 must also learn to bend and be more flexible in its wants, needs and points of view. This relationship principle also becomes obvious as the individual enters the workplace and finds himself working with others in the normal course of business. Money, which comes under the rulership of the 2 vibration, raises its head to acknowledge its importance to the self and its survival. Life definitely changes.

The *Thirties Decade* sways the soul, naturally once again, to the opposing positive polarity and encases the individual in a vibration of self-expression, fulfillment, and integration. Now, the self, having struggled through the maturation process in the valley of fire of the 1 and learning to cooperate, support and share with others while swimming across the watery domain of the 2, catches a breath of fresh air in the social ease of the 3 where 1 and 2 merge to form the first polar triad of integrated self-expression. In a general sense this is a time of ease, fun, communication, artistic expression, social integration, good times and pleasure. The self is neither too young nor too old. The body is still, for the most part, youthful, supple and vibrant, making the experience of life somewhat enjoyable during the thirties decade unless the numbers 1 and 3 are afflicted in the first Challenge position, in which case there will be potential problems with identity, self, health, image, happiness, joy, communication.

Families and the marriage environment are a major focus during this time as a normal manifestation of the merging process of the 1 and 2 to form the 3--the marriage. From the marriage, children are born and the first triad is complete. Father, mother and children, or the husband, wife and their blend, i.e., "us," the marriage bond, all live in an environment of self-expression and social interaction. If all is smooth, loving, and harmonious within this triad, there is a feeling of goodness, wholeness, completeness. However, if either the 1 or the 2, representing the male and female respectively, is absent from the picture, this triad of integrated perfection becomes incomplete and perfection is lost or thwarted. Children may, if not given a full understanding of the importance of male and female energies within this incomplete triangle, become incomplete themselves or harbor deficiencies on an emotional or psychological level. The basic theory of this first polar triad of *integrated perfection* of the 1, 2 and 3 vibrations is that the opportunity for perfected self-expression exists *if* all the parts are connected and energy is flowing smoothly throughout the entire structure.

Metaphysically, the number 3 and its symbolic structure, the *triangle*, represent the expression of perfection. However, if any of the vibratory components are missing, or are negatively expressed, the expression of perfection, itself, becomes incomplete. This is why it is important to understand the cosmic relationship of numbers. Love may not be enough to create individual fulfillment. There needs to be a balanced involvement of energies. If, for example, a child is devoid of the experience and contact with a mother--the yin or female energy--the child may grow

The King's Book of Numerology II: Forecasting - Part 1

to have issues with females. If devoid of a father--the male energy--issues of the yang may be a problem. This is why one parent families are susceptible to problems. There is simply a basic lack of the required masculine or feminine energies to form a balanced, harmonious, perfected state of being. The issues, problems and consequences generated as a result of one parent families are obvious and, many times, sad. Growing boys need masculine energy with which to identify. Growing girls need feminine energy for the same reason. The sole parent may supply enough love but not enough of the missing vibration to create a sense of natural fulfillment, wholeness and completion in the child. Hence, difficulties may emerge as a direct result of not having enough yin and yang energies present in single gender or single parent families. Life experience bears this out. We all need both masculine and feminine energies to be whole.

The *Forties Decade* involves the individual with work, effort, regimentation and structures of all kinds. The limitations, confinements, constrictions and restrictions of life may be quite apparent. One may also realize security on many levels here in this decade or, if there is negatively aspected 4 energy in the life chart (void, challenge, voided challenge or grand voided challenge), there could easily be issues with security, even an absence of it. The windsomeness and waywardness of youth, and the fun and ease of life to this point begin to become reflections, not realities. The order of the day, of the 4 decade, is order, work, service, effort. This can be a strong and solid time period. But the ruling energy is *structure* and all that it represents.

It is during this phase of life that structural issues of the body become noticeable, especially to athletes or people highly involved in physical expression and activity. The body's natural metabolism usually falls markedly during the *forties decade* and one finds himself having to consume less food in order to prevent weight gain. The basic natural furnace within the body just is not putting out as much fire and energy as it used to when it was young. Therefore, one must be concerned with the principles of regimentation, discipline, order, self-control and restraint, especially in a dietary sense if one desires to maintain one's health. If these are observed, developed, and strengthened, the *forties decade* can be wonderfully strong and robust, but if not, life can start to become a struggle and a weight to bear. The number Four does rule struggle, weight and limitation.

It is also during the *forties decade* that a physically active person may realize his body does not heal as fast when it is injured as it did in youth. Losing much of its natural, youthful energy, it doesn't scream to be exercised as much as it was in younger years, so the much needed flow of the body's life energies and fluids are reduced. Again, one must exercise discipline and strength of will to maintain a sense of health and well-being. By the end of the *forties decade*, the individual has

King

passed through the first square of life, having transited each of the cosmic elements of fire, water, air and earth.

The hallmark of the *Fifties Decade* is change, movement, exploration and freedom. Having transited the first square of life, the soul feels or realizes a need for alterations in the life process. Children, most probably, have left the nest, work may or may not have provided a sense of security and, certainly, the body is not the same as it used to be. A feeling of exploration and freedom, perhaps even uncertainty, become awakened. The experiences of people may be expanded as one receives grand children into the family fold or reaches out to others in a business manner as a matter of having acquired a richness and variety of work experience in the marketplace.

In the *Fifties Decade*, the self begins a journey through the second square of life, building upon the foundation of the first. If the first had been constructed well, the second is in good stead. If not, the aspect of change here may become rather dramatic, and the sins of having lived solely in and for the *present* during the first square of life while not considering or simply being oblivious to the future may become readily apparent. It is true that everything happens in the *present* but one must not forget that the *present* may be around for seventy, eighty, ninety or a hundred years, and in order to enjoy one's later life, care must be taken to take care of life during the whole journey, especially in the beginning where the foundation for the rest of life is constructed. If one fails to prepare, one prepares to fail. In life, it is no different. One must live in the *present* but never forsake the *future*. In fact, great care should be taken in the *present* to insure a caring *future*. The *present* is the foundation of the *future*. Buildings built on sand are sure to collapse, while those built on rock survive--strong and solid to the end.

The *Sixties Decade* brings adjustments, responsibilities and additional concerns for family and community. Fathers and mothers often become patriarchs and matriarchs as older family members depart this incarnation, passing their rulership down to the emerging new leaders. Caring for and nurturing others is the primary focus during the sixties.

It is during this time period that many people retire from employment and begin the transition into the remainder of their life. It is interesting to note that the age generally regarded as the retirement benchmark is *sixty-five*, an age which expresses the dominant energy of adjustment (6) encompassing the energy of change and freedom (5) to create a transition energy of *eleven* (6 + 5 = 11), which further places an interest of the individual (1) on himself (1) generating a personal relationship (11/2).

The decades of the seventies and eighties bring one into the arena of analysis and connection respectively, if, of course, the individual lives this long. The *Seventies Decade* focuses on spiritual

The King's Book of Numerology II: Forecasting - Part 1

and religious concerns as the individual, having led a full life to this point, begins to think, wonder, question, analyze, scrutinize, review, examine and reflect on his own life and life's meaning in general . . . hopefully. It is sad that one should have to wait this long to enter this energy field and begin this deepening process. If one is wise and hyperopic, he can begin this process in his youth if he is aware enough, focused enough, and strong enough to overcome the pull of the general tendencies of the other decades. Spirituality does not have to come at the end of life. In fact, life is, itself, a spiritual journey. Most of us simply get caught up in the early part of life with the thrill of surfing the different waves of energy and experience life offers from decade to decade. But we certainly do not have to wait until the end is near to ask ourselves about God and question the meaning of existence. Better to do it when we are young and full of energy and health. If we wait too long, we may never have the chance to discover our spiritual legacy and therefore lose the great spiritual opportunity which the human body and human life afford. As Mystics proclaim, once we lose the human form we may not get it again, and therefore it is incumbent upon us to make the most of it and its opportunity for God realization now while we have the chance. Human life is a priceless gift, not a right. We do not own our bodies. They're on loan to us. We should never lose sight of this fact and use our human existence to make divine progress.

The *Eighties Decade* will bring connections and disconnections--connections with a deeper side of us which we began in the *seventies decade* and a general disconnection with the material world with this body and this life as the life force within us begins to wane. Actions and choices which we initiated early in our life may return to us on this connecting wave of *eight* energy as *eight* has been associated with the law of karma, with the reaping of what we have sown. In fact, the Grim Reaper symbolizes this fact of life but, obviously, he represents a disconnection, not a connection.

The *Nineties Decade* ushers in a perspective of universality and endings. Should one make it this far, concerns are obviously about drawing things to an end and feeling the energies of termination and completion. Philosophy and philanthropy may be strong interests as well during this time period. Public recognition may also be experienced if the life has been founded on meritorious conduct and accomplishment. In any instance, the *Nineties Decade* is the culmination of all the decades before it, the ending of the *Cycle of Binaries*.

King

Age, Crown & Transition Ciphers

Having considered the decade of the age in question in order to arrive at a general understanding of the ten year vibratory veil enshrouding the individual, the next step is to look at the binary format of the actual age of the individual which consists of the age as a root, the *crown*-- the basic, simple cipher(s) of the age reduced to a single number by addition, and the *challenge* -- the result of the subtraction of the ciphers forming the age. The *crown* represents the positive energy of the binary in question; the *challenge*, the negative energy. The *crown* can also be viewed as that which pulls us upward, while the *challenge* weights us down or, in some cases, stabilizes us.

If a person is eight years old, the crown is eight and possesses no challenge. But if a person is fifteen, the *crown* is *six* (1 + 5 = 6) and the *challenge* is *four* (5 - 1 = 4). A person forty-eight years of age will have a crown of *three* (4 + 8 = 12 > 1 + 2 = 3), a transition root of *twelve* and a *challenge* of *four*.

Age 15: Root, Crown & Challenge

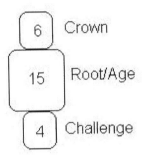

Thus, a fifteen year old person will spend one year in a 6 basic vibration of home, adjustment, matters of the heart, sexuality, sensuality, and responsibility and be challenged with issues of the number 4: structure, discipline, limitations, restrictions, rules, regulations, etc.- principles the emerging and often defiant 1 energy rebels against. The 15 energy creates a base of the self, ego, independence and action (1) focused on freedom, change, experience, experimentation, people and the senses (5) in conjunction with the challenges of rules, regulations, restrictions, regimens, limitations, discipline and self-control (4). In effect, these are the general influences of any 15 year old person. Other factors illustrated in the basic chart come into play, but the vibrations of the 15 - the 1, 4, 5 and 6 - create the framework for the year's activity. And, just to be sure we understand the process, the vibrations of a person's age begin on the birthday of the individual and at the exact minute of birth, continuing until the next birthday when the vibrations change again. In the case of the *Age Timeline*, the next set of vibrations will be the current year plus one as the *age timeline* is also the *chronological time line*.

If a person is 48, not only does there exist a 3 crown in his chart but there also exists a transition root of 12 (4 + 8 = 12) and a 4 challenge. This should be taken into effect when the age is read because it does offer additional information about this year of life. Thus, a person who is 48 years old will be involved in a year's influence of words, communication, ease of living, friends, good times, pleasure and artistic self-expression (3 crown) juxtaposed with work, limitation, security and effort (4 challenge). The 48 vibration (the age itself) will be rooted in work and effort (4) encompassing connection or disconnection, interaction, integration and social involvement (8). This 48 year should bring outward, social influences in work and business. See the following chart.

Age 48: Root, Transition root; Crown & Challenge

There is still more. The single ciphers of 4 and 8 in the 48 cipher combine to form a transition root of 12. This binary is formed by the single ciphers 1 and 2 which represent the yang and yin, the male and female energies, the dual charges of the basic polarity principle. Because each cipher (1 and 2) is equally represented, the final product, the 3, is in balance, which explains why the number 3 is traditionally regarded as a vibration of relative ease - it is a reflection of the balanced energies of the yin and the yang, the female and male aspects of creation. This is symbolically represented by the triangle, the symbolic representation of integrated perfection and harmonized balance.

King

222

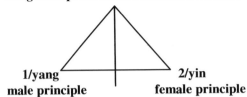

3
integrated perfection/harmonized balance

1/yang
male principle

2/yin
female principle

Forty-eight is not the only double number carrying a *twelve transition root*. *Thirty-nine, fifty-seven, sixty-six, seventy-five, eighty-four* and *ninety-three* all house a transition root of *twelve* and, therefore, should reflect a state of harmonized balance, yielding a *three crown* in reduction--the cosmic cipher of integrated perfection as represented by the preceding diagram. This does not mean a life may not contain difficulties during these ages because each binary does have its inherent challenges, but the *twelve/three triad*, the symbol of integrated perfection housing a state of balance and harmony, should have a mitigating effect on any negative conditions during this age and foster general good feelings in normal conditions.

The same procedure is followed for determining the general influences at any age of life. Analyze the crown, the age itself (the specific root of the crown), any transition roots and challenges. The only exception to the challenges will be the master numbers 11, 22, 33, 44, 55, 66, 77, 88 and 99. These do not maintain a challenge and, therefore, their pulling energy - that which drives them - is not weighted down, anchored or hindered by any challenge vibration. This is one reason master numbers are so powerful - they're basically unencumbered, energetic, dual ciphered powerhouses void of challenge or encumbrance.

Those binaries housing a zero cipher: 10, 20, 30, 40, 50, 60, 70, 80 and 90 have the same root, crown and challenge. Thus, in all ways they are in gestation, preparing the individual for the journey ahead in their respective energy fields. The 10 is pure 1 energy in gestation. The 20 is pure 2 energy in gestation. The 30 is pure 3 energy in gestation and so forth.

Cross Checking--Activation--Correspondences

Cross-Checking is the process of evaluating and referencing one component of a chart with other components in the same chart to determine additional identifying characteristics, conditions, possibilities, validities, verities and accuracies. It is an extremely important and integral concept, not only in analyzing a chart but in the process of forecasting as well. *Activation* is the principle identifying the process of a transiting energy--any timeline cipher--energizing or bringing to life a

The King's Book of Numerology II: Forecasting - Part 1

component in the chart as it *transits* or moves across or through the life of an individual. This *activation* is generated as a result of the transiting energies *matching* or *corresponding to* a component of the individual's Basic and/or Life Matrices. *Correspondences*, therefore, are identical matching energies between transits (energies moving through the chart) and Basic Matrix components (see *The King's Book of Numerology, Volume I, Foundations & Fundamentals*).

The greater number of identical energies in a chart at any given time increases the intensity of the vibration in question. When identical energies occur simultaneously in a chart, the energies are said to be *stacked*. *Stacking* creates great intensity, an excellent example of which was the Towers' Tragedy of 911 (11 September 2001). On that day America witnessed a fourteen stack of 5 energy and a triple stack of 11/2 energy. With such an enormous amount of fire, loss, detachment, freedom, conflict, contention, deceit and duplicity represented by the 5 and 2 ciphers respectively, there was absolutely no way 911 could have been a peaceful day for America.

In furthering our understanding of *correspondences*, if a person is forty-eight years old and retains a *Three* Expression, it will be a relatively comfortable year for the person as long as the three is not afflicted by void, challenge or voided challenge impediments because the number 48 with its 3 crown matches the *Three Expression*. This vibratory match or *correspondence* (identical matching energies) creates a comfortable association through a recognizable, identical duplication of energies and, hence, the result produced is a favorable outcome.

Correspondences should always be determined in the analysis process because they establish the internal connection of the individual with the forces moving through his life. If a person's age matches either of his *Soul* vibrations, this correspondence will generally bring to the individual what he wants and desires, and he will be content and happy. If the age matches the *Nature* vibrations, he will find the way and manner in which he does things flowing smoothly. If the age matches the *Expression*, he will feel good about who he is. A match in the *Lifepath* intensifies his life's lessons and a correspondence in the *Performance/Reality* strengthens and corroborates the performance given in life during that particular year. In effect, the *transiting energy*, in this case the *age*, activates that part of a person's chart which maintains an identical vibration with it. More succinctly, transiting energies *activate* Basic Matrix and Life Matrix energies through identical energy matches or *correspondences*.

Age Timeline Influence

In Chapter Two we learned about life cycle patterns and their two major elements of *causes/influences/themes/issues* and *effects/outcomes/realities/experiences*. The nine life cycle

224

patterns can be applied to the age timeline (and every timeline) to assist us in analyzing a person's life.

In 'reading' the age timeline the chronological age is that aspect which identifies the *causes/influences/themes/issues* operating in the person's life which are the most personal to the individual. The energies of the age timeline do include other people but not to the extent that other timelines do such as the *universal timeline (UTL)* and *personal year timeline (PTL)*. The age timeline is principally about the self and its feelings, thoughts, attitudes, and experiences.

If the chronological age identifies issues and themes, how is the PE [Performance/Experience] generated which represents the *effects/outcomes/realities/experiences* in the age timeline? Simply by adding the Expression to the age timeline. The outcome of these two components is the Age Timeline PE and reality the person will experience during the year. To keep things simple at the present time, we'll simply use simple (single) ciphers to illustrate this point. Because this volume of *The King's Numerology* is about *basic* forecasting, we'll focus principally on single ciphers throughout each timeline and keep the process simple. This will allow us to understand the concepts more fully and lessen any confusion created by dealing with root structures, a subject for later study. The only roots we'll deal with at all are those of each specific age of the person in question. Crowns and challenges we'll keep as single numbers.

Let's say a person has a 5 Expression. To arrive at the PE outcome/reality aspect of the ATL [Age Timeline] during any age we will simply add 5 to the age in question. If our 5 Expression person is age nineteen, for example, we add 5 to 1 (19 in reduction is a 1) to arrive at a 1/6 Influence/Reality set   (1 [age 19 reduced to a single digit] + 5 [the simple Expression of the person] = 6, the PE or outcome energy field).

1 (ATL) + 5 (Expression) = 6 ATL-PE

What does this mean? At age nineteen the individual will experience new beginnings (1) which will play themselves out in matters of the home and heart (6). Because he is 19 years of age, the new beginnings reflected in the 1 crown will be based on the self (1) in power and completion (9). There will also be a feeling of new beginnings (1) juxtaposed with endings and conclusions (9). Male (yang) energy will be highlighted. These energies are *influencing* energies, not *outcome* energies. The *effects/outcomes/realities* and *experiences* energy will be manifested through the PE energy field of the number 6 - the home; responsibilities, adjustments, concerns and activities in the domestic environment; the heart, romance and community as the 1 energy is blended with the 5 Expression energy derived from the natal name of the individual.

And this is what is so profound about the life cycle pattern theory discussed in Chapter Two. This 1/6 modality will repeat itself in nine years and every nine year period after that for the entire life of the individual. Therefore, at age 28, 37, 46, 55, 64, 73, 82, 91 and 100 the same 1/6 LCP (life cycle pattern) will transit the person's life because each of these binaries becomes a 1 through simple reduction. Therefore, God shows us what we can expect to happen in the future if we're looking forward, or confirm what is past if we're looking at our life retrospectively.

A note: the experiences generated in each of the other nine year cycles, although similar, will not exactly duplicate those in another year because other vibratory energies will come into play based on different timelines. However, it can be said with certainty that the general influences and outcomes of the Age Timeline will be present as the nine year cycle returns upon itself. For a clearer view, look at the chart below.

5 Expression: Cycle of Nines

Chronological Age	19	20	21	22	23	24	25	26	27	28
Influence Crown	1	2	3	4	5	6	7	8	9	1
+ 5 Expression	[+5]	[+5]	[+5]	[+5]	[+5]	[+5]	[+5]	[+5]	[+5]	[+5]
Outcome Crown	6	7	8	9	1	2	3	4	5	6

Here we see that at age nineteen and twenty-eight the I/R (influence/reality) set of the 1/6 life cycle pattern is the same. And so it will be for the entire life. The difference is that the issues/outcomes at age twenty-eight will be slightly different from those at age nineteen. As we see by subtraction, the challenges will also be different. The subcap at age 19 is 8 while the subcap at age 28 is 6. Yet, both have 1 crowns. However, the issues/outcomes at age eighty-two, for example, will be similar to those at age twenty-eight because the underlying energies, those of the 2 and 8, will be present in both cases. Eighty-Two is simply the numerical anastrophe or inversion of Twenty-Eight. The same will be true for ages nineteen and ninety-one. This nine year cycle theory pertains to each I/R set within the life cycle pattern. For example, the 2/7 I/R set of the 1/6 LCP (5 Expression) occurs at ages 2, 11, 20, 29, 38, 47, 56, 65, 74, 83 and 92. The 6/9 I/R set of the 1/4 LCP (3 Expression) occurs at ages 6, 15, 24, 33, 42, 51, 60, 69, 78, 87 and 96. So it is with each of the 81 Influence/Reality sets of the Nine Life Cycle Patterns. Each set repeats itself every nine years.

King

With this understanding of the *Cycle of Nines* we can see the truth in Edna St. Vincent Millay's comment regarding life: "It's not true that life is one damn thing after another; it is one damn thing over and over." In effect, life is an ever turning wheel of the same energy patterns - Influence/Reality sets cycling round and round and round throughout life.

It is understanding this recurring *Cycle of Nines* reality that blesses us with prognosticative insight. Life is truly designed and destined. Each of us has a specific blueprint, a divine design which, when studied, can reveal treasures of knowledge, understanding and wisdom. What is the purpose of such a cyclical pattern of recurring energies? Only God knows for sure, but perhaps it is because each of us has specific lessons to learn, debts to reconcile and experiences to encounter in each incarnation related to the specific attributes of the numerical energies manifested in our charts. Regardless of the reason, the fact remains that the energies of our lives keep circling and cycling in a never-ending pattern of identical vibrations.

Pinnacle and Challenge Binary Crowns

As we have studied, binaries have pinnacles and challenges. They also have Pinnacle PEs and Challenge PEs - the pinnacle crowns or "addcaps" (capstones of the addition process) and the challenge crowns or "subcaps" (capstones of the subtraction process). When the Simple Expression is added to any crown, the reality (performance/experience) cipher appears. For example, the 39 cipher maintains a 3 crown pinnacle (addition position or addcap) and a 6 crown challenge (subtraction position or subcap). Therefore, a 1 Expression individual at age 39/12/3 will maintain a 4 Crown Pinnacle PE (1 + 3 = 4) and a 7 Crown Challenge PE (1 + 6 [9-3] = 7). See the diagram below.

Pinnacle/Challenge PE Format: Age 39 with a 1 Expression

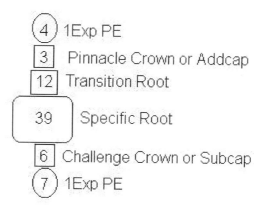

During his thirty-ninth birthday, the 1 Expression individual will be pulled forward by a 3/4 I/R set in his Pinnacle position and restrained by a 6/7 I/R modality in his Challenge position. The pinnacles pull us; the challenges restrain and weight us. Assuming the 1 Expression individual has no negative aspects (voids, challenges or voided challenges) involving the numerical ciphers of this 39 binary in his chart, he can expect the year's energies to pull him forward in the direction of issues relating his self-expression and personal fulfillment (3 crown) as they relate to his work, the job, the home, and all things of structural importance - regimens, rules, regulations, patterns and security issues (4 crown pinnacle PE). This can be regarded as a positive influence. Those energies which will tug at him, restrain him, and weigh him down will be those of the heart, family and domestic environment (6 crown challenge) which will generate realities of a reflective, mental, analytical, reclusive, concerning, perhaps even disturbing or chaotic nature (7 crown challenge PE).

Addcaps & Subcaps

Addcaps (AC) are generated as a result of the addition process and engage us in a positive sense. *Subcaps* (SC) are derived from the subtraction process and represent challenges. Every age from 10 to 99 has an addcap and subcap crown as seen in the chart below except master numbers which house no subcap, thus adding to the power of the master number's addcap crown. This is an invaluable chart for acquiring a quick glimpse of the energies involved at any age from 10 to 99. Simply add the individual's Expression crown to the Age crowns and the Age Timeline PEs become readily apparent.

Binary Crowns: Addcaps & Subcaps

Addcap Crown	1	2	3	4	5	6	7	8	9	1
Teens Decade	10	**11**	12	13	14	15	16	17	18	19
Subcap Crown	1	0	1	2	3	4	5	6	7	8

Addcap Crown	2	3	4	5	6	7	8	9	1	11-2
Twenties Decade	20	21	**22**	23	24	25	26	27	28	29
Subcap Crown	2	1	0	1	2	3	4	5	6	7

Addcap Crown	3	4	5	6	7	8	9	1	11-2	3
Thirties Decade	30	31	32	**33**	34	35	36	37	38	39
Subcap Crown	3	2	1	0	1	2	3	4	5	6

Addcap Crown	4	5	6	7	8	9	1	11-2	3	4
Forties Decade	40	41	42	43	**44**	45	46	47	48	49
Subcap Crown	4	3	2	1	0	1	2	3	4	5

Addcap Crown	5	6	7	8	9	1	11-2	3	4	5
Fifties Decade	50	51	52	53	54	**55**	56	57	58	59
Subcap Crown	5	4	3	2	1	0	1	2	3	4

Addcap Crown	6	7	8	9	1	2	3	4	5	6
Sixties Decade	60	61	62	63	64	65	**66**	67	68	69
Subcap Crown	6	5	4	3	2	1	0	1	2	3

Addcap Crown	7	8	**9**	1	11-2	3	4	5	6	7
Seventies Decade	70	71	72	73	74	75	76	**77**	78	79
Subcap Crown	7	6	5	4	3	2	1	0	1	2

Addcap Crown	8	9	1	11-2	3	4	5	6	7	8
Eighties Decade	80	81	82	83	84	85	86	87	**88**	89
Subcap Crown	8	7	6	5	4	3	2	1	0	1

Addcap Crown	9	1	11-2	3	4	5	6	7	8	9
Nineties Decade	90	91	92	93	94	95	96	97	98	**99**
Subcap Crown	9	8	7	6	5	4	3	2	1	0

Subcap Study

The " Binary Crowns: Addcaps & Subcaps" chart above tells an interesting story. Each of the single crowns 1 through 9 is challenged by itself in its gestation (0) period (10, 20, 30, etc.). The number 1 crown is challenged by every even number (the social numbers 2, 4, 6 and 8), while the number 2 is challenged by every odd number (the creative numbers 1, 3, 5 and 7) with the

The King's Book of Numerology II: Forecasting - Part 1

exception of the number 9 - the Grand Elemental and the gestation binaries. It would seem, therefore, that when God gives us energies of the yang, the self and independence (the 1), He challenges us with its exact opposite - the energy of the yin, others and relationship. When the vibration of females, others and relationship enters our life, it is challenged by its opposite - the creative energies of the odd numbers. The number 1 is the most common challenge of the 90 binaries with 17 placings. The number 2 is the second most common challenge with 15. Therefore, the themes of yin and yang; man and woman, positive and negative, self and others comprise the most abundant challenges for mankind. Interestingly, the number 9 only has 1 subcap challenge, itself, in its 90 gestation period.

Number pairs 3 & 8 have the same challenges, as do 4 & 7, 5 & 6 and 2 & 9. The number 1 is the only cipher that stands out by itself (it's not part of a pair), as well as being the only cipher with all even numbered challenges.

Crown	Subcaps	Total	Notes
1	1 and 2 - 4 - 6 - 8	17	all even challenges
2	2 and 1 - 3 - 5 - 7	15	all odd challenges; same as 9
3	3 and 1 - 2 - 4 - 6	13	same as 8
4	4 and 1 - 2 - 3 - 5	11	same as 7
5	5 and 1 - 2 - 3 - 4	9	same as 6
6	6 and 1 - 2 - 3 - 4	7	same as 5
7	7 and 1 - 2 - 3 - 5	5	same as 4
8	8 and 1 - 2 - 4 - 6	3	same as 3
9	9 and 1 - 3 - 5 - 7	1	same as 2

This subcap theory is a major piece of the forecasting puzzle. It can be used with any cipher, in any position of the numerology chart.

Age Timeline Lifescan Grid

We can now place all of this information into a more simple chart - the *Age Timeline Lifescan Grid*. In effect, the age of any individual represents the causes, influences, themes and issues for the chronological year in question relative to its own timeline. There are other timelines yet to be discussed, and they will also have their cause and theme aspects. In the Age Timeline Lifescan Grid below, the age of the individual or entity is listed in the vertical column on the left. The effects, outcomes, realities and experiences for each Expression are represented by the numbers in the vertical columns to the right of the age column. In effect, the numbers derived from the Age plus the Expression are actually the PE or Performance/Experience - in other words the reality the individual will experience during the age in question. This is the same concept used in the Basic Matrix (*The King's Book of Numerology, Volume I, Foundations & Fundamentals*)

Age + Expression = PE Reality (Performance/Experience)

or

ATL (Age Timeline) + the Expression = the ATL-PE (Age Timeline Reality)

For example, if a person has a 2 Expression (the numbers located across the top in the Age Timeline Lifescan chart below) and is two years old (far left column), the PE or reality will be a 4 (2 + 2 = 4). For a 7 Expression person who is also two years old, the PE will be a 9 (2 + 7 = 9). A six year old with a 1 Expression will have a 7 PE (6 + 1 = 7). Notice in the chart that every nine years the patterns duplicate. The years 1 through 9 have the same numerical patterns as the years 10 through 18, 19 through 27, 28 through 36 and so forth as seen in the Age Timeline I/R Sets above.

With this chart we can generally ascertain the themes and issues a person will be dealing with at any age during his entire lifetime, as well as the outcome and reality the individual will experience in general as a result of the age generated issues and themes. (A review of Chapter Two, "Life Cycle Patterns" may be helpful at this point as the LCPs are *the* major tool in accurate forecasting).

For example, let's take nine children, each with a different Expression 1 through 9 and make them all ten years old. All of them, therefore, will be involved in issues and themes of self, ego, identity, new beginnings, yang/male energies, independence and so forth (the 1 energy). But for each of the nine Expressions, the outcome will be different because their Expressions are different. Let's take a look.

The 1 Expression child will have a PE of 2 (1 + 1 = 2) so he will be dealing with the energy of others, yin/female energy, and relationships. In effect this is the 1/2 LCP discussed previously. The 2 Expression child will experience realities associated with his happiness, health, self-expression, self-fulfillment, communication, image and words - a 1/3 LCP. The 3 Expression PE will carry a

1/4 LCP and the issues of new beginnings will play themselves out in the arena of structures, rules, regulations, organization, the home, personal security and so forth. A 4 Expression person will yield a 1/5 LCP and experience realities of change, detachment, freedom, exploration, experimentation, movement and motion. The 5 Expression individual (1/6 LCP) will find a year saturated with realities focusing on adjustments and responsibilities in the home life, love, nurturing and caring. The 1/7 LCP person (6 Expression) will most likely experience the most turmoil, confusion, heartache and difficulty of the nine Expressions. The 1/7 pattern is one of isolation and separation. It can bring great peace or great chaos; great nobility or great ignobility; great spiritual awakening or great tragedy. The 7 Expression child at age ten will carry a 1/8 LCP and find things connecting or disconnecting during the year. There will be much social interaction. The 1/9 LCP originating from an 8 Expression will experience endings, conclusions, terminations, travel or expansions. The 9 Expression child will manifest a 1/1 LCP and be immersed in new beginnings and male energy of action and independence. For more understanding, a review of the nine life cycle patterns is obviously important (see Chapter Two, *Life Cycle Patterns*).

With the foregoing explanation, look at your own cycles and those of your loved ones in the Age Timeline Lifescan below. Become familiar with the patterns. It may even be a good idea to log the realities during of each year of life and use such information for making future projections or for understanding the past.

Age Timeline Lifescan: 1 to 99

The 9 Basic Expressions

Age Down: causes - influences - themes - issues

Across - PE: effects - outcomes - realities -experiences

Exp. → / Age ↓	1	2	3	4	5	6	7	8	9
1	2	3	4	5	6	7	8	9	1
2	3	4	5	6	7	8	9	1	2
3	4	5	6	7	8	9	1	2	3
4	5	6	7	8	9	1	2	3	4
5	6	7	8	9	1	2	3	4	5
6	7	8	9	1	2	3	4	5	6
7	8	9	1	2	3	4	5	6	7
8	9	1	2	3	4	5	6	7	8
9	1	2	3	4	5	6	7	8	9
10/1	2	3	4	5	6	7	8	9	1
11/2	3	4	5	6	7	8	9	1	2
12/3	4	5	6	7	8	9	1	2	3
13/4	5	6	7	8	9	1	2	3	4
14/5	6	7	8	9	1	2	3	4	5
15/6	7	8	9	1	2	3	4	5	6
16/7	8	9	1	2	3	4	5	6	7
17/8	9	1	2	3	4	5	6	7	8
18/9	1	2	3	4	5	6	7	8	9
19/1	2	3	4	5	6	7	8	9	1
20/2	3	4	5	6	7	8	9	1	2
21/3	4	5	6	7	8	9	1	2	3
22/4	5	6	7	8	9	1	2	3	4
23/5	6	7	8	9	1	2	3	4	5
24/6	7	8	9	1	2	3	4	5	6
25/7	8	9	1	2	3	4	5	6	7
26/8	9	1	2	3	4	5	6	7	8
27/9	1	2	3	4	5	6	7	8	9
28/1	2	3	4	5	6	7	8	9	1
29/2	3	4	5	6	7	8	9	1	2
30/3	4	5	6	7	8	9	1	2	3
31/4	5	6	7	8	9	1	2	3	4
32/5	6	7	8	9	1	2	3	4	5
33/6	7	8	9	1	2	3	4	5	6
34/7	8	9	1	2	3	4	5	6	7
35/8	9	1	2	3	4	5	6	7	8

Exp. → Age ↓	1	2	3	4	5	6	7	8	9
36/9	1	2	3	4	5	6	7	8	9
37/1	2	3	4	5	6	7	8	9	1
38/2	3	4	5	6	7	8	9	1	2
39/3	4	5	6	7	8	9	1	2	3
40/4	5	6	7	8	9	1	2	3	4
41/5	6	7	8	9	1	2	3	4	5
42/6	7	8	9	1	2	3	4	5	6
43/7	8	9	1	2	3	4	5	6	7
44/8	9	1	2	3	4	5	6	7	8
45/9	1	2	3	4	5	6	7	8	9
46/1	2	3	4	5	6	7	8	9	1
47/2	3	4	5	6	7	8	9	1	2
48/3	4	5	6	7	8	9	1	2	3
49/4	5	6	7	8	9	1	2	3	4
50/5	6	7	8	9	1	2	3	4	5
51/6	7	8	9	1	2	3	4	5	6
52/7	8	9	1	2	3	4	5	6	7
53/8	9	1	2	3	4	5	6	7	8
54/9	1	2	3	4	5	6	7	8	9
55/1	2	3	4	5	6	7	8	9	1
56/2	3	4	5	6	7	8	9	1	2
57/3	4	5	6	7	8	9	1	2	3
58/4	5	6	7	8	9	1	2	3	4
59/5	6	7	8	9	1	2	3	4	5
60/6	7	8	9	1	2	3	4	5	6
61/7	8	9	1	2	3	4	5	6	7
62/8	9	1	2	3	4	5	6	7	8
63/9	1	2	3	4	5	6	7	8	9
64/1	2	3	4	5	6	7	8	9	1
65/2	3	4	5	6	7	8	9	1	2
66/3	4	5	6	7	8	9	1	2	3
67/4	5	6	7	8	9	1	2	3	4
68/5	6	7	8	9	1	2	3	4	5
69/6	7	8	9	1	2	3	4	5	6
70/7	8	9	1	2	3	4	5	6	7
71/8	9	1	2	3	4	5	6	7	8
72/9	1	2	3	4	5	6	7	8	9
73/1	2	3	4	5	6	7	8	9	1
74/2	3	4	5	6	7	8	9	1	2
75/3	4	5	6	7	8	9	1	2	3
76/4	5	6	7	8	9	1	2	3	4
77/5	6	7	8	9	1	2	3	4	5
78/6	7	8	9	1	2	3	4	5	6
79/7	8	9	1	2	3	4	5	6	7
80/8	9	1	2	3	4	5	6	7	8

King

Exp. → Age ↓	1	2	3	4	5	6	7	8	9
81/9	1	2	3	4	5	6	7	8	9
82/1	2	3	4	5	6	7	8	9	1
83/2	3	4	5	6	7	8	9	1	2
84/3	4	5	6	7	8	9	1	2	3
85/4	5	6	7	8	9	1	2	3	4
86/5	6	7	8	9	1	2	3	4	5
87/6	7	8	9	1	2	3	4	5	6
88/7	8	9	1	2	3	4	5	6	7
89/8	9	1	2	3	4	5	6	7	8
90/9	1	2	3	4	5	6	7	8	9
91/1	2	3	4	5	6	7	8	9	1
92/2	3	4	5	6	7	8	9	1	2
93/3	4	5	6	7	8	9	1	2	3
94/4	5	6	7	8	9	1	2	3	4
95/5	6	7	8	9	1	2	3	4	5
96/6	7	8	9	1	2	3	4	5	6
97/7	8	9	1	2	3	4	5	6	7
98/8	9	1	2	3	4	5	6	7	8
99/9	1	2	3	4	5	6	7	8	9

Analysis Notes

Simply knowing the age and Expression of an individual will not give us a completely clear picture of what is going on during any age of the person's life. There are other timelines and factors coming into play which will be addressed in the course of this book which, when added to the age timeline, will give us an excellent picture of a person's life.

Nonetheless, the ATL and its PE offer major clues for assessing a person's life and the realities he will experience at any age of the life journey. For now it is best to simply be aware of the age timeline and apply it to your own life and those individuals whose lives you are familiar with in order to develop your assessment skills.

In reading any timeline begin with the simple and then move to the complex. Look at the *crown* of the age in question and its *challenge*. Then address the separate aspects of the binary forming the age itself, remembering that the first number is the most dominate because it represents the decade through which the individual is transiting and the number it is embracing is the focus if its influence. Also remember that the age ciphers describe the influences, causes, themes and issues present within the scope of the ATL.

After assessing the age and its causal themes, then consider the P/E, the performance/reality energy. This will indicate the outcome of the influencing ATL energies as they combine, filter, funnel or pass through the energy field of the individual which is noted by his Expression cipher.

Chapter Eleven

UNIVERSAL YEAR TIMELINE: UTL

The *Universal Year Timeline* or UTL is the second of the three major annual timelines in the King's Numerology system. It adds another vibratory strand to the tapestry of our annual destiny. The Age Timeline, because it is strictly a combination of our age plus our Expression, is the energy "closest to home" so to speak. It is the most personal to us. However, it houses no universal energies, those energies encompassing the whole of humanity and reflected in the calendar day, month and year. The universal timeline houses the most general, annual universal energy common to all mankind (the calendar year) and thus brings into our personal experience more universal experiences - those involving other people who are themselves affected by universal energies.

The basic component of the *Universal Year Timeline* is simply the calendar year in question. For simplicity sake it can be reduced to a single digit. The year 1976, for example, would reduce to a Five

$(1 + 9 + 7 + 6 = 23 > 2 + 3 = 5)$. 2006 would register an 8 crown $(2 + 6 = 8)$, while 1993 would reduce to a pure master 22/4 vibration. Incidentally, this 22 master builder cipher will not repeat itself in the calendar *year* position again until the year 2299! To place this in perspective, in the Twentieth Century alone it duplicated itself seven times: 1939, 1948, 1957, 1966, 1975, 1984 and 1993. What this means is that until the year 2299, the last year of the 23rd Century, there will be no master builder 22 energy present in the final Epoch position of a person's chart (see Epoch timeline). In other words, until 2299 no one born on earth will have, as the final Epoch aspect of their life from generally their late forties and early fifties Age Timeline, the energies of building, constructing, forming, regulating and bringing order to their lives or sharing the master builder energy with others. They may have the 22 elsewhere in their charts but not in the final Epoch portion of their lives.

Calendar dates affect us all because their vibrations are universal. Every year the earth transits through another annual cycle, and each of us is generally influenced by the cosmic energies present in that cycle. Because these energies are universal, and every living entity is affected by them as a natural result of being part of the universal whole, the year represents the first real annual ingress of others into our lives and charts. Through the Universal Year Timeline, we become more actively interactive with other people.

And speaking of charts, as a reminder, each of our numerological year cycles begins on our birthday each year and not on the 1st of January. If person "A" were born on the 1st of January 2003 and person "B" were born on the 31st of December 2003, person "A" would be living the last day of his 2003 year on the very day person "B" would be beginning his 2003 yearly cycle. In effect, "B" would be experiencing his 2003 energies during the 2004 calendar year. This is why, from a forecasting perspective, a calendar year's influence actually extends for twenty-four months (two years), not twelve months (one year). Therefore, when discussing a person or client's yearly cycles it is wise to clarify this point, otherwise there may be some legitimate confusion as to the specific energies operating during the year in question. Annual numerological energies always begin on the anniversary of our birth (our birthday) and go to the next birthday.

The calendar year houses many interesting facts such as the 22 master energy not recurring until the year 2299. Here's another interesting note. The Epoch component of the calendar year (the epoch represents the actual ciphers of the year as opposed to the day and month of the year itself) rules the timeline of life from the late forties to the early fifties and onward to the end of life. For everyone born in the year 2000, the only cipher present in their final Epoch timeline is the number 2! No other numbers exist. Therefore, this begs the question, "What is going to happen to earth to make this aspect of the lives of people born in the year 2000 so simple when they reach their final epoch timeline somewhere in their late 2040s to early 2050s?" In contrast, the year 1999 is comprised of four distinct numbers - the ciphers 1-9-9-9. From the year 1111 there existed complexity in the final Epoch period because of ciphers occupying each of the four places in the year format. But the year 2000 only has a 2 and three zeros. In fact, until the year 2111 there won't be an Epoch without zeros. Zero ciphers will still exist in the Epoch timeline up until then. This will obviously take twenty-one hundred and eleven years to reach this place in time. Even a person born in 2001 will only have a 3 Final Epoch; a person born in 2002 a 4 Final Epoch and so forth. Carrying this further, a person born on 1 January 2000 will only have a simple Lifepath of 4.

There's no complexity in such a lifepath at all. This birthdate, besides having a pure 2 final Epoch, will only have a pure 3 Crown (final) Pinnacle. The Crown Challenge of a 1 January 2000 birthdate will be 1999. Interesting isn't it that the complexity is in the Challenge while the Epoch and Pinnacle manifest a more simple energy?

Here's another interesting fact. The most complex a lifepath could possibly be for a person born in the calendar year 2000 is a 45 and that would be from a birthdate of 31 December (31 + 12 + 2 = 45/9). Yet, the most complex lifepath of the last millennium was a 71, reflective of a person born on 31 December 1999 (31 + 12 + 28 = 71/9). Again, there is a huge shift between the last thousand years of 1 energy of the male and the current thousand years of 2 energy of the female. This is another indication of the immense change in millennia from the 1 to the 2. For more complete information regarding the enormous transitions of earth as it moves into the Second Millennium dominated by yin (female) energy, read *The Age of the Female: A Thousand Years of Yin.*

The ATL/PE (Age Timeline Performance/Experience)

Like the ATL and its PE, the UTL also has a PE, as do all the timelines. The calendar year represents the *causes/influences/themes* and *issues* as they pertain to the timeline tapestry. To determine the *effects/outcomes/*realities and experiences, simply add the simple Expression to the crown of the universal timeline line.

Universal Year Timeline Crown + Expression Crown = UTL/PE

Examples using a 4 Expression:

> 1945 = 1 UTL crown + 4 Expression crown > 5 UTL/PE crown
>
> 1983 = 3 UTL crown + 4 Expression crown > 7 UTL/PE crown
>
> 1997 = 8 UTL crown + 4 Expression crown > 12 > 3 UTL/PE crown

Reading the Universal Timeline

The first part of any timeline Influence/Reality (IR) set outlines the issues and themes present. The PE represents the outcomes or realities - the performances the individual will give as a result of the timeline energy moving through the person's energy field. All timelines will be read the same way. Perhaps extended research will one day indicate more specific explanations for each of the timelines, but for now we can interpret the timeline as the cause and the PE as the effect.

King

Below are *Universal Year Timeline Lifescan* tables for reading the universal year timeline as they apply to the Twentieth and Twenty-First centuries. To determine the addcap PE (outcome and reality energy), simply cross reference the calendar year listed in the left column (the influence and theme energy) with the Expression crowns across the top.

For example, what would a person's PE addcap crown be if he had a 7 Expression and was born in 1963? The answer is 8. How about a person born in 1951 with a 9 Expression? The answer is 7. And a person born in 1994 with a 1 Expression? The answer is a 6 PE. For explanation of the causes and effects, refer to Chapter Two: Life Cycle Patterns.

Universal Year Timeline Lifescan
The 9 Basic Expressions - Addcap Crowns
1900 to 1999

Year Down: causes - influences - themes - issues

Across - PE: effects - outcomes - realities -experiences

Exp. → / Year ↓	1	2	3	4	5	6	7	8	9
1900 > 1	2	3	4	5	6	7	8	9	1
1901 > 2	3	4	5	6	7	8	9	1	2
1902 > 3	4	5	6	7	8	9	1	2	3
1903 > 4	5	6	7	8	9	1	2	3	4
1904 > 5	6	7	8	9	1	2	3	4	5
1905 > 6	7	8	9	1	2	3	4	5	6
1906 > 7	8	9	1	2	3	4	5	6	7
1907 > 8	9	1	2	3	4	5	6	7	8
1908 > 9	1	2	3	4	5	6	7	8	9
1909 > 1	2	3	4	5	6	7	8	9	1
1910 > 2	3	4	5	6	7	8	9	1	2
1911 > 3	4	5	6	7	8	9	1	2	3
1912 > 4	5	6	7	8	9	1	2	3	4
1913 > 5	6	7	8	9	1	2	3	4	5
1914 > 6	7	8	9	1	2	3	4	5	6
1915 > 7	8	9	1	2	3	4	5	6	7
1916 > 8	9	1	2	3	4	5	6	7	8
1917 > 9	1	2	3	4	5	6	7	8	9
1918 > 1	2	3	4	5	6	7	8	9	1
1919 > 2	3	4	5	6	7	8	9	1	2
1920 > 3	4	5	6	7	8	9	1	2	3
1921 > 4	5	6	7	8	9	1	2	3	4

Exp. ➜	1	2	3	4	5	6	7	8	9
Year ⬇									
1922 > 5	6	7	8	9	1	2	3	4	5
1923 > 6	7	8	9	1	2	3	4	5	6
1924 > 7	8	9	1	2	3	4	5	6	7
1925 > 8	9	1	2	3	4	5	6	7	8
1926 > 9	1	2	3	4	5	6	7	8	9
1927 > 1	2	3	4	5	6	7	8	9	1
1928 > 2	3	4	5	6	7	8	9	1	2
1929 > 3	4	5	6	7	8	9	1	2	3
1930 > 4	5	6	7	8	9	1	2	3	4
1931 > 5	6	7	8	9	1	2	3	4	5
1932 > 6	7	8	9	1	2	3	4	5	6
1933 > 7	8	9	1	2	3	4	5	6	7
1934 > 8	9	1	2	3	4	5	6	7	8
1935 > 9	1	2	3	4	5	6	7	8	9
1936 > 1	2	3	4	5	6	7	8	9	1
1937 > 2	3	4	5	6	7	8	9	1	2
1938 > 3	4	5	6	7	8	9	1	2	3
1939 > 4	5	6	7	8	9	1	2	3	4
1940 > 5	6	7	8	9	1	2	3	4	5
1941 > 6	7	8	9	1	2	3	4	5	6
1942 > 7	8	9	1	2	3	4	5	6	7
1943 > 8	9	1	2	3	4	5	6	7	8
1944 > 9	1	2	3	4	5	6	7	8	9
1945 > 1	2	3	4	5	6	7	8	9	1
1946 > 2	3	4	5	6	7	8	9	1	2
1947 > 3	4	5	6	7	8	9	1	2	3
1948 > 4	5	6	7	8	9	1	2	3	4
1949 > 5	6	7	8	9	1	2	3	4	5
1950 > 6	7	8	9	1	2	3	4	5	6
1951 > 7	8	9	1	2	3	4	5	6	7
1952 > 8	9	1	2	3	4	5	6	7	8
1953 > 9	1	2	3	4	5	6	7	8	9
1954 > 1	2	3	4	5	6	7	8	9	1
1955 > 2	3	4	5	6	7	8	9	1	2
1956 > 3	4	5	6	7	8	9	1	2	3
1957 > 4	5	6	7	8	9	1	2	3	4
1958 > 5	6	7	8	9	1	2	3	4	5
1959 > 6	7	8	9	1	2	3	4	5	6
1960 > 7	8	9	1	2	3	4	5	6	7
1961 > 8	9	1	2	3	4	5	6	7	8
1962 > 9	1	2	3	4	5	6	7	8	9
1963 > 1	2	3	4	5	6	7	8	9	1
1964 > 2	3	4	5	6	7	8	9	1	2
1965 > 3	4	5	6	7	8	9	1	2	3
1966 > 4	5	6	7	8	9	1	2	3	4

King

Exp. ➜ Year ⬇	1	2	3	4	5	6	7	8	9
1967 > 5	6	7	8	9	1	2	3	4	5
1968 > 6	7	8	9	1	2	3	4	5	6
1969 > 7	8	9	1	2	3	4	5	6	7
1970 > 8	9	1	2	3	4	5	6	7	8
1971 > 9	1	2	3	4	5	6	7	8	9
1972 > 1	2	3	4	5	6	7	8	9	1
1973 > 2	3	4	5	6	7	8	9	1	2
1974 > 3	4	5	6	7	8	9	1	2	3
1975 > 4	5	6	7	8	9	1	2	3	4
1976 > 5	6	7	8	9	1	2	3	4	5
1977 > 6	7	8	9	1	2	3	4	5	6
1978 > 7	8	9	1	2	3	4	5	6	7
1979 > 8	9	1	2	3	4	5	6	7	8
1980 > 9	1	2	3	4	5	6	7	8	9
1981 > 1	2	3	4	5	6	7	8	9	1
1982 > 2	3	4	5	6	7	8	9	1	2
1983 > 3	4	5	6	7	8	9	1	2	3
1984 > 4	5	6	7	8	9	1	2	3	4
1985 > 5	6	7	8	9	1	2	3	4	5
1986 > 6	7	8	9	1	2	3	4	5	6
1987 > 7	8	9	1	2	3	4	5	6	7
1988 > 8	9	1	2	3	4	5	6	7	8
1989 > 9	1	2	3	4	5	6	7	8	9
1990 > 1	2	3	4	5	6	7	8	9	1
1991 > 2	3	4	5	6	7	8	9	1	2
1992 > 3	4	5	6	7	8	9	1	2	3
1993 > 4	5	6	7	8	9	1	2	3	4
1994 > 5	6	7	8	9	1	2	3	4	5
1995 > 6	7	8	9	1	2	3	4	5	6
1996 > 7	8	9	1	2	3	4	5	6	7
1997 > 8	9	1	2	3	4	5	6	7	8
1998 > 9	1	2	3	4	5	6	7	8	9
1999 > 1	2	3	4	5	6	7	8	9	1

Universal Year Timeline Lifescan
The 9 Basic Expressions - Addcap Crowns
2000 to 2099

Year Down: causes - influences - themes - issues

Across - PE: effects - outcomes - realities -experiences

Exp. ➜ Year ⬇	1	2	3	4	5	6	7	8	9
2000 > 2	3	4	5	6	7	8	9	1	2
2001 > 3	4	5	6	7	8	9	1	2	3
2002 > 4	5	6	7	8	9	1	2	3	4
2003 > 5	6	7	8	9	1	2	3	4	5
2004 > 6	7	8	9	1	2	3	4	5	6
2005 > 7	8	9	1	2	3	4	5	6	7
2006 > 8	9	1	2	3	4	5	6	7	8
2007 > 9	1	2	3	4	5	6	7	8	9
2008 > 1	2	3	4	5	6	7	8	9	1
2009 > 2	3	4	5	6	7	8	9	1	2
2010 > 3	4	5	6	7	8	9	1	2	3
2011 > 4	5	6	7	8	9	1	2	3	4
2012 > 5	6	7	8	9	1	2	3	4	5
2013 > 6	7	8	9	1	2	3	4	5	6
2014 > 7	8	9	1	2	3	4	5	6	7
2015 > 8	9	1	2	3	4	5	6	7	8
2016 > 9	1	2	3	4	5	6	7	8	9
2017 > 1	2	3	4	5	6	7	8	9	1
2018 > 2	3	4	5	6	7	8	9	1	2
2019 > 3	4	5	6	7	8	9	1	2	3
2020 > 4	5	6	7	8	9	1	2	3	4
2021 > 5	6	7	8	9	1	2	3	4	5
2022 > 6	7	8	9	1	2	3	4	5	6
2023 > 7	8	9	1	2	3	4	5	6	7
2024 > 8	9	1	2	3	4	5	6	7	8
2025 > 9	1	2	3	4	5	6	7	8	9
2026 > 1	2	3	4	5	6	7	8	9	1
2027 > 2	3	4	5	6	7	8	9	1	2
2028 > 3	4	5	6	7	8	9	1	2	3
2029 > 4	5	6	7	8	9	1	2	3	4
2030 > 5	6	7	8	9	1	2	3	4	5
2031 > 6	7	8	9	1	2	3	4	5	6
2032 > 7	8	9	1	2	3	4	5	6	7
2033 > 8	9	1	2	3	4	5	6	7	8
2034 > 9	1	2	3	4	5	6	7	8	9
2035 > 1	2	3	4	5	6	7	8	9	1

King

Exp. ➜	1	2	3	4	5	6	7	8	9
Year ⬇									
2036 > 2	3	4	5	6	7	8	9	1	2
2037 > 3	4	5	6	7	8	9	1	2	3
2038 > 4	5	6	7	8	9	1	2	3	4
2039 > 5	6	7	8	9	1	2	3	4	5
2040 > 6	7	8	9	1	2	3	4	5	6
2041 > 7	8	9	1	2	3	4	5	6	7
2042 > 8	9	1	2	3	4	5	6	7	8
2043 > 9	1	2	3	4	5	6	7	8	9
2044 > 1	2	3	4	5	6	7	8	9	1
2045 > 2	3	4	5	6	7	8	9	1	2
2046 > 3	4	5	6	7	8	9	1	2	3
2047 > 4	5	6	7	8	9	1	2	3	4
2048 > 5	6	7	8	9	1	2	3	4	5
2049 > 6	7	8	9	1	2	3	4	5	6
2050 > 7	8	9	1	2	3	4	5	6	7
2051 > 8	9	1	2	3	4	5	6	7	8
2052 > 9	1	2	3	4	5	6	7	8	9
2053 > 1	2	3	4	5	6	7	8	9	1
2054 > 2	3	4	5	6	7	8	9	1	2
2055 > 3	4	5	6	7	8	9	1	2	3
2056 > 4	5	6	7	8	9	1	2	3	4
2057 > 5	6	7	8	9	1	2	3	4	5
2058 > 6	7	8	9	1	2	3	4	5	6
2059 > 7	8	9	1	2	3	4	5	6	7
2060 > 8	9	1	2	3	4	5	6	7	8
2061 > 9	1	2	3	4	5	6	7	8	9
2062 > 1	2	3	4	5	6	7	8	9	1
2063 > 2	3	4	5	6	7	8	9	1	2
2064 > 3	4	5	6	7	8	9	1	2	3
2065 > 4	5	6	7	8	9	1	2	3	4
2066 > 5	6	7	8	9	1	2	3	4	5
2067 > 6	7	8	9	1	2	3	4	5	6
2068 > 7	8	9	1	2	3	4	5	6	7
2069 > 8	9	1	2	3	4	5	6	7	8
2070 > 9	1	2	3	4	5	6	7	8	9
2071 > 1	2	3	4	5	6	7	8	9	1
2072 > 2	3	4	5	6	7	8	9	1	2
2073 > 3	4	5	6	7	8	9	1	2	3
2074 > 4	5	6	7	8	9	1	2	3	4
2075 > 5	6	7	8	9	1	2	3	4	5
2076 > 6	7	8	9	1	2	3	4	5	6
2077 > 7	8	9	1	2	3	4	5	6	7
2078 > 8	9	1	2	3	4	5	6	7	8
2079 > 9	1	2	3	4	5	6	7	8	9
2080 > 1	2	3	4	5	6	7	8	9	1

Exp. → / Year ↓	1	2	3	4	5	6	7	8	9
2081 > 2	3	4	5	6	7	8	9	1	2
2082 > 3	4	5	6	7	8	9	1	2	3
2083 > 4	5	6	7	8	9	1	2	3	4
2084 > 5	6	7	8	9	1	2	3	4	5
2085 > 6	7	8	9	1	2	3	4	5	6
2086 > 7	8	9	1	2	3	4	5	6	7
2087 > 8	9	1	2	3	4	5	6	7	8
2088 > 9	1	2	3	4	5	6	7	8	9
2089 > 1	2	3	4	5	6	7	8	9	1
2090 > 2	3	4	5	6	7	8	9	1	2
2091 > 3	4	5	6	7	8	9	1	2	3
2092 > 4	5	6	7	8	9	1	2	3	4
2093 > 5	6	7	8	9	1	2	3	4	5
2094 > 6	7	8	9	1	2	3	4	5	6
2095 > 7	8	9	1	2	3	4	5	6	7
2096 > 8	9	1	2	3	4	5	6	7	8
2097 > 9	1	2	3	4	5	6	7	8	9
2098 > 1	2	3	4	5	6	7	8	9	1
2099 > 2	3	4	5	6	7	8	9	1	2

Universal Year Timeline - Subcaps

It is logical that if numbers can be added together to generate influences and outcomes, they can be subtracted as well to generate influences and outcomes. As we've discussed earlier, the addcaps can be viewed as representing events, circumstances, situations, etc. viewable above the service waters of a person's life, while the subcaps can be seen as representing those events, conditions, concerns and issues below the surface and out of view of the normal public and, hence, more of a personal issue. These can be considered challenges of the individual.

Creating subcaps is more involved because the subtraction process is more complicated with multiple numbers than the addition process, as a study of the subcap binary lifescans reveals. Therefore, in this first forecasting edition of *The King's Book of Numerology*, the simplest subcap creation procedure will be addressed: a simple binary subcap formation for the 1900s and a simple subcap creation for the first century of the 2nd millennium.

Universal Year Timeline Lifescan
The 9 Basic Expressions - Subcap Binaries
1900 to 1999

Year Down: causes - influences - themes - issues

Across - PE: effects - outcomes - realities -experiences

Exp. → / Year ↓	1	2	3	4	5	6	7	8	9
1900 > 19 > 8	9	1	2	3	4	5	6	7	8
1901 > 11 > 0	1	2	3	4	5	6	7	8	9
1902 > 12 > 1	2	3	4	5	6	7	8	9	1
1903 > 13 > 2	3	4	5	6	7	8	9	1	2
1904 > 14 > 3	4	5	6	7	8	9	1	2	3
1905 > 15 > 4	5	6	7	8	9	1	2	3	4
1906 > 16 > 5	6	7	8	9	1	2	3	4	5
1907 > 17 > 6	7	8	9	1	2	3	4	5	6
1908 > 18 > 7	8	9	1	2	3	4	5	6	7
1909 > 19 > 8	9	1	2	3	4	5	6	7	8
1910 > 11 > 0	1	2	3	4	5	6	7	8	9
1911 > 12 > 1	2	3	4	5	6	7	8	9	1
1912 > 13 > 2	3	4	5	6	7	8	9	1	2
1913 > 14 > 3	4	5	6	7	8	9	1	2	3
1914 > 15 > 4	5	6	7	8	9	1	2	3	4
1915 > 16 > 5	6	7	8	9	1	2	3	4	5
1916 > 17 > 6	7	8	9	1	2	3	4	5	6
1917 > 18 > 7	8	9	1	2	3	4	5	6	7
1918 > 19 > 8	9	1	2	3	4	5	6	7	8
1919 > 20 > 2	3	4	5	6	7	8	9	1	2
1920 > 12 > 1	2	3	4	5	6	7	8	9	1
1921 > 13 > 2	3	4	5	6	7	8	9	1	2
1922 > 14 > 3	4	5	6	7	8	9	1	2	3
1923 > 15 > 4	5	6	7	8	9	1	2	3	4
1924 > 16 > 5	6	7	8	9	1	2	3	4	5
1925 > 17 > 6	7	8	9	1	2	3	4	5	6
1926 > 18 > 7	8	9	1	2	3	4	5	6	7
1927 > 19 > 8	9	1	2	3	4	5	6	7	8
1928 > 20 > 2	3	4	5	6	7	8	9	1	2
1929 > 21 > 1	2	3	4	5	6	7	8	9	1
1930 > 13 > 2	3	4	5	6	7	8	9	1	2
1931 > 14 > 3	4	5	6	7	8	9	1	2	3
1932 > 15 > 4	5	6	7	8	9	1	2	3	4
1933 > 16 > 5	6	7	8	9	1	2	3	4	5
1934 > 17 > 6	7	8	9	1	2	3	4	5	6
1935 > 18 > 7	8	9	1	2	3	4	5	6	7

Exp. ➜ Year ⬇	1	2	3	4	5	6	7	8	9
1936 > 19 > 8	9	1	2	3	4	5	6	7	8
1937 > 20 > 2	3	4	5	6	7	8	9	1	2
1938 > 21 > 1	2	3	4	5	6	7	8	9	1
1939 > 22 > 0	1	2	3	4	5	6	7	8	9
1940 > 14 > 3	4	5	6	7	8	9	1	2	3
1941 > 15 > 4	5	6	7	8	9	1	2	3	4
1942 > 16 > 5	6	7	8	9	1	2	3	4	5
1943 > 17 > 6	7	8	9	1	2	3	4	5	6
1944 > 18 > 7	8	9	1	2	3	4	5	6	7
1945 > 19 > 8	9	1	2	3	4	5	6	7	8
1946 > 20 > 2	3	4	5	6	7	8	9	1	2
1947 > 21 > 1	2	3	4	5	6	7	8	9	1
1948 > 22 > 0	1	2	3	4	5	6	7	8	9
1949 > 23 > 1	2	3	4	5	6	7	8	9	1
1950 > 15 > 4	5	6	7	8	9	1	2	3	4
1951 > 16 > 5	6	7	8	9	1	2	3	4	5
1952 > 17 > 6	7	8	9	1	2	3	4	5	6
1953 > 18 > 7	8	9	1	2	3	4	5	6	7
1954 > 19 > 8	9	1	2	3	4	5	6	7	8
1955 > 20 > 2	3	4	5	6	7	8	9	1	2
1956 > 21 > 1	2	3	4	5	6	7	8	9	1
1957 > 22 > 0	1	2	3	4	5	6	7	8	9
1958 > 23 > 1	2	3	4	5	6	7	8	9	1
1959 > 24 > 2	3	4	5	6	7	8	9	1	2
1960 > 16 > 5	6	7	8	9	1	2	3	4	5
1961 > 17 > 6	7	8	9	1	2	3	4	5	6
1962 > 18 > 7	8	9	1	2	3	4	5	6	7
1963 > 19 > 8	9	1	2	3	4	5	6	7	8
1964 > 20 > 2	3	4	5	6	7	8	9	1	2
1965 > 21 > 1	2	3	4	5	6	7	8	9	1
1966 > 22 > 0	1	2	3	4	5	6	7	8	9
1967 > 23 > 1	2	3	4	5	6	7	8	9	1
1968 > 24 > 2	3	4	5	6	7	8	9	1	2
1969 > 25 > 3	4	5	6	7	8	9	1	2	3
1970 > 17 > 6	7	8	9	1	2	3	4	5	6
1971 > 18 > 7	8	9	1	2	3	4	5	6	7
1972 > 19 > 8	9	1	2	3	4	5	6	7	8
1973 > 20 > 2	3	4	5	6	7	8	9	1	2
1974 > 21 > 1	2	3	4	5	6	7	8	9	1
1975 > 22 > 0	1	2	3	4	5	6	7	8	9
1976 > 23 > 1	2	3	4	5	6	7	8	9	1
1977 > 24 > 2	3	4	5	6	7	8	9	1	2
1978 > 25 > 3	4	5	6	7	8	9	1	2	3
1979 > 26 > 4	5	6	7	8	9	1	2	3	4
1980 > 18 > 7	8	9	1	2	3	4	5	6	7

King

Exp. ➜ Year ⬇	1	2	3	4	5	6	7	8	9
1981 > 19 > 8	9	1	2	3	4	5	6	7	8
1982 > 20 > 2	3	4	5	6	7	8	9	1	2
1983 > 21 > 1	2	3	4	5	6	7	8	9	1
1984 > 22 > 0	1	2	3	4	5	6	7	8	9
1985 > 23 > 1	2	3	4	5	6	7	8	9	1
1986 > 24 > 2	3	4	5	6	7	8	9	1	2
1987 > 25 > 3	4	5	6	7	8	9	1	2	3
1988 > 26 > 4	5	6	7	8	9	1	2	3	4
1989 > 27 > 5	6	7	8	9	1	2	3	4	5
1990 > 19 > 8	9	1	2	3	4	5	6	7	8
1991 > 20 > 2	3	4	5	6	7	8	9	1	2
1992 > 21 > 1	2	3	4	5	6	7	8	9	1
1993 > 22 > 0	1	2	3	4	5	6	7	8	9
1994 > 23 > 1	2	3	4	5	6	7	8	9	1
1995 > 24 > 2	3	4	5	6	7	8	9	1	2
1996 > 25 > 3	4	5	6	7	8	9	1	2	3
1997 > 26 > 4	5	6	7	8	9	1	2	3	4
1998 > 27 > 5	6	7	8	9	1	2	3	4	5
1999 > 28 > 6	7	8	9	1	2	3	4	5	6

Universal Year Timeline Lifescan

The 9 Basic Expressions - Simple Subcaps

2000 to 2099

Year Down: causes - influences - themes - issues

Across - PE: effects - outcomes - realities -experiences

Exp. ➜ Year ⬇	1	2	3	4	5	6	7	8	9
2000 > 2	3	4	5	6	7	8	9	1	2
2001 > 1	2	3	4	5	6	7	8	9	1
2002 > 0	1	2	3	4	5	6	7	8	9
2003 > 1	2	3	4	5	6	7	8	9	1
2004 > 2	3	4	5	6	7	8	9	1	2
2005 > 3	4	5	6	7	8	9	1	2	3
2006 > 4	5	6	7	8	9	1	2	3	4
2007 > 5	6	7	8	9	1	2	3	4	5
2008 > 6 [home/hearth/heart]	7	8	9	1	2	3	4	5	6
2009 > 7 [global recession]	8	9	1	2	3	4	5	6	7

Exp. →	1	2	3	4	5	6	7	8	9
Year ↓									
2010 > 8	9	1	2	3	4	5	6	7	8
2011 > 9	1	2	3	4	5	6	7	8	9
2012 > 10 > 1	2	3	4	5	6	7	8	9	1
2013 > 11 > 0	1	2	3	4	5	6	7	8	9
2014 > 12 > 1	2	3	4	5	6	7	8	9	1
2015 > 13 > 2	3	4	5	6	7	8	9	1	2
2016 > 14 > 3	4	5	6	7	8	9	1	2	3
2017 > 15 > 4	5	6	7	8	9	1	2	3	4
2018 > 16 > 5	6	7	8	9	1	2	3	4	5
2019 > 17 > 6	7	8	9	1	2	3	4	5	6
2020 > 18 > 7	8	9	1	2	3	4	5	6	7
2021 > 19 > 8	9	1	2	3	4	5	6	7	8
2022 > 20 > 2	3	4	5	6	7	8	9	1	2
2023 > 21 > 1	2	3	4	5	6	7	8	9	1
2024 > 22 > 0	1	2	3	4	5	6	7	8	9
2025 > 23 > 1	2	3	4	5	6	7	8	9	1
2026 > 24 > 2	3	4	5	6	7	8	9	1	2
2027 > 25 > 3	4	5	6	7	8	9	1	2	3
2028 > 26 > 4	5	6	7	8	9	1	2	3	4
2029 > 27 > 5	6	7	8	9	1	2	3	4	5
2030 > 28 > 6	7	8	9	1	2	3	4	5	6
2031 > 29 > 7	8	9	1	2	3	4	5	6	7
2032 > 30 > 3	4	5	6	7	8	9	1	2	3
2033 > 31 > 2	3	4	5	6	7	8	9	1	2
2034 > 32 > 1	2	3	4	5	6	7	8	9	1
2035 > 33 > 0	1	2	3	4	5	6	7	8	9
2036 > 34 > 1	2	3	4	5	6	7	8	9	1
2037 > 35 > 2	3	4	5	6	7	8	9	1	2
2038 > 36 > 3	4	5	6	7	8	9	1	2	3
2039 > 37 > 4	5	6	7	8	9	1	2	3	4
2040 > 38 > 5	6	7	8	9	1	2	3	4	5
2041 > 39 > 6	7	8	9	1	2	3	4	5	6
2042 > 40 > 4	5	6	7	8	9	1	2	3	4
2043 > 41 > 3	4	5	6	7	8	9	1	2	3
2044 > 42 > 2	3	4	5	6	7	8	9	1	2
2045 > 43 > 1	2	3	4	5	6	7	8	9	1
2046 > 44 > 0	1	2	3	4	5	6	7	8	9
2047 > 45 > 1	2	3	4	5	6	7	8	9	1
2048 > 46 > 2	3	4	5	6	7	8	9	1	2
2049 > 47 > 3	4	5	6	7	8	9	1	2	3
2050 > 48 > 4	5	6	7	8	9	1	2	3	4
2051 > 49 > 5 [* change]	6	7	8	9	1	2	3	4	5
2052 > 50 > 5 [* change]	6	7	8	9	1	2	3	4	5
2053 > 51 > 4	5	6	7	8	9	1	2	3	4
2054 > 52 > 3	4	5	6	7	8	9	1	2	3

King

Exp. →	1	2	3	4	5	6	7	8	9
Year ↓									
2055 > 53 > 2	3	4	5	6	7	8	9	1	2
2056 > 54 > 1	2	3	4	5	6	7	8	9	1
2057 > 55 > 0	1	2	3	4	5	6	7	8	9
2058 > 56 > 1	2	3	4	5	6	7	8	9	1
2059 > 57 > 2	3	4	5	6	7	8	9	1	2
2060 > 58 > 3	4	5	6	7	8	9	1	2	3
2061 > 59 > 4	5	6	7	8	9	1	2	3	4
2062 > 60 > 6	7	8	9	1	2	3	4	5	6
2063 > 61 > 5	6	7	8	9	1	2	3	4	5
2064 > 62 > 4	5	6	7	8	9	1	2	3	4
2065 > 63 > 3	4	5	6	7	8	9	1	2	3
2066 > 64 > 2	3	4	5	6	7	8	9	1	2
2067 > 65 > 1	2	3	4	5	6	7	8	9	1
2068 > 66 > 0	1	2	3	4	5	6	7	8	9
2069 > 67 > 1	2	3	4	5	6	7	8	9	1
2070 > 68 > 2	3	4	5	6	7	8	9	1	2
2071 > 69 > 3	4	5	6	7	8	9	1	2	3
2072 > 70 > 7	8	9	1	2	3	4	5	6	7
2073 > 71 > 6	7	8	9	1	2	3	4	5	6
2074 > 72 > 5	6	7	8	9	1	2	3	4	5
2075 > 73 > 4	5	6	7	8	9	1	2	3	4
2076 > 74 > 3	4	5	6	7	8	9	1	2	3
2077 > 75 > 2	3	4	5	6	7	8	9	1	2
2078 > 76 > 1	2	3	4	5	6	7	8	9	1
2079 > 77 > 0	1	2	3	4	5	6	7	8	9
2080 > 78 > 1	2	3	4	5	6	7	8	9	1
2081 > 79 > 2	3	4	5	6	7	8	9	1	2
2082 > 80 > 8	9	1	2	3	4	5	6	7	8
2083 > 81 > 7	8	9	1	2	3	4	5	6	7
2084 > 82 > 6	7	8	9	1	2	3	4	5	6
2085 > 83 > 5	6	7	8	9	1	2	3	4	5
2086 > 84 > 4	5	6	7	8	9	1	2	3	4
2087 > 85 > 3	4	5	6	7	8	9	1	2	3
2088 > 86 > 2	3	4	5	6	7	8	9	1	2
2089 > 87 > 1	2	3	4	5	6	7	8	9	1
2090 > 88 > 0	1	2	3	4	5	6	7	8	9
2091 > 89 > 1	2	3	4	5	6	7	8	9	1
2092 > 90 > 9	1	2	3	4	5	6	7	8	9
2093 > 91 > 8	9	1	2	3	4	5	6	7	8
2094 > 92 > 7	8	9	1	2	3	4	5	6	7
2095 > 93 > 6	7	8	9	1	2	3	4	5	6
2096 > 94 > 5	6	7	8	9	1	2	3	4	5
2097 > 95 > 4	5	6	7	8	9	1	2	3	4
2098 > 96 > 3	4	5	6	7	8	9	1	2	3
2099 > 97 > 2	3	4	5	6	7	8	9	1	2

Notes

Notice that the years 2008 and 2009 show a 6 and 7 subcap respectively. 2008 was the year in which the housing market became severely challenged and depressed. People lost their homes, divorces and family issues were quite common. The number 6 rules the domestic environment, the heart, love life, family and the domicile. Plus, the 6 subcap is a derivative of the 2 and 8 - the energies of relationship and money. See the connection? Remember our discussion of *pinnacle, challenge and epoch pillars* in Chapter Three?

The year 2009 with its 7 subcap was the year of global recession. This 7 is derived from the pillars 2 and 9. The number 9 rules the global arena, and the world was, indeed, undergoing a recession during this time as signified by the 7. The inherent global tension was in the 11-2 crown.

Notice, too, the successive years of 2051 and 2052, both of which carry 5 subcaps, the only two successive years in the first century of the 2nd Millennium to do so. Their addcaps respectively are 8 and 9. These energies portend a twenty-four month timeline of global change, shifting, movement, motion and uncertainty, especially the year 2052 with its 9 addcap. The numbers 9 and 5 rule the universal stage and people in general more than any two numbers. Remember our earlier discussion of the simplicity of those people born in the year 2000 and how the 2 energy occurring as the final epoch illustrated extreme simplicity? How will that simple 2 epoch energy play itself out in the years 2051 and 2052 given the association of the numerical factors involved? Thus, 2051 and 2052 pose interesting scenarios on a global level. This period of time is still within the extended gestation period of the 2nd Millennium, a period which will not run its full course until the year 2100, the beginning of the 22nd Century.

Universal Year Timeline Lifescan - Binary Subcaps

The question now arises, "What of the binary subcaps created as a result of the addition of annual ciphers comprising each year [numbers added left to right] of the 2nd Millennium?" This offers another glimpse of the intricacy and complexity of life through numbers, giving multiple subcaps a chance to emerge. In the following chart, the single numbers of each year have been added together to create a binary [where applicable] which further generates its own subcap. Notice that the number of subcaps grows as the millennium progresses.

Universal Year Timeline Lifescan
The 9 Basic Expressions - Binary Subcaps
2000 to 2099

Year Down: causes - influences - themes - issues

Across - PE: effects - outcomes - realities -experiences

Exp. → / Year ↓	1	2	3	4	5	6	7	8	9
2000 > no binary subcap	-	-	-	-	-	-	-	-	-
2001 > no binary subcap	-	-	-	-	-	-	-	-	-
2002 > no binary subcap	-	-	-	-	-	-	-	-	-
2003 > no binary subcap	-	-	-	-	-	-	-	-	-
2004 > no binary subcap	-	-	-	-	-	-	-	-	-
2005 > no binary subcap	-	-	-	-	-	-	-	-	-
2006 > no binary subcap	-	-	-	-	-	-	-	-	-
2007 > no binary subcap	-	-	-	-	-	-	-	-	-
2008 > no binary subcap	-	-	-	-	-	-	-	-	-
2009 > 11 > 0	-	-	-	-	-	-	-	-	-
2010 > no binary subcap	-	-	-	-	-	-	-	-	-
2011 > no binary subcap	-	-	-	-	-	-	-	-	-
2012 > no binary subcap	-	-	-	-	-	-	-	-	-
2013 > no binary subcap	-	-	-	-	-	-	-	-	-
2014 > no binary subcap	-	-	-	-	-	-	-	-	-
2015 > no binary subcap	-	-	-	-	-	-	-	-	-
2016 > no binary subcap	-	-	-	-	-	-	-	-	-
2017 > 10 > 1	2	3	4	5	6	7	8	9	1
2018 > 11 > 0	-	-	-	-	-	-	-	-	-
2019 > 12 > 1	2	3	4	5	6	7	8	9	1
2020 > no binary subcap	-	-	-	-	-	-	-	-	-
2021 > no binary subcap	-	-	-	-	-	-	-	-	-
2022 > no binary subcap	-	-	-	-	-	-	-	-	-
2023 > no binary subcap	-	-	-	-	-	-	-	-	-
2024 > no binary subcap	-	-	-	-	-	-	-	-	-
2025 > no binary subcap	-	-	-	-	-	-	-	-	-
2026 > 10 > 1	2	3	4	5	6	7	8	9	1
2027 > 11 > 0	-	-	-	-	-	-	-	-	-
2028 > 12 > 1	2	3	4	5	6	7	8	9	1
2029 > 13 > 2	3	4	5	6	7	8	9	1	2
2030 > no binary subcap	-	-	-	-	-	-	-	-	-
2031 > no binary subcap	-	-	-	-	-	-	-	-	-
2032 > no binary subcap	-	-	-	-	-	-	-	-	-
2033 > no binary subcap	-	-	-	-	-	-	-	-	-
2034 > no binary subcap	-	-	-	-	-	-	-	-	-
2035 > 10 > 1	2	3	4	5	6	7	8	9	1

Exp. ➜ Year ⬇	1	2	3	4	5	6	7	8	9
2036 > 11 > 0	-	-	-	-	-	-	-	-	-
2037 > 12 > 1	2	3	4	5	6	7	8	9	1
2038 > 13 > 2	3	4	5	6	7	8	9	1	2
2039 > 14 > 3	4	5	6	7	8	9	1	2	3
2040 > no binary subcap	-	-	-	-	-	-	-	-	-
2041 > no binary subcap	-	-	-	-	-	-	-	-	-
2042 > no binary subcap	-	-	-	-	-	-	-	-	-
2043 > no binary subcap	-	-	-	-	-	-	-	-	-
2044 > 10 > 1	2	3	4	5	6	7	8	9	1
2045 > 11 > 0	-	-	-	-	-	-	-	-	-
2046 > 12 > 1	2	3	4	5	6	7	8	9	1
2047 > 13 > 2	3	4	5	6	7	8	9	1	2
2048 > 14 > 3	4	5	6	7	8	9	1	2	3
2049 > 15 > 4	5	6	7	8	9	1	2	3	4
2050 > no binary subcap	-	-	-	-	-	-	-	-	-
2051 > no binary subcap	-	-	-	-	-	-	-	-	-
2052 > no binary subcap	-	-	-	-	-	-	-	-	-
2053 > 10 > 1	2	3	4	5	6	7	8	9	1
2054 > 11 > 0	-	-	-	-	-	-	-	-	-
2055 > 12 > 1	2	3	4	5	6	7	8	9	1
2056 > 13 > 2	3	4	5	6	7	8	9	1	2
2057 > 14 > 3	4	5	6	7	8	9	1	2	3
2058 > 15 > 4	5	6	7	8	9	1	2	3	4
2059 > 16 > 5	6	7	8	9	1	2	3	4	5
2060 > no binary subcap	-	-	-	-	-	-	-	-	-
2061 > no binary subcap	-	-	-	-	-	-	-	-	-
2062 > 10 > 1	2	3	4	5	6	7	8	9	1
2063 > 11 > 0	-	-	-	-	-	-	-	-	-
2064 > 12 > 1	2	3	4	5	6	7	8	9	1
2065 > 13 > 2	3	4	5	6	7	8	9	1	2
2066 > 14 > 3	4	5	6	7	8	9	1	2	3
2067 > 15 > 4	5	6	7	8	9	1	2	3	4
2068 > 16 > 5	6	7	8	9	1	2	3	4	5
2069 > 17 > 6	7	8	9	1	2	3	4	5	6
2070 > no binary subcap	-	-	-	-	-	-	-	-	-
2071 > 10 > 1	2	3	4	5	6	7	8	9	1
2072 > 11 > 0	-	-	-	-	-	-	-	-	-
2073 > 12 > 1	2	3	4	5	6	7	8	9	1
2074 > 13 > 2	3	4	5	6	7	8	9	1	2
2075 > 14 > 3	4	5	6	7	8	9	1	2	3
2076 > 15 > 4	5	6	7	8	9	1	2	3	4
2077 > 16 > 5	6	7	8	9	1	2	3	4	5
2078 > 17 > 6	7	8	9	1	2	3	4	5	6
2079 > 18 > 7	8	9	1	2	3	4	5	6	7
2080 > 10 > 1	2	3	4	5	6	7	8	9	1

King

Exp. ➔	1	2	3	4	5	6	7	8	9
Year ⬇									
2081 > 11 > 0	-	-	-	-	-	-	-	-	-
2082 > 12 > 1	2	3	4	5	6	7	8	9	1
2083 > 13 > 2	3	4	5	6	7	8	9	1	2
2084 > 14 > 3	4	5	6	7	8	9	1	2	3
2085 > 15 > 4	5	6	7	8	9	1	2	3	4
2086 > 16 > 5	6	7	8	9	1	2	3	4	5
2087 > 17 > 6	7	8	9	1	2	3	4	5	6
2088 > 18 > 7	8	9	1	2	3	4	5	6	7
2089 > 19 > 8	9	1	2	3	4	5	6	7	8
2090 > 11 > 0	-	-	-	-	-	-	-	-	-
2091 > 12 > 1	2	3	4	5	6	7	8	9	1
2092 > 13 > 2	3	4	5	6	7	8	9	1	2
2093 > 14 > 3	4	5	6	7	8	9	1	2	3
2094 > 15 > 4	5	6	7	8	9	1	2	3	4
2095 > 16 > 5	6	7	8	9	1	2	3	4	5
2096 > 17 > 6	7	8	9	1	2	3	4	5	6
2097 > 18 > 7	8	9	1	2	3	4	5	6	7
2098 > 19 > 8	9	1	2	3	4	5	6	7	8
2099 > 20 > 2	3	4	5	6	7	8	9	1	2

Chapter Twelve

PERSONAL YEAR TIMELINE- PTL

The *Personal Year Timeline*, like the *Age* and *Universal Timelines*, is a potent tool in the forecasting process. In fact, these three timelines and their PEs give the most conclusive and definitive information about a person's life on a year-to-year basis.

The Personal Year Timeline, or PTL, provides each of us with the main lessons, issues and themes during the particular natal year in question, bringing a variety of people, events and circumstances into our lives. The PTL is unique because it's a blend of personal and universal data. The ATL is as purely "us" as it can be - defined by our age. The UTL is simply the calendar year, but the PTL involves our own day and month of birth plus the calendar year [when it's activated on our birthday].

The Personal Year Timeline, like all timelines, runs in nine year cycles and manifests crown, challenge, and root forms in most cases. The only time a root would not appear in the PTL is when there are simply too few digits to create one. For example, a PTL date format of 2 February 2000 would only possess three numbers which total a sum of 6 which does not possess any root structure:

(2 February 2000 > 2 + 2 + 2 = 6).

Calculating the Personal Year Timeline

The Personal Year Timeline is determined by adding the day and month of the subject's natal birth data to the current calendar year. For instance, during the year 1998, any person born on 7 May would have a 3 Personal Year which would begin on his birthday on 7 May, and continue until his next birthday in 1999, at which time his Personal Year would sequentially advance to a 4 PTL.

King

In this first computation, each of the three calendar components is reduced to a single digit, added together and reduced to a single digit.

Day of birth		Month of birth		Calendar Year			Personal Year
7		May		1998			
7		5		27			
7	+	5	+	9	=	21	2 + 1 = **3**

In this second computation, the calendar ciphers are simply added from left to right and reduced to a single digit. This yields a *general* root of 39, a transition root of 12 and crown of 3.

$$7 + 5 + 1 + 9 + 9 + 8 = 39 > 12 > 3$$

In this case the general root and the specific root are identical (see *The King's Book of Numerology, Volume I, Foundations & Fundamentals*). The *specific* root is obtained by adding the specific values of the calendar components: $7 + 5 + 27 = 39$.

A third method of computing the personal year timeline is to "stack 'em and add 'em."

Calendar year	1998
Month of birth	+ 5
Day of birth	+ 7
	2010
	2 + 1 = 3
Personal Year	**3**

Using these three methods we determine that 7 May 1998 has roots of 39, 21 and 12 to support its 3 crown. It also has two challenges: 6 and 1. The 6 is derived from the subtraction of the two ciphers in the 39 General root (9 - 3), and the 1 results from the subtraction of the 1 and 2 in the 12 and 21 roots. The primary challenge is the 6; the secondary challenge is the 1.

This 39/12/3 *Personal Year Timeline* is one which will carry lessons in the general categories of self-expression, self-integration, image, politics, art, words, language, communication, pleasure, enjoyment, marriage, children, friends, fun, health, beauty and relative ease. However, as all coins of the numerical realm have two sides, issues of disease, dis-ease, inharmony, inappropriate pleasures involving spiritually untoward liaisons, abusive communication, marital problems, and difficulties with children could also present themselves. Additionally, the attributes of the 3 will be drawn to conclusion or expansion in the public spotlight as a result of the 9 focus in the thirties decade.

Since 3 and 9 are both artistic and communicative ciphers, there should be much creativity throughout this 39th year. The 12 and 21 binaries foretell of the self in relationship - the 1 embracing the 2, and relationship encompassing the self - the 2 embracing the 1.   New relationships are a definite possibility, as is the ending of a marriage or other significant partnership.   Too, the 1 and 2 represent energies of the yang and yin, so male and female issues will also be brought into focus this year. The 6 primary challenge will bring issues of love, matters of the heart, family, domestic responsibilities and adjustments to bear on the individual. The 1 secondary challenge will focus on yang energies of leadership, authority and creativity, as well as the self and its identity, independence, needs and wants.

As a matter of note, the 3 is, generally, the cipher carrying the most fulfilling and pleasurable experiences, the easiest of loads, and the least difficult lessons in life.   If there is any cipher denoting ease, it is the three. It is the salve of the nine basic numbers and has a remarkable tendency to dilute problems and concerns, most likely because 3 is the energy of self-fulfillment, and when an individual is fulfilled and generally content, life's worries don't seem to be as bothersome. However, if the 3 is negatively aspected by void or challenge ciphers, it can be quite challenging because it deals directly with the integration of life in its three basic components: body, mind and spirit. It is not uncommon to find 3 energy present in charts at the time of death. The 3 rules the spirit of life and its integration, and when life becomes disintegrated, it dies. If too much 3

King

occurs in a chart, it can manifest as extreme vanity and self-obsession, as well as a sense of entitlement and privilege. The negatively aspected 3 also portends health issues, disease, dis-ease, inharmony, verbal discord and problems with children.

It must also be remembered that the PTL influencing energy represents the issues and themes of what one is to learn in regards to the particular vibration in question during its annual cycle. It does not represent the outcome or result of the year's theme energies. Outcomes and results are always indicated by the PE. Too, when we *learn about* a subject, we often are engaged by all aspects of it, so it is probable that positive and negative issues will come to the fore during any given personal year timeline.

When we regard the PTL, we can think of it as being a *subscript* of the basic life script denoted in the Lifepath. Since the Lifepath focuses on our main lesson during this incarnation and is composed of day, month and year aspects, so the personal year timeline - also composed of day, month and year aspects - focuses on our annual lesson within the greater context of the dominating Lifepath curriculum.

Personal years run in nine years cycles. However, because the individual will transit other vibratory fields during his life [pinnacles, challenges, epochs, name timelines, letter timelines], it is safe to say that no single year's PTL experience will be exactly like another. Experiences will be similar but not identical. For example, let's say a person lives on three different continents [the three Epochs] during the course of an eighty-seven year life. The weather of the first continent [1st Epoch] is cold, harsh, foreboding, unkind. He lives there for thirty years. The second continent [2nd Epoch] is less abrasive, somewhat more temperate, but still unappealing. He lives there for twenty-seven years. The third continent [3rd Epoch] on which he lives out the remainder of his eighty-seven years is warm, inviting, embracing, kind, and beautiful. Because the PTL, ATL and UTL follow nine year cycles, their recurring issues and themes will be affected by each of the environments of the three continents on which our subject lives during his life. Yet, the experiences of each of the three main annually transiting timelines (PTL, ATL, UTL) will definitely be influenced by the weather and geographical composition of each of the three continents [vibratory fields] and, therefore, be different to some degree. Having a bad hair day is somehow easier to cope with in a sunny, warm, pleasant, free and inviting environment than in harsh, severe, freezing cold, tempest-tossed, storm-filled, rusty iron environs.

Our lives are just like this example of living on three continents during a lifetime. The first continent of our lives is defined by our day of birth, the second continent by our month of birth, and the third continent by our year of birth. If each of these vibrational continents reflects a

The King's Book of Numerology II: Forecasting - Part 1

different numerical vibration, the influences and realities associated with the PTL, ATL and UTL will be different. If the numerical vibrations of the three continents are the same, the lessons of the PTL, ATL and UTL will be quite similar. For example, if a person were born on the 7th of July in the year 2005, the three continents of his life would be a 7, 7, 7. Hence, there would be little major change in "continental" energies. Were a person born on the 3rd of February in the year 2005, the continental energies (Epochs) will be 3, 2 and 7 respectively - a much different pattern showing greater change than the 7, 7, 7 pattern. Therefore, one must be careful not to conclude that just because these three major timelines [PTL, ATL and UTL] and their influences recur every nine years their lessons will be identical.

Personal Year Timeline Scan: Simple Version

Charting the simple PTL-PE is easy. Simply add the Simple Expression to the single cipher of the Personal Year Timeline and reduce to a single digit, just as we did for the ATL and UTL. This will give us the influences and outcomes for the personal year timeline. Let's take some examples.

Example #1: 8 Expression person born on 27 February. The hypothetical calendar year is 2004 (27 - 2 - 2004). The PTL is 8 and the PTL-PE is 7. The would be written as 8/7. This combination would also generate a 6/5 Challenge.

$$2 + 7 + 2 + 2 + 4 = 17 > 1 + 7 = 8 \text{ PTL}$$

$$8 \text{ PTL} + 8 \text{ Expression} = 16 > 7 \text{ PTL-PE.}$$

Challenge calculation
$$17 > 7 - 1 = 6 \text{ Challenge}$$

$$6 \text{ Challenge} + 8 \text{ Exp.} = 14 > 5 \text{ Challenge PE}$$

King

This 8/7 PTL-PE influence/reality set will most likely generate social and/or business interactions, connections, disconnections and circulation issues (8) creating possible concerns, stresses, difficulties, and ignominies of the heart. Positively aspected in an individual with an elevated consciousness, such an 8/7 I/R set will create deep spiritual connections.

The 6/5 Challenge associated with this sequence means there will be changes, movement, motion, shifts, detachments, uncertainties, and freedom (5) stemming from adjustments and responsibilities made in matters of love, the heart, the domicile and the community. (6).

Example #2: 6 Expression individual born on 5 July. The hypothetical calendar year is 2010 (5 - 7 - 2010). The PTL is 6; the PTL-PE is 3. This is written 6/3. The Challenge combination would be a 4/1.

$$5 + 7 + 2 + 1 = 15 > 1 + 5 = 6 \text{ PTL}$$

$$6 \text{ PTL} + 6 \text{ Expression} = 12 > 1 + 2 = 3 \text{ PTL-PE}$$

Challenge Calculation

$$15 > 5 - 1 = 4 \text{ Challenge}$$

$$4 \text{ Challenge} + 6 \text{ Exp.} = 1 \text{ Challenge PE}$$

In this 6/3 PTL-PE the influencing energies focus on love, nurturing, the home, family, community, responsibilities and adjustments. The outcome is the 3 energy of ease, pleasure, good times, friends, communication, artistic endeavors, creative expression, children and possible marriage. Since the 3 vibration normally is positive, this 6/3 pattern may well bring positive outcomes to love issues. Without question, love and pleasure are the operating energies. If negatively aspected, the potential outcome would be discomfort, disease, dis-ease, medical care, difficulties with children, unkind words, disappointment, unhappiness, sadness.

The 4/1 Challenge reflects new beginnings whose origins are security, work, the house, job or employment. There could be an emergence of new routines, new patterns, new rules, new order - something new that is based in structures, foundations, frameworks, security, and stability.

Example #3. 5 Expression person born on 3 March; hypothetical calendar year is 2006 (3 - 3 - 2006). PTL is a 5; PTL-PE is a 1. This is written 5/1. The Challenge I/R is 3/8.

$$3 + 3 + 2 + 6 = 14 > 1 + 4 = 5 \text{ PTL}$$

$$5 \text{ PTL} + 5 \text{ Expression} = 10 > 1 + 0 = 1 \text{ PTL-PE}$$

$$14 > 4 - 1 = 3 \text{ Challenge}$$

$$3 \text{ Challenge} + 5 \text{ Exp.} = 8 \text{ Challenge PE}$$

This is going to be a dynamic year for this 5 individual. The personal year's energies are saturated in change, motion, movement, detachment, loss, experience, and freedom as reflected in the 5 PTL. The 1 PTL-PE forecasts new beginnings, solo journeys, and creative enterprises. The 1 in this position reflects the start of a new nine year cycle in the outcome/reality position of the I/R set. Both the 5 and 1 are fire signs, so there will be much heat and action during this year, heat and action which create shifts and starts. These energies will also chasten, purify, detach, and liberate.

One main concern with 5 energy is that, although it is traditionally regarded as the energy of freedom, it is also the energy of slavery - the other side of the freedom coin. Care must always be taken to incorporate the thought of consequence to action before an action is initiated. A lack of reasonable thought and shallow judgment could result in unhealthy outcomes and realities. Life doesn't always give second chances and one wrong move could be fatal or everlastingly tragic, sorrowful, and lamentable. Freedom is not license carte blanche, i.e., license without consequence. Freedom is action taken in consideration of consequence, and while the 5 energy is certainly the most potentially liberating and freeing, it is arguably also the most dangerous, enslaving, rebellious and incarcerating. To be sure, freedom is not free. If one gets too carried away with excitement without exercising caution, restraint, proper discrimination, discipline or judgment, the costs and effects can be, and oftentimes are, devastating. As 5 is that vibration standing at the midpoint of the nine basic energies (1-4 and 6-9), it is definitely a two edged sword whose razored edges can sever the shackles of slavery, thereby making one free, or cut the flesh of the body into pieces, creating mayhem and slavery.

The 3/8 Challenge heralds success, interactions, connections or disconnections (8) in personal expression, fulfillment, words, art, communication, the law and children (3). Art (3) integrates (8)

King

with this vibration - any kind of art: visual, literary, vocal, musical, martial, painting, drawing, sculpting.

Example #4: 1 Expression; birthdate - 4 December; hypothetical year - 2012.
The PTL is a 3; PE is a 4. The full PTL-PE to be written as 1/4. The Challenge is a 1/2.

$$4 + 1 + 2 + 2 + 1 + 2 = 12 > 3 \text{ PTL}$$

$$1 \text{ Expression} + 3 \text{ PTL} = 4 \text{ PTL-PE}$$

$$\text{Challenge calculation}$$
$$12 > 2 - 1 = 1 \text{ Challenge}$$

$$1 \text{ Challenge} + 1 \text{ Exp.} = 2 \text{ Challenge PE}$$

The 1/4 PTL-PE addresses new beginnings (1) in structures of some kind (4). It can also be interpreted as the self (1) involved in work, service, organization, effort, limitation, restriction, and discipline (4). This is a time when foundations take form (4) as a result of an insurgence of new ideas, new energies, new thoughts and actions (1). It is also the beginning of a new nine year influence/theme cycle, as the 1 energy is the vibration of initiation.

The 1/2 I/R set in the Challenge position of this numerical combination reveals new beginnings (1) in relationship (2). It can also translate as the self (1) in support of others (2). Certainly, there is action (1) creating reaction (2); action (1) bringing opposing parts of the whole into balance (2). It is also leadership (1) embracing followership (2).

What personal year are you in? Add the day and month of your birth together along with the current calendar year. Remember, however, the calendar year does not personally start for you until your birthday. So if it's March of a certain year, say 2005, and your birthday isn't until August, your new personal 2005 year does not start until August. Use the previous calendar year for your calculations - in this case 2004. Always keep in mind that our numerological year does not begin until our birthday. The only person who would begin their personal year on January 1st is the person who is born on January 1st. If you're born on December 31st, then your personal year begins on December 31st, even though December 31st is the final day of the calendar year.

After you determine your PTL crown by adding all the numbers and reducing to a single digit, add your Simple Expression and reduce to a single digit again to arrive at your PTL-PE. The following chart makes finding your PE easy. Simply cross reference the PTL crown in the left column with the Expression crown in the right column. Last, compute your Challenge vibration. Thus, you should have two I/R sets: a PTL-PE and its corresponding Challenge modality.

Personal Year Timeline Scan

The 81 Influence/Reality Sets

PTL Down: causes - influences - themes - issues

PE Across: effects - outcomes - realities -experiences

Exp. ➔ PTL ⬇	1	2	3	4	5	6	7	8	9
1	2	3	4	5	6	7	8	9	1
2	3	4	5	6	7	8	9	1	2
3	4	5	6	7	8	9	1	2	3
4	5	6	7	8	9	1	2	3	4
5	6	7	8	9	1	2	3	4	5
6	7	8	9	1	2	3	4	5	6
7	8	9	1	2	3	4	5	6	7
8	9	1	2	3	4	5	6	7	8
9	1	2	3	4	5	6	7	8	9

Chapter Thirteen

ANNUAL CYCLE PATTERN - ACP

The *Annual Cycle Pattern*, or ACP, is a powerful forecasting tool to help assess the energies and issues of any natal year. This triumvirate structure is comprised of the Age Timeline [ATL], Universal Timeline [UTL] and the Personal Year Timeline [PTL]. In simplistic terms we can view the Age Timeline as just "us," the Universal Timeline as the "world" and the Personal Year Timeline as "us" and the "world" in concert. The "us" can be changed to other pronouns such as *I, me* or *we*, and the "world" to "others" or "them." Regardless of grammatical nuances, the ATL is the most personal timeline; the UTL is the most universal and the PTL is a combination of the two.

Timeline Application: Annual Forecast

We can use the three major timelines to generate a fairly accurate annual forecast. There is still much more to study regarding forecasting, yet these three timelines can give us an excellent indication of the energies present in any given year.

Let's use this example: a person who is 36 years of age in 2002; born on 8 February 1966 and maintaining a 7 Expression. Therefore, The Age Timeline (ATL) is 36 with a 9 addcap pinnacle and a 3 subcap challenge. The Universal Timeline (UTL) is 4 (2002 reduced to a single digit). It has no subcap challenge. The Personal Year Timeline is a 5 addcap with a 14 *general root* (8 + 2 + 2 + 2 = 14 > 5) giving it a 3 subcap challenge (4 -1 = 3).

Below is a tabulation of the three major timelines as they apply to our friend who has a 7 Expression. To arrive at the PEs for each timeline we'll simply add 7 to each of them. We'll also add 7 to the ATL and PTL subcap crowns to determine the subcap PEs.

King

Annual Forecast Using the Three Major Timelines

7 Expression; Birthday: 8 February; Age - 36; Year - 2002 [born 1966]

Timeline	Roots	Addcap	Subcap
ATL	36	9	3
P/E	-----	7	1
UTL	2002	4	-0-
P/E	-----	2	-0-
PTL	14	5	3
P/E	-----	3	1

ATL/PE

The ATL/PE is a 9/7. This gives us some major clues and drastically begins to clarify the year's experiences. The 9 rules conclusions, endings, expansions, education, the public stage, notoriety, travel and all things universal. The 7 governs concerns, stress, study, teaching, reflection, introspection, separation, isolation, examination, internalization, spirituality, analysis, turmoil, possible chaos [if negatively aspected] and peace, stillness, centeredness [the latter will be the case if the individual operates from a spiritual point of view]. One scenario is that something will be ending in this person's life, and it will create deep thought and concern (in the least) or great mental distress and discomfort for the individual. Another scenario is that there could be education activity (9) in a course of study (7) or an exposure (9) of something hidden (7). A third scenario could be long distant (9) suffering or turmoil (7). A fourth could be knowledge or wisdom gained (7) through contact with the public, either being the dispenser or recipient of the knowledge. It is not an unlikely supposition that troubles and turmoils arising in or from the public arena will occur.

The 3/1 Challenge accompanying this 9/7 ATL/PE indicates negative self-expression issues. A 3 Challenge is about unhappiness and a lack of personal fulfillment. In this case the 3 is playing itself out in the realm of the 1, the self and its ego. A marriage could be undergoing challenges which in turn generate concerns of self-worth or personal isolation. There could very possibly be health issues in the person's life or in the life of a male figure or a person with strong 1 energy in their chart because 3 rules health, beauty, disease, dis-ease, image, words, speech, communication,

The King's Book of Numerology II: Forecasting - Part 1

and 1 rules the self and all things yang. This could also equate to criticism (3) from a male (1), an authority figure (1) or any person (regardless of gender) who maintains a 1 energy in his or her Basic Matrix.

UTL/PE

The UTL/PE is a 4/2 I/R set. This indicates an influence of security, stability, work, service, toil, plodding along, staying the course, the job, house, routines, patterns, rules, regulations, principles of honesty, devotion, order, trust and loyalty (4) playing themselves out in the arena of relationships, support, others, balance, fairness, females and female energy, being the helper and partner (2). This 4/2 modality definitely indicates something going on in the work and relationship aspects of the individual's life. The 4 serves and the 2 helps. This could involve the stability and security of relationships, contractual issues of others, the devotion of a female or partner, the process of serving and helping other people. Because 4 rules stability, if positively aspected this will be a year of maintenance. Yet, if negatively aspect by void or challenge position or both, this year will force the individual to focus on the positive aspects of the 4 and 2 to remain stable.

PTL/PE

The PTL/PE gives us more definitive clues. The 14/5 energy addresses losses, changes, detachments, motion, movement, freedom, and uncertainties playing themselves out in the arena of one's happiness, joy, self-fulfillment, self-expression, friends, health, and beauty (3). Something's definitely shifting (5) in the individual's happiness and well-being (3). This 5/3 pattern could also indicate something positive. Just because we lose something or something is taken away from us, doesn't mean the thing, person or experience removed is bad. We may have a cancer removed from our body, a wart from our nose, a bad habit of cursing replaced by more positive language. Whatever happens under this vibration, however, will involve change in one's happiness, self-expression, marriage, children or health. A 5/3 pattern can be highly indicative of experiences (5) in pleasure (3) or a variety (5) of pleasurable experiences (3), but such an outcome is more commonly the result of a 23/5 or a 32/5, not a 14/5. The 14/5 absolutely suggests loss and detachment of some kind.

The 3/1 attending challenge to this PTL/PE intensifies the 3/1 pattern in the ATL/PE. This is an example of *stacking* - the occurrence of simultaneous identical energies within a numerology chart. When stacking occurs, intensity occurs. It's like adding fire to fire. Here again in this 3/1 pattern we have individual concerns of personal identity, self-worth, value, and independence springing forth from an afflicted 3 energy of unhappiness and a lack of ease - a double dose of 3/1 energy because of the stacking.

If any of the above single ciphers or I/R sets appear in the *Challenge* position of the chart at the time they transit the person's life, or if they are *void*, the outcome will most definitely be quite difficult for the individual. Nonetheless, they are lessons the soul needs - experiences deemed necessary by God himself. Who are we to argue or take issue with a person's destiny or the hand that created it? We can sympathize and empathize, but we cannot change a person's destiny. We can certainly help him understand it, show him the salutary effects of maintaining a positive outlook in terms of balancing karmas and reconciling prior debts, have compassion and understanding for him, but we cannot change what has been written for him. As Saint Charan Singh has stated: *What has to happen has already happened, and what has happened, had to happen.* Such is the divine design of life.

ACP Timeline Text Grid

Placing brief keywords or phrases to the right of the timelines offers a quick glimpse of the year's influences and outcomes. To lessen confusion, one grid below addresses addcaps; the other, subcaps.

ACP: Addcap

Timeline	Roots	Addcap	Influence/Outcomes
ATL	36	9	Expansions, endings, conclusions, travel, public, art, education
P/E	-----	7	Introspection, recession, withdrawal, study, peace, chaos, testing
UTL	2002	4	Work, service, security, stability, roots, order, rules, transformation
P/E	-----	2	Yin, others, balance, partnership, competition, division, deceit
PTL	14	5	Change, movement, motion, loss, detachment, uncertainty, freedom
P/E	-----	3	Communication, image, children, health, beauty, disease, pleasure

ACP: Subcap

Timeline	Roots	Subcap	Influence/Outcomes
ATL	36	3	Communication, image, children, health, beauty, disease, pleasure
P/E	-----	1	Yang, self, identity, independence, leadership, authority figures
UTL	2002	-0-	- None -
P/E	-----	-0-	- None -
PTL	14	3	Communication, image, children, health, beauty, disease, pleasure
P/E	-----	1	Yang, self, identity, independence, leadership, authority figures

Subcaps in the Basic Matrix Umbrella

Subcaps are not only applicable to the Annual Cycle Patterns. By applying the concept of subcaps to the Expression and Lifepath of a person, we can obtain a deeper understanding of the person himself and his life's script. For this example, we'll use our 7 Expression person who was born on 8 February 1966 which would yield a 32 General Lifepath root ($8 + 2 + 1 + 9 + 6 + 6 = 32$). We'll give him a 61 General Expression root for his 7 Expression crown (see *The King's Book of Numerology, Volume I*). This yields a 5 Expression subcap challenge in his name and a 1 challenge in his Lifepath. Because each of these is a derivative of the General root, we'll classify them as *general subcap challenges* (GSC).

Basic Matrix Component	Roots	General Subcap Challenge
Expression	61	5
Lifepath	32	1

This general subcap challenge tells us that our 7 Expression person, while being introspective, reflective, analytical, quiet, private, reclusive, inwardly driven, modest and discerning (all attributes of the 7 energy) is also personally challenged by a feeling of freedom, exploration, experimentation, detachment, motion, movement, change and the senses within the love environment as depicted by the 6 cipher of the sixties decade. This is a lifetime challenge.

King

By looking at the "Binary Crowns: Addcaps & Subcaps" chart below, we see that the only other binary of the 7 Expression associated with a 5 challenge is the number 16 (61 in reverse). The 16/7 cipher is the great purifier as we know, and it is this 5 challenge in the 16 and 61 ciphers that has an impact on creating either saints or sinners. Those souls striving to express the high ideals of a spiritual life will transmute the 5 challenge energy into self-control of their passions and desires (creating freedom from the senses) while those less disposed will tend to indulge their senses rather than restrain them and therefore run the risk of becoming enslaved by them. This 5 challenge in the 16 and 61 ciphers potentially makes one prone to indulgence, experimenting, wandering, cheating, being unfaithful and rebellious. It is this lack of self-restraint and sensual indulgence stemming from actions (1) in love or lust (6) that can cause the person under this vibratory influence to fall, suffering disgrace, ignominy, and ignobility in the process. A clear picture of this is reflected in the number 16 card of the Major Arcana of the Tarot deck, the Tower.

The 32/5 Lifepath of our 7 Expression person maintains a 1 challenge. This indicates issues with the self, its image and identity, authority figures or concerns, personal worth, independence, accountability and responsibility. In some capacity, the individual will be involved with his own issues or with other people who also have 1 energy in their charts. Like the Expression challenge, this too will last for the entire life.

Binary Crowns: Addcaps & Subcaps

Crowns >	1	2	3	4	5	6	7	8	9
Addcap Crowns	1	2	3	4	5	6	7	8	9
Age/Binaries	10	11	12	13	14	15	16	17	18
Subcap Crowns	1	0	1	2	3	4	5	6	7
Addcap Crowns	1	2	3	4	5	6	7	8	9
Age/Binaries	19	20	21	22	23	24	25	26	27
Subcap Crowns	8	2	1	0	1	2	3	4	5
Addcap Crowns	1	2	3	4	5	6	7	8	9
Age/Binaries	28	29	30	31	32	33	34	35	36
Subcap Crowns	6	7	3	2	1	0	1	2	3
Addcap Crowns	1	2	3	4	5	6	7	8	9
Age/Binaries	37	38	39	40	41	42	43	44	45
Subcap Crowns	4	5	6	4	3	2	1	0	1
Addcap Crowns	1	2	3	4	5	6	7	8	9
Age/Binaries	46	47	48	49	50	51	52	53	54
Subcap Crowns	2	3	4	5	5	4	3	2	1
Addcap Crowns	1	2	3	4	5	6	7	8	9
Age/Binaries	55	56	57	58	59	60	61	62	63
Subcap Crowns	0	1	2	3	4	6	5	4	3
Addcap Crowns	1	2	3	4	5	6	7	8	9
Age/Binaries	64	65	66	67	68	69	70	71	72
Subcap Crowns	2	1	0	1	2	3	7	6	5
Addcap Crowns	1	2	3	4	5	6	7	8	9
Age/Binaries	73	74	75	76	77	78	79	80	81
Subcap Crowns	4	3	2	1	0	1	2	8	7
Addcap Crowns	1	2	3	4	5	6	7	8	9
Age/Binaries	82	83	84	85	86	87	88	89	90
Subcap Crowns	6	5	4	3	2	1	0	1	9
Addcap Crowns	1	2	3	4	5	6	7	8	9
Age/Binaries	91	92	93	94	95	96	97	98	99
Subcap Crowns	8	7	6	5	4	3	2	1	0

King

PE Funnels and Filters

In order to generate a Performance/Experience outcome energy field, the influencing energy must combine, mix with, filter or funnel through a second energy field. The three timelines of the ACP [ATL, UTL, PTL] all filter through the Expression to create their PE. The Expression, Soul, Nature, Names [of the Expression] and Letters [of the Expression] all filter through the Lifepath to create their PE. The following graphic will add a visual perspective to this concept.

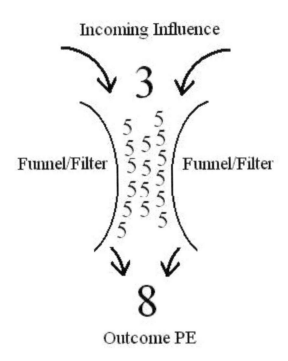

As is clearly visible, the 8 PE is generated with the 3 passing through the energy field of the 5 which makes the 8 rich in 5 energy. If the influencing cipher were a 2 and the PE an 8, the 2 would have to funnel through the energy field of the 6 to create the 8. Thus, the 8 would have very different properties. The 8 PE derived from the 3 would be very active, diverse, motion-oriented, free and dynamic while an 8 PE derived from the number 2 would be rich in family, love, relationship, sensual, domestic, nurturing energy. Thus, the funnel/filter energy must always be considered when assessing the Outcome PE energy field. All 8s are not alike. We know this because it has ten binary roots, as do all single ciphers. By the same token, all 8 PEs are not like. The funnel/filter structure from which the 8 or any PE was generated as the influencing cipher passed through it must be taken into account. The same is true for all PEs.

Influencing Energy Cipher + Filter/Funnel Cipher > PE cipher

Annual Life Cycle Pattern

One of the major benefits of knowing the ACPs is that they repeat themselves every nine years, thus allowing us to create an *Annual Life Cycle Pattern* which reveals a full life scan of the ATL, UTL and PTL working in unison. This recurring aspect allows us to prepare and plan for the future and not get broadsided by energy waves that could imbalance us. Just remember that these recurring annual cycle patterns will be interrelated with their epochs, pinnacles, challenges, name and letter timelines as the person transits his life. All timelines need to be taken into account when forecasting the potentials within the destiny of an individual at any given point in time.

Using the previous example of a 7 Expression person born on 8 February 1966, we can generate an Annual Life Cycle Pattern for the entire life of the individual. To use the chart, simply reduce the current age to a crown, find its location in the top row [the age will be listed in the column below it] and consult the Annual Cycle Pattern in the same column farther down. It would be helpful to make note of any voids in the chart by marking the voided cipher with a "v" such as: 1v, 2v, 3v, etc. whether it occupies an influence or outcome position. To establish the chart, start with age 1 - the year following the person's birth, generate the ATL, UTL and PTL and work forward in sequence.

Annual Life Cycle Pattern
Subject: 7 Expression; Born 8 February 1966
Major Timelines return every Nine (9) years.

Age	1	2	3	4	5	6	7	8	9
Age	10/1	11/2	12/3	13/4	14/5	15/6	16/7	17/8	18/9
Age	19/1	20/2	21/3	22/4	23/5	24/6	25/7	26/8	27/9
Age	28/1	29/2	30/3	31/4	32/5	33/6	34/7	35/8	36/9
Age	37/1	38/2	39/3	40/4	41/5	42/6	43/7	44/8	45/9
Age	46/1	47/2	48/3	49/4	50/5	51/6	52/7	53/8	54/9
Age	55/1	56/2	57/3	58/4	59/5	60/6	61/7	62/8	63/9
Age	64/1	65/2	66/3	67/4	68/5	69/6	70/7	71/8	72/9
Age	73/1	74/2	75/3	76/4	77/5	78/6	79/7	80/8	81/9
Age	82/1	83/2	84/3	85/4	86/5	87/6	88/7	89/8	90/9
Age	91/1	92/2	93/3	94/4	95/5	96/6	97/7	98/8	99/9
ATL	1	2	3	4	5	6	7	8	9
ATL PE	8	9	1	2	3	4	5	6	7
UTL	5	6	7	8	9	1	2	3	4
UTL PE	3	4	5	6	7	8	9	1	2
PTL	6	7	8	9	1	2	3	4	5
PTL PE	4	5	6	7	8	9	1	2	3

Timeline Analysis Summary

The three major timelines transiting a person's chart on an annual basis are the Age timeline (ATL), Universal timeline (UTL), and Personal Year timeline (PTL). They give us an excellent blueprint of the annual destiny cycle operating in a person's life. These three timelines are the mainstay of the annual forecasting process. As the other timelines are introduced into the mix, a clear picture of the individual's destiny will emerge.

As far as the analysis process is concerned, begin always with the crown of each timeline and then proceed to the roots. Be simple minded. Think in simple terms. List the attributes of each number; write them down if necessary to obtain a clear picture of each cipher. Think of the *crown* (either addcap or subcap) as drawing its life-force from its root structure. What energies are in the roots of the crowns? Be sensitive to decades and the number upon which they focus. Bring your own intuition to bear on the meanings presented by each number. Are there harmonies and inharmonies between the ciphers? How do all of these ciphers correspond with the Basic Matrix, Life Matrix, Name Timeline, Letter Timeline? Is there any stacking? Much of this may seem confusing at first, but continual practice will yield positive results. The study of numerology is a journey, not a race. Be patient, enjoy the process.

Chapter Fourteen

THE CHART

It is now time to put our numerology education to practice, using everything we have learned from both *The King's Book of Numerology: Volume I - Foundations and Fundamentals* and *The King's Book of Numerology II: Forecasting - Part I* to construct a basic numerology chart. We'll create this chart, this life blueprint, for our traveling companion, Richard Johnston Roe, born 6 December 1999, using his first birthday as a point of genesis.

A. Basic Matrix

The first item is to generate a Basic Matrix [personal profile] template for RJ showing the crowns and root structure of the seven components of his life's blueprint/destiny: 1. Lifepath 2. Expression
3. Performance/Experience [PE] 4. Soul 5. Material Soul 6. Nature 7. Material Nature. List any voids. Once the Basic Matrix is configured, analyze the crowns to assess the general field of play for each component and then analyze the roots of each crown to see how they add "color" and nuance to it and what their general and specific energies reveal. Next, check for master numbers; the number of odd numbered energies [1-3-5-7-9] which depict aspects of internalization, and then determine the even numbered energies [2-4-6-8] concentrating on relationship and social interaction. Are there sets of opposites appearing in the matrix: 1 and 2; 4 and 5; 7 and 8? What harmonies exist - 1 and 7; 2 and 6; 4 and 8; 5 and 9? Is the artistic triad 3-6-9 contained in the matrix? Is there an abundance of more than one numerical cipher? RJ's chart, for example, shows two 1s and two 7s. If there are voids in the Expression, do they show up in the Basic Matrix? If they do not, a *grand void* will be created. It is also important to check the *focus number* in each binary and trinary root structure to assess the intensity of that number. The focus cipher is the last number in the binary or trinary set. The more times the focus number appears, the greater its

King

intensity and influence. Once this is done, spend some time contemplating on the interrelationship of the numbers and their energies and how they apply to the life in question. Utilize both reason and intuition to arrive at the potentials of the chart.

[Note: a blank numerology chart form concludes this chapter.]

Basic Matrix
Richard Johnston Roe
Born: 6 December 1999

Roots ⇩	Lifepath	Expression	PE	Soul	M/S	Nature	M/N	Voids
Simple	1	7	8	6	7	1	2	7
General	37	97	134	33	70	64	101	na
Specific	46	214	260	60	106	154	200	na
Transition	10-19	16	35	-0-	-0-	10-19	11-38	na

Basic Matrix Terms

Expression	The actor/actress full potentials, assets and liabilities
Lifepath	The life script, path in life, lessons to learn, energy world
Performance/Experience - PE	The role one will play on life's stage; the performance; reality
Soul	Core desires, needs, wants, motivations
Material Soul - MS	Second set of core desires
Nature	The personality and manner of doing things
Material Nature - MN	Second set of personality traits
Voids	Missing energies in the natal name

B. Life Cycle Pattern:

Establish the Life Cycle Pattern of the individual. Because RJ's Expression is a 7, his LCP is a 1/8. It would be helpful to mark any voids with a "v" designation.

LCP	1/8		7 Expression							
Influence/Cause	1	2	3	4	5	6	7v	8	9	Influence/Cause
[+ Expression Filter]	[+7]	[+7]	[+7]	[+7]	[+7]	[+7]	[+7]	[+7]	[+7]	[+ Expression Filter]
Outcome/Effect	8	9	1	2	3	4	5	6	7v	Outcome/Effect

C. The Specific Inclusion

After constructing the Specific Inclusion, check for voids, master numbers and high percentages relative to a particular house. RJ has a 33 in his 5th House indicating greatly diverse communication skills. Many actors, singers and communicators have 33 in their 3rd or 5th House.

The King's Book of Numerology II: Forecasting - Part 1

Master numbers 11, 22 and 44 may appear in different houses. Master numbers in the Inclusion are strong factors in the chart and need consideration. Percentages over 40% in a particular house also warrant merit, as do a large number of genera in a particular house. Exceptional people often have a master number(s) or a high percentage of a number in their charts.

RJ: Inclusion Notes   33 in the 5th House

Richard Johnston Roe: Specific Inclusion

Basic No./House	No. of Genera	Specific Value	Percentage
1s	3 (A, J, S)	30	30/214 = 14.0%
2s	1 (T)	20	20/214 = 9.3%
3s	1 (C)	3	3/214 = 1.4%
4s	1 (D)	4	4/214 = 1.7%
5s	3 (2Ns, E)	**33**	33/214 = 15.4%
6s	3 (3 0s)	45	45/214 = 21.0%
7s	0 Void	0	0
8s	2 (2 Hs)	16	16/214 = 7.5%
9s	4 (3 Rs, I)	63	63/214 = 29.4%
Totals	**18 Letters**	**214 Specific Value**	**100%** [round off]

D. Name Timeline

The number of names in the Expression varies. American tradition usually has three names: first, middle, last. Yet, it's not uncommon for European Expressions to only have two names: a first and surname. Note all names. If a person has a "Jr." suffix, use it separately as "Jr.," not "Junior." Too, make sure if "Jr." is part of the natal name, use it in calculating the Expression [J=1; R=9]. If a person has a II, III or IV behind their name, translate the II to a "B," the III to a "C" and the IV to a "D" when establishing the Expression. As a note of accuracy, the last number of the name timeline of the last name should equal the General Expression of the individual. RJ's last name "Roe" shows a timeline from age 78 to 97. His General Expression is a 97. If these numbers to do match, there's a mistake. Recalculate. Too, make sure all the names are natal names, not married or nicknames, at least for the accuracy of the timeline. Extra names are like veils. They have some affect on the life but the name at birth establishes the destiny. If a person lives beyond the final number in his Expression, the energies cycle back to the first name.

King

Name Timeline Matrix
Richard Johnston Roe - 6 December 1999
[7 Void] [Filter is 1 LP]

	First	**Middle**	**Last**
Names > > >	Richard	Johnston	Roe
Timeline	Birth to 43	44 to 77	78 to 97
General	43	34	20
Simple	7v	7v	2
Expression (+ 1 LP Filter) =	[+1]	[+1]	[+1]
Name Timeline PE	8	8	3

E. Letter Timeline

There are different grid formats to lay out the Letter Timeline. A horizontal grid with the letters moving naturally left to right as one would read the name is optimum, but using a vertical grid is also effective. Here we get a good glimpse of the letter, its timeline, value and performance/experience. After the final letter timeline is transited, the chart cycles back to the first letter of the first name if the person is still living.

Letter Timeline
Richard Johnston Roe - 6 December 1999
[7 Void] [Filter is 1-LP]

Letter	Timeline	Letter Value & Term		LP		PE
R	Birth-9	9	+	1	=	1
I	10-18	9	+	1	=	1
C	19-21	3	+	1	=	4
H	22-29	8	+	1	=	9
A	30	1	+	1	=	2
R	31-39	9	+	1	=	1
D	40-43	4	+	1	=	5
J	44	1	+	1	=	2
O	45-50	6	+	1	=	7
H	51-58	8	+	1	=	9
N	59-63	5	+	1	=	6
S	64	1	+	1	=	2
T	65-66	2	+	1	=	3
O	67-72	6	+	1	=	7
N	73-77	5	+	1	=	6
R	78-86	9	+	1	=	1
O	87-92	6	+	1	=	7
E	93-97	5	+	1	=	6

F. Decade Timeline

A small grid such as this one can be used to show the Decade Timeline and its PE.

RJ's Decade Timeline
[Filter is his 7 Expression]

Decade	IR Set	Decade	IR Set	Decade	IR Set
Teens	1/8	40s	4/2	70s	7/5
20s	2/9	50s	5/3	80s	8/6
30s	3/1	60s	6/4	90s	9/7
				Century	1/8

Notes:

G. Life Matrix: Simple Version

Richard Johnston Roe - 6 December 1999
[Lifepath: 1 Expression: 7 PE: 8 Soul: 6 Material Soul: 7 Nature: 1 Material Nature: 2 Void: 7]

Note: For Epoch calculation we'll use the simple 27 year method.

Epochs	1st: Day	2nd: Month	3rd:Year
Ages	Birth to 27	28 to 54	55 on
Epochs	6/4	3/1	1/8

Periods	1st	2nd	3rd	4th
Age	Birth to 35	36 to 44	45 to 53	54 to end
Pinnacle	9/7v	4/2	4/2	7v/5
Challenge	3/1 & 6/4	2/9 & 7v/5	1/8	4/2 & 5/3

280

LIFE MATRIX

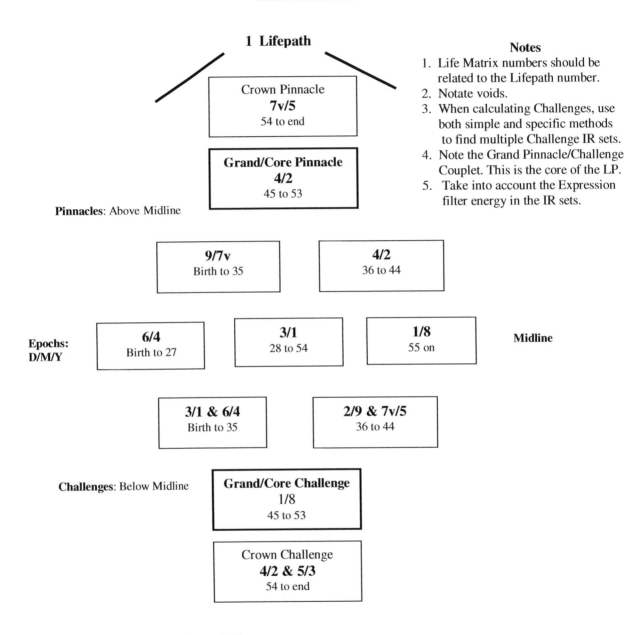

H. Annual Cycle Pattern Annual Forecast

Placing the data from the three major annual timelines: Age Timeline [ATL], Universal Timeline [UTL] and the Personal Year Timeline [PTL] into a grid gives us a quick glimpse of the year's energies. Remember, however, to cross reference these timelines with the other timelines in the chart as well as the Basic Matrix components. Too, the ACP begins on the birthday of the individual and continues to the next year's birthday. It does not begin on 1 January. We'll chart RJ's

ACP for his first birthday. Since he was born in 1999, his first birthday is in 2000. Note that his UTL and PTL are the same. This is because the day and month of his birth, 6 December, equal a 9 [review ACP calculations if necessary]. This duplicate UTL/PE and PTL/PE set is an example of *stacking*. Once again, the timelines reference *influences*, the PEs reference *outcomes*.

ACP ANNUAL FORECAST
Richard Johnston Roe
DOB: 6 December 1999
[Filter is his 7 Expression]

[Lifepath: 1 Expression: 7 PE: 8 Soul: 6 Material Soul: 7 Nature: 1 Material Nature: 2 Void: 7]

From
6 December 2000 to 6 December 2001

Timelines		
ATL	1	Yang energy [male], self, ego, new beginnings, independent, identity, starts
P/E	8	Social interaction, connection/disconnection, flow, wealth, comfort
UTL	2	Yin energy [female], others, relationship, partnership, opposition, balance
PE	9	Expansion, exposure, endings, public, recognition, art, universality, travel
PTL	2	Yin energy [female], others, relationship, partnership, opposition, balance
P/E	9	Expansion, exposure, endings, public, recognition, art, universality, travel

I. Annual Life Cycle Pattern

As we've discussed, this is a great tool in the forecasting process. Notice that RJ's 7 void becomes quite active in those years with a 6, 7, 8 and 9 crown. This will be problematic for him during his 1st and 4th Pinnacles and his 2nd Challenge because it will create stacking. It is not active during his crown years 1 through 5. Stacking is the concentration of simultaneous identical numbers or IR Sets [Influence/Reality] during a given time period thus increasing the intensity of the ciphers in question.

For example, because of the particular arrangement of his birth data, every year of his life as far as his ACPs are concerned, RJ will have stacking in his UTL and PTL. When correlated with the same IR sets in other parts of his life, this will definitely create more stacking and, hence, more intensity.

King

282

Annual Life Cycle Pattern
Richard Johnston Roe
DOB: 6 December 1999
[Filter is his 7 Expression]

Age	1	2	3	4	5	6	7	8	9
Age	10/1	11/2	12/3	13/4	14/5	15/6	16/7	17/8	18/9
Age	19/1	20/2	21/3	22/4	23/5	24/6	25/7	26/8	27/9
Age	28/1	29/2	30/3	31/4	32/5	33/6	34/7	35/8	36/9
Age	37/1	38/2	39/3	40/4	41/5	42/6	43/7	44/8	45/9
Age	46/1	47/2	48/3	49/4	50/5	51/6	52/7	53/8	54/9
Age	55/1	56/2	57/3	58/4	59/5	60/6	61/7	62/8	63/9
Age	64/1	65/2	66/3	67/4	68/5	69/6	70/7	71/8	72/9
Age	73/1	74/2	75/3	76/4	77/5	78/6	79/7	80/8	81/9
Age	82/1	83/2	84/3	85/4	86/5	87/6	88/7	89/8	90/9
Age	91/1	92/2	93/3	94/4	95/5	96/6	97/7	98/8	99/9

	1	2	3	4	5	6	7	8	9
ATL	1	2	3	4	5	6	7v	8	9
ATL PE	8	9	1	2	3	4	5	6	7v
UTL	2	3	4	5	6	7v	8	9	1
UTL PE	9	1	2	3	4	5	6	7v	8
PTL	2	3	4	5	6	7v	8	9	1
PTL PE	9	1	2	3	4	5	6	7v	8

The King's Book of Numerology II: Forecasting - Part 1

THE KING'S NUMEROLOGYtm
BASIC CHART

A. Basic Matrix

Name: Birthday:

Roots ⇩	Lifepath	Expression	PE	Soul	M/S	Nature	M/N	Voids
Simple								
General								
Specific								
Transition								

Basic Matrix Terms

Expression	The actor/actress full potentials, assets and liabilities
Lifepath	The life script, path in life, lessons to learn, energy world
Performance/Experience - PE	The role one will play on life's stage; the performance; reality
Soul	Core desires, needs, wants, motivations
Material Soul - MS	Second set of core desires
Nature	The personality and manner of doing things
Material Nature - MN	Second set of personality traits
Voids	Missing energies in the natal name

B. Life Cycle Pattern:

LCP	1/		-- Expression							
Influence/Cause	1	2	3	4	5	6	7v	8	9	Influence/Cause
[+ Expression Filter]	[+]	[+]	[+]	[+]	[+]	[+]	[+]	[+]	[+]	[+ Expression Filter]
Outcome/Effect										Outcome/Effect

C. The Specific Inclusion

Name: Birthdate

Basic No./House	No. of Genera	Specific Value	Percentage
1s			
2s			
3s			
4s			
5s			
6s			
7s			
8s			
9s			
Totals	**-- Letters**	**--- Specific Value**	**100%** [round off]

King

284

D. Name Timeline Matrix

Name: Date of Birth

[-- Void(s)]   [Filter is -- LP]

	First	Middle	Last
Names > > >			
Timeline			
General			
Simple			
Expression (+LP Filter) =	[+]	[+]	[+]
Name Timeline PE			

E. Letter Timeline

Name: Birthdate:

[-- Void(s)]   [Filter is -- LP]

Letter	Timeline	Letter Value & Term		LP		PE
	Birth-		+		=	
			+		=	
			+		=	
			+		=	
			+		=	
			+		=	
			+		=	
			+		=	
			+		=	
			+		=	
			+		=	
			+		=	
			+		=	
			+		=	
			+		=	
			+		=	
			+		=	
			+		=	
			+		=	
			+		=	

F. Decade Timeline

[Filter is -- Expression]

Decade	IR Set	Decade	IR Set	Decade	IR Set
Teens	1/	40s	4/	70s	7/
20s	2/	50s	5/	80s	8/
30s	3/	60s	6/	90s	9/
				Century	1/

G. Life Matrix: Simple Version

Name: Birthdate

[Lifepath: -- Expression: -- PE: -- Soul: - Material Soul: -- Nature: -- Material Nature: -- Void: --]

Note: For Epoch calculation we'll use the simple 27 year method.

Epochs	1st: Day	2nd: Month	3rd:Year
Ages	Birth to 27	28 to 54	55 on
Epochs			

Periods	1st	2nd	3rd	4th
Age				
Pinnacle				
Challenge				

286

LIFE MATRIX

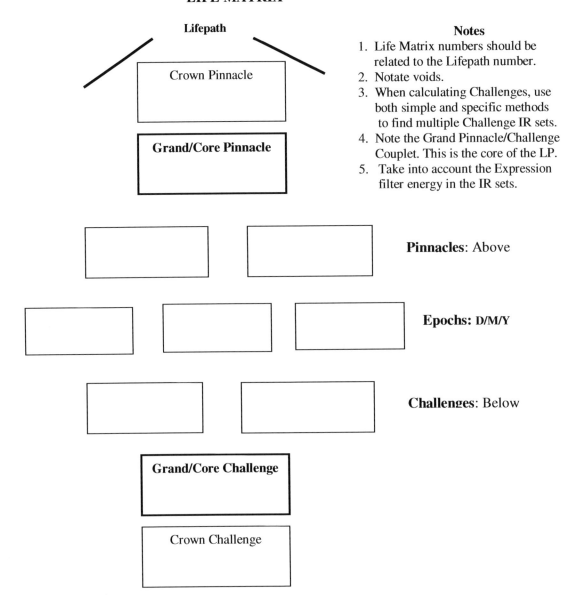

Lifepath

Crown Pinnacle

Grand/Core Pinnacle

Pinnacles: Above

Epochs: D/M/Y

Challenges: Below

Grand/Core Challenge

Crown Challenge

Notes
1. Life Matrix numbers should be related to the Lifepath number.
2. Notate voids.
3. When calculating Challenges, use both simple and specific methods to find multiple Challenge IR sets.
4. Note the Grand Pinnacle/Challenge Couplet. This is the core of the LP.
5. Take into account the Expression filter energy in the IR sets.

H. Annual Cycle Pattern Annual Forecast

ACP ANNUAL FORECAST

Name   Birthdate

[Filter is   -- Expression]

[Lifepath: -- Expression: --   PE: --   Soul: -   Material Soul: --   Nature: --   Material Nature: --   Void: --]

From
Day____/Month____/Year_____   to Day_____/Month_____/Year_____

Timelines		
ATL		
P/E		
UTL		
PE		
PTL		
P/E		

I. Annual Life Cycle Pattern

Annual Life Cycle Pattern

Name   Birthdate

[Filter is -- Expression]

Age	1	2	3	4	5	6	7	8	9
Age	10/1	11/2	12/3	13/4	14/5	15/6	16/7	17/8	18/9
Age	19/1	20/2	21/3	22/4	23/5	24/6	25/7	26/8	27/9
Age	28/1	29/2	30/3	31/4	32/5	33/6	34/7	35/8	36/9
Age	37/1	38/2	39/3	40/4	41/5	42/6	43/7	44/8	45/9
Age	46/1	47/2	48/3	49/4	50/5	51/6	52/7	53/8	54/9
Age	55/1	56/2	57/3	58/4	59/5	60/6	61/7	62/8	63/9
Age	64/1	65/2	66/3	67/4	68/5	69/6	70/7	71/8	72/9
Age	73/1	74/2	75/3	76/4	77/5	78/6	79/7	80/8	81/9
Age	82/1	83/2	84/3	85/4	86/5	87/6	88/7	89/8	90/9
Age	91/1	92/2	93/3	94/4	95/5	96/6	97/7	98/8	99/9
ATL									
ATL PE									
UTL									
UTL PE									
PTL									
PTL PE									

King

Summary

And thus we come to a temporary pause in our King's Numerology journey. There is much to learn of life through numbers but too much knowledge too soon is not conducive to the learning process. These first two volumes: *The King's Book of Numerology: Volume I - Foundations & Fundamentals* and *The King's Book of Numerology II: Forecasting - Part I* have created a blueprint for understanding the blueprints of our lives and destinies, as well as a foundation for continued research and study. As we who know, numerology is a divine science and art of extraordinary dimension, revealing secrets of life that common consciousness does not possess.

Please remember that such work demands not just exceptional knowledge but responsibility, wisdom and understanding, especially of karmic law. It is a great privilege to be given the sight of God's handiwork, and any violation of its use will bring divine disciplinary measures. Do not doubt this statement. We reap what we sow. If we sow good seed, we will reap a good harvest, but if we sow bad seed, we will unavoidably reap a bad harvest. As 15th/16th Century Saint Ravidas says, *The fruit of action unfailingly overtakes the doer.* Saint Dadu of the 16th Century states: *What you have not done will never befall you. Only what you have done will befall you.* Saint Sawan Singh of the 20th Century corroborates: *Whatever we are reaping now, we, ourselves, have sown before.* Therefore, the divine admonition is to keep numerology work pure and noble. Use it to help yourself and others but use it wisely, being always grateful for its gifts and vision.

God Speed.

Richard Andrew King

The King's Book of Numerology II

Forecasting - Part 1

by

Richard Andrew King

Richard King Publications
PO Box 3621
Laguna Hills, CA 92654
www.richardking.net

Richard Andrew King
~ Books ~
www.richardking.net

The King's Book of Numerology
Volume 1-Foundations & Fundamentals

The King's Book of Numerology, Volume 1-Foundations & Fundamentals provides complete descriptions of Basic Numbers, Double Numbers, Purifier Numbers, Master Numbers, the Letters in Simple and Specific form as well as the Basic Matrix, the numerological blueprint of our lives.
~
"*The King's Book of Numerology* series contains new information that informs and predicts more completely and accurately than any previously published numerological work. It brings back the empowered sciences of long ago, information long since lost upon this plane." ~ G. Shaver

"The best numerology book I've ever read." ~ M.W.

"I've learned as much about numerology from *The King's Book of Numerology* the last few days than I have in my past five years of study." ~ Frank M.

The King's Book of Numerology II
Forecasting - Part 1

The King's Book of Numerology II: Forecasting - Part 1 is dedicated to opening the door to the divine blueprint of our lives. That plan, that divine blueprint of destiny, is exact, precise, unchangeable, unalterable and . . . knowable, at least in general terms. Once this awareness of a predetermined fate becomes established through application of numbers and their truths, our understanding and consciousness of life will, no doubt, change. We will begin to see ourselves as part of an immense spiritual super-structure far beyond our current ability to comprehend, understand or perceive. Life will take on new meaning and, perhaps, we will even begin to awaken to greater spiritual truths. Subjects covered: Life Cycle Patterns, The Pinnacle/Challenge Matrix, Epoch Timeline, Voids, Case Studies and much more.

Blueprint of a Princess
Diana Frances Spencer - Queen of Hearts

The tragic death of Princess Diana of Wales - the most famous, the most photographed, the most written about woman of the modern world and possibly of all time - was one of the most shocking and saddening events of the late Twentieth Century. Not since the assassination of American President John Fitzgerald Kennedy in 1963, has such an event captured the attention of the world. On that ill-fated Sunday of 31 August 1997, and the following week until her funeral, there was much discussion and reflection of the Queen of Hearts, the People's Princess, England's Rose. But in all of the media news coverage, there was no discussion given to the cosmic aspects of her life and death. This book is dedicated to addressing those issues through The King's Numerology. Its purpose and hope is to offer some consolation and explanation as to that one question so poignantly written on a card of condolence left with the multitude of flowers before the gates of Buckingham Palace. . . "Why?"

~

"After learning from King's numerological teaching, it is impossible to conceive of going back to that 'twilight naive and foggy' state of being where one can only guess or hint at the truths, motivations and directions of one's life that is Pre-King. Not only do I recommend this book, but I suggest it and his other numerology books as absolutely necessary for the library of anyone even remotely interested in the science of numerology." ~ Hunter Stowers

99 Poems of the Spirit

99 Poems of the Spirit draws from the writings of Perfect Saints, Masters, Mystics and Sacred Scriptures. Designed to lift the consciousness, mind and heart, all of the poems are original works by Richard Andrew King. Their purpose is to help connect the reader with the mystic side of life in order to enhance the process of self-realization while advancing on the spiritual path and climbing the ladder leading to the ultimate attainment of God Realization. It is a treasure chest of poetic spiritual gems offered to excite, educate and stimulate the mind and soul in the glorious journey of spiritual ascent.

Messages from the Masters
Timeless Truths for Spiritual Seekers

In a time where there is more need for enlightenment than ever before, *Messages from the Masters: Timeless Truths for Spiritual Seekers* offers timeless truths for genuine seekers thirsty for spiritual nectar.

Masters are the PhDs of the universe, the Light Bearers of the Divine Flame. Their knowledge and wisdom are supreme. They have no equal. Although appearing human, they are not. Masters are the exalted Sons of God. Their chief duty is to rescue souls, liberating them from the maniacal maelstrom and madness of the material world and returning them to their eternal Home with the Lord.

Messages from the Masters is a rich source of hundreds of quotes from a cavalcade of nine Perfect Saints throughout the last six hundred years: Guru Ravidas, Kabir, Guru Nanak, Tulsi Sahib, Swami Ji Maharaj, Baba Jaimal Singh, Sawan Singh, Jagat Singh and Charan Singh. The messages in this book focus on the importance of the Divine Diet, the priceless Human Form, Reincarnation, the World, the Negative Power and Soul Food.

Warning! *Messages from the Masters* is not for the faint of heart or the worldly-minded. Masters come into the world to sever our attachment to it, not make it a paradise. Although the epitome of love and wisdom, they shoot straight from the hip, pull no punches, favor no religion. Their universal message of soul liberation is reflected in the statement of Saint Maharaj Charan Singh: *Just live in the creation and get out of it*!

The Age of the Female
A Thousand Years of Yin

The Age of the Female: A Thousand Years of Yin highlights the profound and extraordinary ascent of the female in the modern world, placing her center stage in the global spotlight as presidents and leaders of nations, titans of industry, corporate executives, military generals, media magnets, doctors, lawyers and a whole host of other prestigious titles normally associated with the male. Why has her rise to prominence been so rapid, especially in consideration of historic time? Why also has there been an increased interest in other people's lives in our society, in competitive athletics, personal data collection and the exploration of space and other worlds? *The Age of the Female: A Thousand Years of Yin* answers these questions. It is an insightful and exciting read into these mysteries, offering compelling and irrefutable evidence through the ancient science and art of numerology that, indeed, the age of the female has arrived and the next thousand years belong, not to him, but to her.

The Age of the Female II
Heroines of the Shift

The Age of the Female II: Heroines of the Shift continues the remarkable journey of the female's ascent in the modern world of the 2nd Millennium. This installment is a general read in five chapters honoring the accomplishments of women in categories of female firsts, female Nobel laureates, female athletes, female icons and female quotations. The achievements of the women featured in *The Age of the Female II: Heroines of the Shift* are deserving of respect and admiration. Their lives, challenges and successes are motivational catalysts for every individual to be the best he or she can be and to honor the very essence of what it is to be human. *The Age of the Female II: Heroines of the Shift* is intended to be an inspiring and educational read for everyone, not just women but men, too, offering knowledge and insight of the depth, power and daring-do of women as their Yin energy rises upon the global stage in this millennium which destiny has irrefutably marked as the Age of the Female.

King

To order books, go to

www.RichardKing.Net

Contact

Richard Andrew King

PO Box 3621

Laguna Hills, CA 92654

www.RichardKing.Net

296

298

39623012R00172

Made in the USA
Lexington, KY
03 March 2015